Hoofbeats and Society

HOOFBEATS
and
SOCIETY

STUDIES OF HUMAN-HORSE INTERACTIONS

Elizabeth Atwood Lawrence

INDIANA UNIVERSITY PRESS
BLOOMINGTON

Chapter 2 was originally published in *Great
Plains Quarterly* 1 (Spring 1981): 81–94, and is reprinted here with
the permission of the editor.

Manufactured in the United States of America

Library of Congress Cataloging in Publication Data
Lawrence, Elizabeth Atwood, 1929–
  Hoofbeats and society.

  Bibliography: p.
  Includes index.
  1. Horses—Social aspects.   2. Horsemen and horse-
women. I. Title.
SF284.4.L39 1985   798   84-48296
ISBN 0-253-32843-8

To
my family
and
for
Goldie and Bonney

CONTENTS

Preface

"Gypsy gold does not chink and glitter. It gleams in the sun and neighs in the dark" (Vesey–Fitzgerald 1965:29). Within this Romany maxim are encapsulated the strong symbolic meanings with which the horse has become imbued for a particular group of people. The fact that "a Gypsy without a horse is no genuine Gypsy" (McDowell 1970:103; Clebert 1963:103; Erdös 1959:3) articulates a theme which frequently recurs throughout the history and culture of mankind: the bonds which unite people with horses do not represent utilitarian relationships alone, though they may first arise out of these, but are soon transformed into affective ones as well. Horses, as will be shown in the chapters that follow, frequently come to have intense symbolic power for those who interact with them.

Associated with the equine capacity for providing traction and transport have always been the horse's extreme sensitivity and an unusual potentiality for fine-tuned communication with people. In its role as a living vehicle, carrying human beings forward into space, the horse has provided new dimensions of physical experience and sensation, and, by means of shared kinetic processes—the physical and mental merging of two species—has awakened us to fresh aspects of perception through its special qualities of pace and rhythm. The horse provides satisfaction for our profound fascination with motion, and has near-universal appeal to the human senses of sight, sound, and touch. Like other creatures that can be included in Lévi-Strauss's concept that animals are "good to think" (1963:89), horses can become vivid images in human cognitive processes, and frequently serve as meaningful constructs in ordering social relations between people and the world about them.

The image of the horse is complex and multidimensional. The elements it symbolizes in human thought are diverse and at times may even appear contradictory. That is not unusual, as Firth, drawing upon the work of Turner (1967:45–52), points out, for "a very important property of symbols" is "their capacity for a single symbol to encapsulate many meanings—to represent many different things, in different contexts or at different levels of understanding in the same general context" (1975:190).

Various facets of the human-horse relationship are explored in this book, and all share the theme of the transformation of the horse by different groups of people into a form which communicates their particular values and expresses a truth about their society that is not easily articulated by other means. There is in each case an adaptive use of the contingencies of the horse/human or horse/rider situation in order to make significant statements about the people's own condition—particularly their view of themselves with regard to the passage of time and their status in the scheme of life which they envision. The contemporary Crow Indians, for example, find in the horse a distillation of the qualities that are most meaningful in their culture, encompassing both past and present. The equine animal is an important element in the way they define themselves as a social entity and the way they relate to the dominant culture. Americans are able to identify in the White Stallion of the Prairies an object which serves well to express their collective feelings about westward expansion and their ambivalence toward it. The Stallion is a powerful symbol that makes people look backward in time and weigh past values against those of the present. In the cowboy sport of rodeo, horse events are structured so as to represent the wild-to-tame transition inherent in the conquest of the New World frontier. The Winning of the West, which is recapitulated in rodeo, looms large in American consciousness, where it is strongly associated with nostalgia for an earlier time. Interactions between the mounted officer and his horse and between the police horse/rider unit and the public serve to symbolically communicate the force of the social order itself. These interactions are a rich source of data about the predicament that the passage of time has brought to citizens in the modern city. In all of these instances, as discussed in detail in the respective chapters devoted to them, perceptions of horses are not static symbols. On the contrary, they involve dynamic feedback, for people's conceptual views of horses become active forces in stimulating the very social interaction which they reflect.

The studies which constitute this book, with the exception of the chapter on the White Mustang and the references to Gypsies, are based upon my own field research as a cultural anthropologist, supplemented by use of material from my background as a practicing veterinarian. For the first chapter, that on the horse in Crow Indian life and culture, I conducted the field work between the years of 1976 and 1980 inclusive, as a participant observer on the Crow Indian Reservation, Crow

Agency, Montana. The third chapter, dealing with human/horse relationships as reflected in the contests and performances of rodeo, is the
result of extensive field work on the rodeo circuit and with the associated ranch/rodeo complex undertaken in the Great Plains states,
particularly Montana and Wyoming, from 1975 through 1979. The
fourth chapter describes the results of field data obtained in my work
with the mounted police in the years 1981 through 1983. In carrying out
this project, interviews were held with mounted officers themselves,
both at their barracks and on their beats, with various personnel who
worked with them and their horses, and with members of the public
who were on the street or who lived in districts where the mounted unit
patrolled. Most of my work was done in one particular large Eastern
city; it was supplemented with data obtained from another smaller
Eastern city.

In the second chapter, I have brought to bear upon the legend of
the Pacing White Mustang my own knowledge and creative thinking
about horses, resulting from many years of experience interacting with
them as a horsewoman and as a veterinarian. Combining this with my
interest in, and study of, the mystique of the American West, and with
various literary and folkloric sources dealing with the frontier, I have
produced a kind of structuralist symbolic study of the Stallion which
has unified these interests. I first wrote the essay upon which this
chapter is based in 1978.

Brief descriptions of Gypsies are included, because this group's
traditional view of horses and interaction with them, as they have been
recorded, reflect intensity of social meaning and symbolism centering
on the animal in a way that may be used to elucidate and expand my
own studies. The Gypsies' relationship with horses in the past has
become legendary, and perhaps time-honored to the point of being
stereotypic. Nevertheless, a consideration of it helps to bring into
focus some of the elements which are of universal importance in inter-
preting the meaning of the horse in human societies. Thus a new dimension of understanding is added by reference to Gypsy lore.

The final chapter contains not only a drawing together of the
studies which constitute this book but also the development of many of
my own creative ideas about horses and their meaning in human experience. These ideas have been gradually formulated over the years in
which I have interacted with horses and during which I have pondered
deeply the question of what makes horses so intensely appealing and

profoundly significant to many people in different societies. My own inquiries into the subject of human/horse relationships are supplemented by the use of a variety of relevant sources, which shed light on the phenomenon of the compelling bond between people and horses that still remains a source of satisfaction in our modern era. I have suggested some of the special symbolic meanings attributed to the horse, particularly with regard to the marking out of time and states of transition in human life.

The role of animals in society is an important field of concern to the social scientist, and one to which I hope the present volume will make significant contribution. Often information about human/animal interactions leads to insights about the nature of a particular society which may not be clearly elucidated through study of other aspects of their culture. With understanding of the character of animal relationships peculiar to a society comes a deeper knowledge about that society's ethos. Much is revealed about the ways in which a group of individuals interact with their environment. In many cases, bonds which people form with animals are becoming increasingly important in the context of the contemporary world. That is especially true of the horse, signifying, as it does for many people, a slower pace and a more natural tempo of life. In the face of the complexity of modern mechanized existence and the alienation from nature which it implies, the human response of reaching out to interact with other creatures is universally meaningful and even vital.

ELIZABETH ATWOOD LAWRENCE

REFERENCES

Block, Martin
    1939 *Gypsies: Their Life and Their Customs.* New York: D. Appleton-
    Century.
Clebert, Jean-Paul
    1963 *The Gypsies.* London: Vista.
Erdös, Kamill
    1959 "Gypsy Horse Dealers in Hungary." *Journal of the Gypsy Lore
    Society* 38, nos. 1–2: 1–6.

Firth, Raymond
    1975   *Symbols: Public and Private.* Ithaca: Cornell University Press.
Lévi-Strauss, Claude
    1963   *Totemism.* Boston: Beacon.
McDowell, Bart
    1970   *Gypsies: Wanderers of the World.* Washington: National Geographic Society.
Turner, Victor
    1967   *The Forest of Symbols.* Ithaca: Cornell University Press.
Vesey-Fitzgerald, Brian
    1965   *Animal Anthology.* London: Newnes.

Acknowledgments

To the Crow people, with their friendliness and love for horses, I am deeply grateful. Many wonderful individuals helped me and were always willing to "talk horse." Special thanks go to Joseph Medicine Crow, Robert Yellowtail, Lloyd and Miriam Old Coyote, the Real Bird family, Dexter Williams, and the Crow Agency 4-H Club leaders. Charles Bradley, Jr. was particularly kind and generous in sharing his data on the history of the Crow Indians. My sincere appreciation goes to the Crow Fair committee members, particularly the rodeo officials and stock contractor, for their cooperation. I am grateful to the Professional Rodeo Cowboys Association for its many courtesies in allowing me to be a part of the cowboy sport, and to the many rodeo people who provided such willing assistance. I want to thank all the mounted police officers and personnel who so graciously spent time giving me information about their work, and especially Sergeant Bob Molloy, whose enthusiastic help was invaluable to my project. To the editors of the *Great Plains Quarterly* go my thanks for permission to republish my work on "The White Mustang of the Prairies." Permission was kindly granted by the University of Tennessee Press to use material in Chapter Three which was first published in my book *Rodeo: An Anthropologist Looks at the Wild and the Tame.* The encouragement provided by Professor Edward Norbeck is acknowledged with gratitude. And in countless ways Priscilla, Mark, and Robert Lawrence have helped to make this work possible.

Hoofbeats and Society

The Horse in Crow Indian Culture, Past and Present

1

Introduction

Today's traveler has only to enter the confines of the Crow Indian Reservation in southeastern Montana when, almost immediately, horses appear everywhere in sight. Free horses are seen grazing along every expanse of grassland and, much to the chagrin of local white residents, even along unfenced highways. In areas of thicker settlements, no matter how closely the houses may be spaced, there is a tethered pony or two in evidence. In every direction, both old and young are observed on their mounts, the children usually two astride one horse, often without saddles. There is a relaxed harmony, a sense of belonging, between people and animals; riders and mounts move as one. In the parks or along the streets, young horsemen and horsewomen gather to talk or laugh together, often extending the reins of their bridles so that the horses can graze during visits. On summer evenings riders are always to be seen watering their grateful mounts along the shores of the Little Big Horn River, presenting a peaceful and pastoral scene which belies that river's bloody fame. On any weekend in the spring or summer, there is sure to be a rodeo, horse race, mounted parade, or 4-H equestrian event scheduled nearby. In the third week in August, there is the eagerly awaited annual Crow Fair, in which the horse plays a dominant role throughout the whole celebration.

Conversation with any of these equestrians soon reveals that to them an Indian, particularly a Crow Indian, is "a horseback." Man and mount are inseparable. During my field work among the Crows, it became immediately and strikingly evident that the horse is today a vitally important factor in the life and culture of these people, both physically and on a symbolic level. This study is concerned with describing the many ways in which the horse functions in Crow society at the present time, and with elucidating the significance of the remarkable reawakening and resurgence of horse interest in recent years among the Crows. Not only does this concern for horses represent a survival from the old horse culture of these Plains people, harking back to the time of their economic dependence upon the animals, but it also represents something which continues to have deep meaning to the Crows in the modern world.

Past and present frequently seem to merge for the Crows and are intimately related in thought. In order, therefore, to discuss and probe today's relationships between horse and Crow, it is appropriate first to describe the horse's role in the history of the Plains Indians and to use that as a background in the attempt to understand contemporary human/equine interactions and their meanings among the Crow people.

The Horse in Plains Indian History, with Special Reference to the Crows

Acquisition of the Horse

The strength of impact of the advent of the horse upon Plains Indian culture is a factor which can hardly be overemphasized, for it revolutionized almost every phase of life for those peoples, who were to become known as "Horse Indians." Their prowess in horsemanship became legendary, and their partnership with the powerful new animal, which it is said they at first mistook for a creature half beast and half man, became one of the closest relationships of interdependence between mankind and animals known to history.

Among Plains Indian groups who were so profoundly affected by the acquisition of the horse, the Crows were preeminent. In the words of a modern-day Crow speaking of his people's association with the horse, "We took to each other like long-lost brothers." Indeed, this observation is borne out historically by the rapidity with which the

[2]

Crows, like other Plains tribes, learned to master the new animal and developed into one of the world's foremost equestrian societies.

As precisely as can be dated by historians from observations recorded in early sources such as La Verendrye (Burpee 1920, 1927), Maximilian (Wied-Neuewied 1906), and Larocque (Burpee 1910), the Crows must have obtained their first horses in about 1730–35, probably from the Shoshonis in Salt Lake country. There are disputes and differing theories about the exact origin of the first Crow horses and, of course, many legends about them. All agree, however, on the fact that the Crow people, whose grassland home in the northern Great Plains was particularly suitable for horse pasturage, became undisputed experts in horsemastership. The horse age in their culture dates approximately from 1750 to 1880.

Effects of the Horse

Though it is evident that the acquisition of the horse permeated and modified virtually every phase of Plains Indian life and culture, Clark Wissler, long considered the classic authority on the subject, concluded that

> while the horse, along with other European influences may have intensified and more completely diffused the various traits, there is no good evidence at hand to support the view that the horse led to the development of important traits. In other words, from a qualitative point of view the culture of the Plains would have been much the same without the horse. [1914:16]

Wissler looked upon the horse as a "new and superior dog," which, by replacing that animal in the culture, only accomplished more efficiently what the dog had done before (1914:18). Followers of his thought, such as Ewers, who in his monograph (1955) stated that he had reached the same conclusion as Wissler, and Murdock, who said of the horse in relation to the Crows: "So perfectly was it adapted to their needs that it intensified rather than modified their native mode of life" (1934:267), perpetuated Wissler's concept that "as an intensifier of original Plains traits, the horse presents its strongest claim" (1914:18). Anthropologists who adhere to this school of thought refer to the horse as a "tool," unrealistically regarding this living herbivorous animal as an object which could be brought out when needed, mainly for transportation, and which was otherwise not a vital factor to be reckoned with. As Wilson states, "The critical question is whether the horse provided a more efficient hunting tool or a new source of energy to Plains technology" (1963:358). His belief in the horse as a new source of energy places him with those whose positions challenge Wissler's, such as Kroeber, who expressed doubt that the traits which characterized the posthorse Plains culture were already present in the prehorse Plains culture (1939:76–77), and with Mishkin, who emphasized the whole horse-herding complex as an innovative determinant in Plains Indian life (1940).

Wissler's idea, which dominated anthropological literature for a long time, ignored the significant differences between dogs and horses and the many influential factors involved in horse husbandry. For, while the dog did at first act as a burden bearer in pulling the travois, making the moving of camp easier for the nomadic Plains Indians, it should not be necessary to point out that the size, temperament, and needs of the canine are vastly different from those of the equine. The dog, when not being used for the transportation of goods, could fit smoothly and unobtrusively into the everyday lives of the people. It was adaptable as a companion, particularly for children, and probably as a game hunter and watchdog. Most important, it could hunt its own food or subsist on the scraps or surplus of its master, sharing the meat that was important in the human diet. Then, too, the dog has in general a more submissive nature than the horse, at least at the outset, and would in all probability bear the burdens of its mistress willingly, without any reward except the owner's regard and its share of food. Respect for the dog's services brought serious injunctions against abusing, killing, or eating dogs for some Plains tribes. This tradition persists among many Crows, who believe that because of the past help given to their people by the dog, they will be punished if they harm or kill a dog. Crows today deride their old enemies, the Cheyennes, for their lack of such a prohibition. When Cheyenne people come to the Crow Reservation, Crows may be heard to say, "Hold on to your dogs; here come the dog eaters!"

Upon initial contact with the horse, Plains Indians did relate the new animal to the dog, as the only domesticated animal with which they were familiar. This association is linguistically evident, for the original Crow word for "my dog" became the word for "my horse," and subsequently the word designating "my dog" was modified to being stated as "my real dog." But much of the perceived resemblance must have dwindled in the era that followed the initial impact. The equine species, in contrast to the canine, was huge, beautiful, and wild, powerful and resistant to taming and training, and still a challenge to handle or ride even if acquired when already trained. A horse would not as readily acquiesce to its tasks without extensive effort and skill on the part of the handler. Thus the horse, once trained and ridden, would be a source of great pride to the owner-trainer. The feeling of accomplishment and psychological sense of power experienced by the much smaller person at having subdued the larger and more massive animal would have deeply affected the Indian mind and attitude. As the Bible states, no man by taking thought can add to his stature; yet by mounting a horse, he does.

Certainly the state of exultation which is characteristic of the mounted man must have had a profound effect upon the Plains Indians' psyche, imparting a new sensation of mastery and self-confidence, which fitted these equestrians for the epithet "lords of the Plains." An early fur trader, Alexander Henry, realized in 1803 the psychological effect of the horse on the Indians with whom he traded when he complained that the acquisition of this animal had already made the natives "too indolent, insolent, and independent" (Coues 1897:225–26). This view may be biased, but it is certain that the possession of the horse, by strengthening them psychologically as well as economically and militarily, made the Plains people much less submissive in attitude than they would have been on foot. As daring and ferocious equestrian raiders, they became a far more serious and persistent threat to white expansion. No mere doglike creature could have brought about this transformation. Once the Indians acquired horses and adapted to them, a sense of oneness with these animals fitted into their existing belief in the unity of all life and permeated into virtually every phase of their life and culture. It must be emphasized that the very sensation of motion itself would have been new to these heretofore pedestrian people. Mounted, they became a human/animal unit with vast potential; the speed and rhythm of the horse became part of the rider, and the force of the man enhanced the power of the horse. Association with the horse quickened the tempo of life and contributed to an intensified aggressiveness, which made "proud and defiant" the classic description of the native horsemen of the Plains.

Differing from the dog in another important respect, the horse is a grass-eating animal, requiring for its maintenance extensive and constantly available pasturage. As more and more of the equine creatures were desired and obtained, the Plainsmen were faced with a fresh set of demands upon their lives, which dictated that for every horse owned, sufficient grassland must be near at hand. Thenceforth the new requirements of horse husbandry vastly altered the lifestyle and movements of the tribe. Prehorse patterns of nomadism for the hunter-gatherer Plains tribes had been determined by availability of game, particularly bison, and to a lesser degree by the ripening of certain plants used for consumption. Posthorse nomadism had to be regulated by available pastureland. When the grass had been eaten by the herd of horses in one area, it was necessary to move camp. The best grasslands had to be constantly sought. This new pressure intensified the need for use of land and undoubtedly reinforced old rivalries between Plains tribes. The Crows, for example, with a relatively small population in their grassy and game-rich home territory, were surrounded by traditional foes, notably the powerful horse-owning tribes of Sioux, Cheyenne, and Arapaho. Earlier in their history, the Crows had placed territorial distance between themselves and their allies, the Hidatsa and Mandan, when they split from these sedentary groups to take up the nomadic hunter-gatherer way of life.

Winter camp had to be carefully planned in posthorse times, in order to insure a climate sufficiently mild to prevent unsheltered horses from freezing and to provide suitable rangeland in which the animals could paw through the snow to eat the grass below. Cottonwood bark, the staple winter food for horses on the Plains, had to be available near such campsites. The number of individuals who could camp together, summer or winter, was determined by horse ownership. Not only was the size of a camping group limited by the number of horses which the land could sustain, but also, to some extent, the designation of individuals who could camp together was determined by new fields of economic activity ushered in by the horse culture. For example, equine caretakers had to be included with each camp. Generally these were specially trained young boys, preferably nephews of the horse owners; thus the need for horse care influenced reassignment of kinship groups to various camps. It was considered a special day in the life of a small boy when he was given the status of horse herder (Roe 1955:260).

It was necessary for horse herds to be constantly guarded against raiders, predators, and possible escape. Animals had to be watched for

[6]

sickness, and young foals needed special protection. Horses were sometimes groomed and were often decorated for the warpath or special ceremony, for horsemen took pride in their mounts' appearance. Horses needed to be herded to new grassland when a pasture was depleted. In addition, skilled and experienced trainers were essential within each group to take charge of their specialized task. Riding teachers were necessary, as children were taught to be proficient equestrians. Makers of riding and transport gear were in demand. Horse medicine men, who had been given special knowledge in a dream or vision, or who had obtained such skill from a relative— usually an uncle or grandfather who had once received it supernaturally—were essential for curing. Sometimes a horse gave a revelation to a shaman or medicine man (Roe 1955:261). Only a few veterinary specialists had the power to heal, and their services were valuable. Not only did they have remedies for sick or wounded horses, but they could revive an exhausted animal or make a charger more swift for the race (Lowie 1924:333–34). Some medicines could impart endurance to a horse, protect it against arrows or bullets, or calm a balky mount. The expertise of those in control of such powers was much desired to insure the success of horse raids and safety in the buffalo hunt. Surgeons were needed for their skill as castrators of stallions, and the services of those with the ability to perform this operation with few fatalities were eagerly sought.

Specialized horse roles were influential in camping arrangements. The possessor of a good buffalo horse—the most highly prized and essential element in the bison-hunting economy of the Plains—was expected to share use of this valued mount with a certain number of people, ordinarily his kin or the poor. Thus the buffalo horse, in being essential for obtaining subsistence for a designated number of families, would determine the location of those families during hunting season. Another effect of such an arrangement was that the owner of the animal had certain authority over those who shared his horse, and the dependent families would be expected to follow his orders. To appreciate the importance of the buffalo horse, one must realize that long, laborious training was needed to compel even a naturally daring horse to act so much against its nature as to approach a huge, terrifying beast like the bison close enough for the rider to shoot the fatal arrow. The marvel of the feat is compounded by the fact that both hands of the hunter were occupied in the kill, so no mouth contact could be used.

[7]

The mount had to learn to respond to voice and leg pressure and to rely on past experience. Despite exhaustion and possibly pain from wounds received in a struggle, a good buffalo horse would bring its rider safely home. It is no wonder, then, that such a horse would receive the special care and protection—verging on veneration—appropriate to its value.

Plains Indians as Pastoralists

Taking into account the far-reaching influence of horse herding and husbandry upon the lives, movements, and culture of the Plains Indians, it is possible to designate them as *nomadic pastoralists.* The tradition of viewing them strictly as hunters or hunter-gatherers is open to revision in the light of their horse-tending complex. Classifying these peoples in the hunter category perpetuates Wissler's view that the use of the horse only intensified and expanded hunting patterns that were already present on the Plains, and ignores the important effects of the horse-herding element.

Modified nomadic pastoralists is a more accurate term, for among Plains tribes such as the Crow, horses were not kept for meat. On the contrary, there was a Crow taboo against eating horse flesh, because of a close relationship to the animal. Other Plains groups, such as the Comanche, used the horse as a secondary but regular source of meat (Mishkin 1940:23). But as Lowie points out, though the Crows did not eat the horses they tended or milk the mares, as did the Mongol and Turkish horse pastoralists, who subsisted directly from their herds, horse husbandry was still intimately bound up with their livelihood (1935:228; 1954:45). Buffalo meat was the prime source of food, as well as of other items used in daily life, and the hunting of the buffalo was an exclusively equestrian endeavor once horses had been acquired. Thus people, horse, and buffalo were intimately linked together in the Plains hunting complex. Mishkin suggests the term *nonparasitic pastoralism* for the Plains, to distinguish it from pastoralism in which herds are maintained for food. He points out that Plains Indian pastoralism is similar in type to the reindeer pastoralism of the Tungus and Yakut in Siberia, and unlike that of the Chuckchee and Koryak, who live on their reindeer (1940:23). Wilson expresses a similar view when he states that "it was horse pastoralism, not the buffalo hunt, which gave the post-horse Plains technology its specific character" (1963:366). Since horse pastoralism so profoundly affected Plains Indian culture, the many facets of its influence must be considered in elucidating the traditional Plains way of life of the past and in understanding the roots of behavior and attitudes with regard to the horse which are still discernible in the present.

Plains Indian pastoralism is a case unto itself; in that the horse was used as an intermediary agent. Control over the procurement of subsistence—that is, the killing of wild buffalo—was made possible through use of a domesticated animal, the horse. The American bison native to the Plains was an animal virtually impossible to domesticate (Garretson 1938; Haines 1970; Roe 1970), while the horse was already domesticated when acquired. The pattern formed by the Indians involving the two species was their own particular adjustment to the unique environmental conditions with which they were confronted. The fact that it was the intermediary animal and not the food animal which was herded does not preclude looking upon Plains tribes as pastoralists.

Though a detailed study placing Plains horse pastoralists in world perspective is beyond the scope of this work, a brief comparison with one group of pastoralists brings to light much that is significant. In his classic ethnography of the cattle-herding Nuer of Africa, Evans-Pritchard describes these people as having "the herdsman's outlook on the world" (1974:16). The same might be said of the Plains Indians, whose horses, like Nuer cattle, were regarded as their dearest possessions (Linderman 1930; Curtis 1909). In both groups men would gladly risk their lives to defend their herds or pillage those of their neighbors. In Nuer and Plains society alike, the animal concerned became the chief occasion for strife, and dwindling herds acted as a stimulus for war. To steal the animal is laudable in each culture, with raiding as an important means of acquisition. In each social system the respective animal was used for compensation and paying of debts. Nuer cattle *are* the essential food supply, whereas Plains horses were essential *to* the food supply, but in both cases the animals represent the most important social asset. Both are valued for prestige and ostentation. As symbols of rank and wealth, both are frequently redistributed—Plains horses in various types of gift-giving ceremonies, and Nuer cattle on many significant occasions, particularly marriage.

Just as Nuer identify with cattle in many ways, such as having their kinship ties stated in terms of cattle, and even comparing the horn-cutting operation to their own initiation into manhood (Evans-

Pritchard 1974:38), so the Plains horsemen identified with the mounts they rode for war and hunting. Grass and water availability determine Nuer migration (Evans-Pritchard 1974:57–59), just as the same elements determined Plains transhumance. The Nuer have a mixed pastoral-horticultural economy, but their land is more suited for cattle husbandry than horticulture; their environmental conditions thus coincide with the bias of their interests, according to Evans-Pritchard (1974:57). The same can be said of some Plains tribes, as well. The Crow homeland, for example, is a naturally excellent horse-grazing area, and though some horticulture could be practiced there, Crows much preferred the life of equestrian nomadism (Medicine Crow 1939; Nabokov 1967; Linderman 1930). As a significant element of what Evans-Pritchard terms the "pastoral mentality," the Nuer "regard horticulture as toil forced upon them by poverty of stock, for at heart they are herdsmen, and the only labor in which they delight is care of cattle" (1974:16).

This outlook in some respects is similar to that of traditional Plains Indians such as the Crows, among whom horticulture was, and still is, regarded as degrading (Medicine Crow 1939). For them, work involving horse care and husbandry has long been considered to be the most prestigious occupation (Curtis 1909; Roe 1955). Among the Nuer, Evans-Pritchard noted, the nomadic pastoral life "nurtures the qualities of the shepherd—courage, love of fighting, and contempt of hunger and hardship—rather than shapes the industrious character of the peasant" (1974:26).

Such an insight regarding the shaping of society could be applicable to the Plains Indians. Indeed, it focuses on a significant root of conflict in ideology between native Americans and non-Indian culture. This disparity in ethos has been the basis of misunderstanding and consequent hostility from the time of Anglo-European contact to the defeat and subjugation of the Indians, down through the present day. It was particularly instrumental in causing the tragedy wrought by those who set out to "solve the Indian problem" on Plains reservations by transforming the natives into farmers. For example, the United States government instructions regarding the Crows in the early reservation period stated: "They should be taught, if not required, to exchange these ponies . . . and this mode of life (roving on ponies) for one confined to so much of the soil as they can cultivate and turn to their support" (Bradley 1970:12). It is not surprising that such an injunction engendered bitterness and frustration in those whose lives and culture had been shaped as nomadic horse pastoralists, as well as hunters.

The Horse in Trade

In addition to the demands of herding, the trade network influenced and directed the migratory movements of Plains Indians. This network, at the height of the horse culture, not only required the use of but revolved around the equine species. Extensive trade was carried on by some Plains groups, both with other tribes and with Anglo-Europeans. Early traders left records of this activity by the nomadic Crows. Tribesmen often exchanged products of the buffalo hunt for the agricultural produce of the sedentary Mandan and Hidatsa (Nabokov 1967:120). The efficiency of the mounted hunt gave the equestrians a surplus, and horses made transportation of the surplus goods possible. By 1800 the Crows were journeying annually to Mandan villages to trade (Hyde 1959); thus the horse-influenced trade route was affecting seasonal cycles of movement for the Crows at that time. Though raiding, as will be discussed, became a prime source of horses for Plains tribes at the height of the horse era, horses were still frequently traded, particularly for highly desirable items. All parties appreciated the value of the equine species, and exchange rates were high. The horse, because of its importance in Indian life and culture, became "the preferred standard of value" (Lowie 1954:45), and the worth of other goods was measured in terms of its numbers. Oral tradition carried down to the present day among the Crows indicates that Crow horses were particularly sought after, being of reputed high quality.

The Horse in Transportation

For the Plains Indians, the impact of the horse on transportation was overwhelming. The large and powerful animal enabled the nomadic people to make longer, faster, easier, and more comfortable trips. The Crows made use of the travois to carry disabled people (Lowie 1954:44). The young, old, and infirm were spared many hardships of travel and possible abandonment (Medicine Crow 1939:18). Horse transport brought the added convenience of heavier lodge poles than could be pulled by dog travois, enabling people to have larger and more commodious teepees (Curtis 1909). Crows still speak of this benefit with gratitude. The great increase in distance which the equestrian Indians could travel vastly extended their knowledge and awareness of a world that had been beyond their reach with dog traction. Their physical domain expanded as new sights were seen, previously unexplored areas were discovered, and alien people were contacted.

Through new contacts, the sphere of each tribe was widened and diffusion of its culture traits expedited, so that horse transportation undoubtedly contributed to making the individual Plains Indian groups more homogeneous. Mental aspects of the horse revolution have often been ignored, yet it is impossible to overstate the awesome influence upon the mind and imagination which horse transportation brought about for people previously on foot. Fresh ideas could arise through the stimulation of new experiences. The limitlessness of many changing horizons now explored by riders must have had a marked effect on the psyche, maturing the mind and enriching it with new power and potentiality, matching the expanded outer domain, now visualized, with an extended scope of inner awareness.

The Horse in the Hunt

The advent of the horse revolutionized the Plains hunting complex. As mentioned previously, Wissler's (1914) view of the horse asserted that the animal only reinforced already existing traits of the culture, including hunting. In the case of the Crows, that would mean that these people in prehorse times had already abandoned their former semisedentary horticultural life by separating from the Hidatsa to take up nomadic hunting. But historians have not determined at exactly what date this change in lifestyle occurred. Timing for this event is of considerable significance, however, because there is a strong possibility that the horse was causally involved. As Ewers (1955:8) points out, Denig (1961:19) and Bradley (1896–1923:179) independently date the separation of the Crow from the Hidatsa at about 1776, or a few years earlier. Ewers states: "It is probable that the Crow Indians did not become actively engaged in this trade (with Europeans) until they had acquired enough horses to make it practical for them to leave the Hidatsa and become nomadic hunters" (1955:8). Most interestingly, then, the horse has here been credited with bringing about for the Crows the vast cultural change from semisedentary horticultural life to nomadic hunting and gathering. Further, some evidence indicating an

[12]

even later date than formerly supposed for this change places some Crows still living in the former way in about 1801 (Le Raye 1908:172–73). Since at about this same date large numbers of horses were acquired by the Crows, this coincidence suggests a causal relationship (Mishkin 1940:23).

Plains Indian hunting was transformed by becoming an equestrian endeavor. The mounted hunt bore little resemblance to the formerly used technique of surrounding game, in which large numbers of people on foot were needed to stampede the buffalo or other animals. Mounted, in contrast, a small number of skilled horsemen could hunt game with greater efficiency and provide a long-lasting supply of meat for people of their encampment. On horseback, the time consumed in hunting and transporting meat was greatly reduced (Ewers 1955). Increased efficiency of hunting improved the diet by making meat more plentiful. Additionally, because of smaller manpower requirements for the mounted hunt, individuals not involved in the pursuit of game were freed to engage in other occupations.

A significant element of the mounted buffalo hunt is that it came to be looked upon as "sport" as well as necessity—an exercise in skill and daring. This phenomenon of the hunt as an exciting, challenging, exhilarating, and somewhat competitive equestrian endeavor became deeply rooted in Plains Indian culture, shaping concepts and behavior patterns that are tenacious. At the height of the horse era, the bison-hunting complex became imbued with the attributes of thrilling and dangerous adventure involving exhibition of masculine prowess—a contest for glory, praise, and prestige. Above all the chase came to be associated with throwing off the yoke of toil and escaping from the restrictions on body and mind which are imposed by scheduled labor.

In addition to the actual physical role it played in bringing about the new form of obtaining meat, the horse became symbolically linked with the spirit of boldness and freedom, the fierce pride in being nomadic hunters which characterized Plains tribesmen. Deeply inculcated into Crow culture from equestrian times was a strong value placed on these traits and an aversion to agriculture and related types of labor. As a Crow wrote of his people:

> The American native has been stereotyped as . . . built for activity and not for labor. The Crow typified this concept. Routine work was incidental to the Crow ere the days of his vast domain was shorn of its

richness. There was no need for organized or specialized labor. When needed, choice meats were easily procured, as "flesh on the hoof" stalked at camp's edge. . . . The common adage "no work, no food" had no serious connotations to the Crows, as it was their fortune to have owned a splendid land. [Medicine Crow 1939:vii]

Relating to their environment during the period of the great bison herds, mounted Plains tribes such as the Crow came to expect the gratification of their needs that their bountiful homeland provided. Exploiting its rich abundance on horseback, they did not develop the attitude of patient waiting for the fruits of their labors that is characteristic of agricultural peoples. Farming was now an alien experience to the Crows, and the philosophy of "sow now and reap later" was not preeminent in their outlook.

The Horse in War

Although intertribal conflicts were common before the coming of the horse (Ewers 1975), the increased contact between tribes made possible by mounted transportation increased the likelihood of war. Old rivalries were intensified among contenders for the best hunting grounds and pasturelands. As the horse became inextricably woven into the Plains Indian war complex, the prized battle steed whose speed, endurance, and agility made victory possible and insured a warrior's survival took on a value equaled only by that of the buffalo horse. Mounted warfare on the Plains took on an epic grandeur not achieved by tribesmen on foot. Its rich panoply of color, excitement, danger, and glory has been celebrated in art, drama, literature, and history and continues to stir the imagination of the world.

Contemporary Plains people look back with pride upon their tribal warrior traditions, and for them the memory of that era is indelible. Recollections of the old days of battle have become a legacy for the Crows, who are descended from the centaurlike warriors who were their forebears, and these remembrances are cherished within their society, even in the modern setting. There is among many tribespeople a desire to relive those times, and bitterness from their loss still rankles in their hearts.

Plains Indian battle was adapted to the horse; warrior and mount were inseparable. The mounted foray, or war party, became the rule.

After the acquisition of horses, bows and shields were made lighter in order to be carried more easily by mounted fighters. War steeds were painted and decorated to insure success and were given special charms for their endurance and safety. Whatever the motive for battle—old hatreds, territory, revenge, glory, horse raiding, or protest against white encroachment—horse and man were a military unit that became legendary. United States Army generals who were called upon to oppose this formidable mounted adversary during the Plains Indian wars signified their respect by calling it the finest light cavalry in the world.

Despite the fact that awe-inspired whites referred to fighting ranks of Plains Indian warriors as cavalry, however, they were mistakenly projecting their own military tactics upon the hostiles. For it is noteworthy that in battle each Plains Indian warrior fought as an individual, and concerted military action in the European sense did not follow from planned war strategy. Today, Crow Indian informants say they relate individualistic fighting to the past military defeats of their tribe. Historically, individualism has been a strong component of Crow culture (Marquis 1928; Nabokov 1967; Linderman 1930), and it has characterized traditional life in many spheres. In war, there was no real central authority. Though young warriors would listen to and heed the advice of older and more experienced men who had earned the title of war chief through certain prescribed feats of bravery and skill, they were not forced to do so (Nabokov 1967).

A warrior's independence of his fellows in battle focused him more keenly upon a close relationship with his mount. Though a friend or kinsman would be expected to help in case of trouble, it was ultimately the horse upon which his success, and often his life, would depend as he undertook his personal war exploits. Frequently, that led to a warrior's viewing his horse as an extension of himself. His feeling of oneness with the animal often caused him to identify with it. This sense of identity is strikingly apparent, for example, in George Catlin's painting of a Crow chief, in which warrior and horse resemble each other so closely (see illustration page 16). Not only do horse and man wear identical headdresses and matching accoutrements, but mane and hair blow back in like manner. Mount and rider are intimately attuned in a visible unity of forward motion. A sense of identity is evident in Crow traditions such as striking the face of a man's horse to insult the owner and extreme personal grief at the death of one's war horse (Curtis 1909).

The painting *Crow Chief on Horse-back in Rich Costume* by George Catlin (1796–1822) is a striking illustration of the strong sense of identity existing between a Plains warrior and his mount. Courtesy Department of Library Services, American Museum of Natural History.

The Horse and Women

Acquisition of the horse altered the status of women among the Crows, particularly because their society was matrilineal. Teepees and other camp goods were the women's property and domain, and women were responsible for moving them. Women, with their dogs to help, were the chief burden bearers in prehorse times. With the use of the horse as a pack animal, women were freed to a large extent from carrying their goods. Horses, in making life easier, doubtless elevated female status in society. Larocque wrote of the Crows in 1805: "The women are indebted solely to having their horses for the ease they enjoy more than their neighbors." He went on to say of the Crows, "They are always on horseback . . . everybody rides, men, women, and children. The females ride astride as the men do" (Burpee 1910:59–60). Crow women were noted for being fine riders. They had ownership of

[16]

horses and saddlery and took pride in them. Ornate bridles and other equine equipment fashioned by Crow women earned lavish praise from early observers (Curtis 1909) and became a tradition that remains to the present day. Unlike the women in some other tribes, Crow women played games on horseback, raced with each other, and sometimes shared the joys of the hunt (Linderman 1932).

Spiritual and Aesthetic Aspects of the Horse

The importance of the horse in Plains Indian life was reflected in spiritual and aesthetic aspects of their culture. For as people whose ethos dictated belief in the brotherhood of mankind with animals, and who looked upon their fellow creatures as coworkers and intermediaries between themselves and the supernatural, their minds had already been prepared for the reverence and near-veneration with which they came to regard this new animal. The intimate and life-sustaining partnership of the Crows with the equine species reinforced old traditions. Horses could impart vital information to people, and they sometimes spoke through visions and dreams, imparting supernatural and curative power to their human associates (Roe 1955; Ewers 1955). The Plains tribesmen's relationship with the horse became the epitome of human unity with the animal world. The horse was more than a vehicle of transportation, for it shared the glory of its own rhythm and motion with riders as no other creature had ever done. The animal not only carried people through space, it brought them forward into new times, both physically and spiritually.

Plenty-Coup, the most respected chief of the Crows, told his biographer in his own words how he and his fellow warriors felt when they went out on a war party:

> To be alone with our war-horses at such a time teaches them to understand us, and us to understand them. My horse fights with me and fasts with me, because if he is to carry me in battle he must know my heart and I must know his or we shall never become brothers. I have been told that the white man, who is almost a god, and yet a great fool, does not believe that the horse has a spirit (soul). This cannot be true. I have many times seen my horse's soul in his eyes. And this day on that knoll I knew my horse understood. I saw his soul in his eyes. [Linderman 1930:100]

A feeling of reciprocity permeates the Plains Indian world view, and accordingly, in return for the many benefits conferred upon them by the horse, it was customary to lavish the animal with care and attention. A boy herder would say to his charges: "You are my gods. I take good care of you" (Roe 1955:261). The natives' concern for their mounts did not escape the attention of some of the earliest white observers. Maximilian, for example, recorded in 1843 that the Crows "possessed more horses than any other tribe of the Missouri, and . . . send them in winter to the Wind River, to feed on a certain shrub, which soon fattens them" (Wied-Neuewied 1906). Another noted that the Crows "are very fond of their horses and take good care of them; as soon as a horse has a sore back he is not used until he is healed; no price will induce a man to part with his favorite horse on whom he places confidence for security either in attack or flight" (Burpee 1910:64–65). Ewers (1955:47) and Roe (1955:262–63) cite numerous examples of other Indian tribes' treating their horses less humanely. Crow belief dictates that a person will be punished in revenge for harming or killing horses and rewarded for giving them good care. In this regard, Curtis records the narratives of some of the "great men of the tribe," telling how they had won their high positions. One related the following:

> I was a poor boy. I had one mare and I cared for her like a babe. I took her to water and to places where the grass was fresh. I had a vision in which she transformed herself into a spirit-man and made known to me the secrets of multiplying the herd. You see the great drove I have now. If you are patient and care for the horses as you would a child, the spirit-horse will pity you and you will prosper. [1909:60]

Sometimes another animal species intervenes between people and horses. For example, as recorded by an early ethnographer, a Crow informant said, "See where I have cut flesh from my arms and wrists in the shape of hoof-prints. Of the spirits above a Blackbird came to me in my vision and showed me how to capture horses from the enemy" (Curtis 1909:59). I discovered continuity between Curtis's finding and my own regarding the association of the blackbird with horses when a present-day Crow told me: "The red-winged blackbird is always fooling around horses. It likes horses and rides on their backs. It represents them among people." This man said that his grandfather had received his horse medicine from such a bird and had passed it on to him. He himself came to possess great power over horses by virtue of this medicine. He related vividly many instances in which he successfully

[18]

utilized this ability to control horses: stopping a runaway horse in its tracks, asking a horse to carry a message to someone two hundred yards away, causing a mount to stop kicking and bucking, and being able to calm a harness horse when damage to his wagon occurred in the middle of a swiftly moving stream.

Another contemporary informant related to me a supernatural horse incident from far back in the Crow past. The story, he said, had been told to him by his grandfather, who had learned of it from his grandfather. A young girl had given especially solicitous care and attention to an old pregnant mare, and because of that she had been taken into the animal's confidence. Later in the girl's life she became an adept midwife, whose services were anxiously sought in cases of difficult childbirth. The valuable knowledge that she made use of to help in these instances, she later revealed, had been imparted to her by the mare in return for the regard she had shown for the animal.

A sacred horse dance was performed by members of a certain society among the Crow Indians. Those who participated in this ceremony were known to possess a powerful substance which could restore horses to normal when exhausted. The secret ingredient they used had come to them originally through a vision. It was especially useful when riders were on the warpath, to make worn-out mounts fresh again, or to cause a treated horse to win a race. Adoption into the horse medicine-owning society and possession of the associated medicine bundle could bring about prosperity through the ownership of many horses, for members were enabled to more easily capture as well as cure horses (Lowie 1924:329–34).

Just as Plains Indians dealt with horses in ceremonies, saw them in dreams and visions, sang of them in lullabyes and songs, and told of them in stories, so horses were often painted on rocks, buffalo robes, shields, and teepees (Alexander 1939; Warner 1975:90–121; Feder 1965:25–50). It was natural to turn to this admired animal as a prime subject for artistic expression. Some of the finest art of the Plains natives from the horse era onward depicts the equine animal (Alexander 1938; Feder 1965). Horse images, whether painted or sketched, were often given a three-dimensional aspect, whereas likenesses of people often seem flat. Significantly, many of the drawings of humans appear identical, with few distinguishing characteristics, whereas their mounts were portrayed more individualistically, with differing patterns and colors. Horses were shown as possessing spirit, their postures evidencing motion and fluidity, grace and speed, while human forms seem stiff and characterless by comparison (Alexander 1938, 1939; Blish 1967).

The Horse as a Measure of Wealth and Prestige

Taking into account the many ways in which the horse influenced Plains Indian life and the extremely high regard in which the tribespeople, particularly the Crows, held the animal, it was natural that in these societies horses became the measure of wealth. Fees for services such as curing or naming were paid in horses. Fines were exacted and punishments meted out in terms of horses. Prices for goods exchanged were set in numbers of horses. A wife was obtained through payment of a certain number of horses, and her social status was thereby determined according to how many horses were paid to her father by her husband. Possession of a large herd of horses by a prospective bridegroom was generally an indication of bravery. Since the animals were often obtained by raiding, a man who was skilled and daring could afford to give enough horses to the family of a desirable woman to win her in marriage.

The custom of buying a wife with horses, as opposed to being barbarous, as Anglo-Europeans have claimed, was in reality a successful mechanism for a society in which life was rigorous, dangers were many, and physical strength was essential. Wealth as measured in numbers of surplus horses carried the implication that the possessor had the most vital characteristics to fit him for existence on the Plains. According to Lowie, "The introduction of horses revolutionized the natives' economic conceptions," for "it created great differences in wealth and correlatively in prestige." Rank and social standing came to depend upon numbers of horses owned. The prestige of those who could afford to do so was greatly enhanced by lending or giving away mounts to those less fortunate. Paupers were people who "trudged afoot" when moving camp, while "favored tribesmen" owned large herds of horses (1963: 44–45).

As the standard of value in the Crow tribe, representing riches, horses became the most highly treasured and desirable objects for gift giving. During important occasions and in the context of many rituals, horses were presented to persons to be honored, as symbols of good feeling and esteem. Among the Crows, for example, horses were given away to people at adoptions, marriages, child-naming ceremonies, and tobacco society initiations. A proud father would make a gift of a horse at the time of his son's first brave deed. Horses might be presented to the needy or to participants' families at those times. Mounts were exchanged in other contexts simply to express kinship ties, as in the Crow tradition of recognizing close affiliation with a man's brother-in-law, who was often the recipient of a fine horse.

Horse Raiding

Although breeding, trading, purchasing, and gift giving accounted for the acquisition of some horses, generally there were not sufficient resources available to the Plains Indians to buy or trade for enough mounts to fill their needs and desires. For most tribes, horse raiding was an important source for obtaining this precious commodity. Elucidation of some of the reasons for the primacy of horse raiding is crucial to understanding the full importance of the horse to the cultural value system and way of life of Plains tribes. From a practical point of view, raising enough foals to fill the demands of the horse economy would have been difficult. Certainly some foals were born and raised, as stallions ran with mares, but with seasonal nomadic migrations, the rigors of cold winters with scarce food and no shelter, lurking predators and thieves, disease, and injury, there was little possibility of maintaining herds through replacement husbandry.

For a breeding operation to have been successful, foals would have had to be laboriously cared for and trained and would not have been fully usable until four or five years of age. Thus the first few years of life would be expensive in time, effort, and subsistence, with little or no return to the owner. How much easier and more productive, then, to rely for the main supply upon obtaining full-grown animals, already trained, from an enemy camp or white settlement! This practice is in keeping, too, with the customary outlook of the Crows, which, they say, still emphasizes immediate concerns rather than discipline for future goals. As one contemporary Crow explained his people's traditional view: "It is more honorable for a Crow to steal bacon than to raise a hog."

Horse stealing among Plains tribes was a complicated phenomenon, and one that became deeply entrenched in the culture. As an aggressive act, the horse raid was intimately tied into the Plains Indian war complex. The animal became the incentive, as well as the instrument, for battle; war and the seizing of enemy horses were indistinguishable in ethic and technique. The surprise attack with a quick getaway was the important strategy in both, and the merit of each act was directly in proportion to the amount of danger incurred in its accomplishment. Since, to tribes such as the Crow, warfare had always been thought of as a kind of "dangerous game" (Medicine Crow 1939:63), rather than an all-out struggle for conquest or annihilation, the horse-raiding foray fit well into the pattern.

Reckless daring and stealth were the prerequisites in planning a horse raid on an enemy camp, and praise was earned in proportion to the chances taken. Lowie asks, but does not answer, the question "Why did a Crow risk his neck to cut loose a picketed horse in the midst of the hostile camp when he could easily have driven off a whole herd from the outskirts?" (1920:356). The explanation seems to be that he did so to court danger and risk injury and death, in order to live up to the expectations of a demanding culture. Also, it is true that the finest and most highly prized animals were those tethered near the owner's teepee for safety, often with the rope tied around the hand or foot of the sleeping warrior to prevent theft of his most important possession (Ewers 1955; Nabokov 1967). Such closely guarded animals were the fleet and highly trained buffalo horses or the spirited and fearless war mounts, on whom the hunter and warrior depended for meat and survival. How much more useful would such horses be to their captors than many mounts taken from "the outskirts!" Little wonder that one of the highest honors in the rating system for a man's achievement of rank and chieftainship among the Crows was the theft of a tethered horse from the enemy (Nabokov 1967; Linderman 1930). Though prestige would come to a man who stole horses from the enemy under any conditions, and glory might accrue to a man who drove off a whole herd, the coup of the "cut horse" was an important stepping stone to highest honors and rank (Curtis 1909).

The horse raid, during the flowering of the Plains horse culture, became virtually a way of life, an all-encompassing goal and passion to young warriors in Crow society. All other deeds came to pale beside it. Horses were the most important booty, desirable as symbols of power and victory over the foe as well as for their usefulness. At the fateful moment, seconds before he dashed recklessly into the enemy's stronghold to seize horses, a warrior aspiring to glory would often make a sacred vow to undergo the sacrifice of participating in the sun dance if only he would be granted success in his feat (Nabokov 1967; Marquis 1928).

Revenge was often a strong motive for Plains warfare, and a horse raid perpetrated by members of a hostile tribe demanded a reprisal. Recovery of a warrior's own horses previously stolen by a foe was even more important than stealing new ones. Horse raiding became life's most exciting adventure for a warrior or for a man who wished to improve his status. It was a key to proving his manhood. If successful, it would gain him the accolades of society, the pride of his family, the admiration of women, a chance to advance his rank, and perhaps enough horses to give him wealth and prestige. Along with the passing of the buffalo hunt, the end of the horse raid was one of the most deeply lamented privations experienced when native Americans of the Plains were confined to reservation life and forced to obey government injunctions which forbade it.

Crow Horses in the Reservation Period

Once settled into the drab and monotonous life on the reservation, with the excitement of their free-roving days of buffalo hunts and horse raids only a memory, the Crows experienced diminution of their herds. The number of Crow horses dwindled from about fifteen thousand in 1880 to only a little less than a thousand in the late 1920s (Bradley 1970), following the United States government's program to rid the reservation rangeland of Crow horses. In 1934, when morale among the Indians was at low ebb, a man named Robert Yellowtail became the only native Crow ever to hold the office of superintendent of the Crow Reservation. As is true with so many of his tribesmen, horses are uppermost in his mind, and he still lives on his working ranch, with horses everywhere in sight. "Crows have always been close to horses," he told me. "Without them we're sunk. Today Crows still love horses. To separate us from horses, you might as well take one of our family away. It is inculcated in the spiritual makeup of the Crow people from the time they are little. Crows are like Arabs, with horses all around them, and they love them like members of their family."

Realizing the central importance of horses in Crow life and culture, when he came to office Yellowtail knew that the key to revitalizing his dispirited people was to bring back Crow horses. For this purpose he established a program which resulted in not only an increase in numbers of horses but also an improvement in their quality. The superintendent managed to import high-grade purebred stallions— "Morgans, Percherons, some racing Thoroughbreds," and "the best blue-ribbon Quarter Horses," he recalls, with which to improve the rough range stock still remaining on the reservation. "With the fine breeding stock they now possess," he claimed in 1934, "Crow horses are going to make history in Montana" (1937:3).

Being a rancher himself, the Crow superintendent was aware of the affinity of Crows for livestock raising, particularly horse husbandry, as opposed to their disinclination toward the occupation of growing crops, which the government had tried to force upon them. Thus he was instrumental in the movement to emphasize Indian ranching and phase out farming on the reservation (Bradley 1970). His program worked not only to provide the good horses that are necessary to successful ranching but also to breathe life into a people who were still the products of traditional Plains Indian horse culture.

With fine horses once more upon the scene in their homeland, the Crows' old spirit of pride in their horses was revived. This feeling ultimately came to be expressed as a kind of ethnic identity and started a new trend of horse interest, which has continued steadily upward from that time. As a Crow delegate to Washington during Yellowtail's term of office in 1937 phrased it:

> Fine horses meant everything to us Crows—they still do. It was like this: you wanted good horses for yourself, and not only that, you wanted them for your relatives too, because you want your relatives to have things as nice as you do. And to get good horses you used to steal them from other tribes or from the whites. I guess the Crows were about the best horse-choosers and stealers in that part of the country; at least we think we were. It wasn't the same as stealing is now, you understand; it was an honorable thing to do—it was like war. We don't steal horses anymore, but we sure still like them. We Crows like to feel we are riding the best and that all our relatives and friends are riding the best too. That feeling goes even for automobiles. But a beautiful horse is the best. [Yellowtail 1937:39]

The Horse in Contemporary
Crow Indian Life and Culture

Crow Horses as a Source of Ethnic Pride

During field work among the Crows, I found that the horse remains today as a tangible symbol of Crow ethnicity and as one of their society's strongest expressions of a resurgence of pride in being Indian. As a vital part of Crow culture during their past history, the horse has become a focal point in the struggle to preserve Indian identity in the face of constant encroachment by the dominant culture. The Crows today retain many aspects of traditional life. Ninety-three percent of the reservation population, according to the records of the Crow Indian Bilingual Agency, speak their native language. Perpetuation of rituals such as the pipe ceremony, tobacco seed ceremony, sun dance, individual vision quest, and purification in the sweat lodge reflects the old ways. The Crow clan system continues to operate, in spite of pressures to conform to the white social system.

In conversation with many Crows, they often reveal that the past is very real to them, almost interchangeable with the present, not historically segmented as in the non-Indian world. Often events which occurred last week or fifty years ago, or in the distant past, are described in the same time frame, and dates seem to have little meaning. The Indians constantly express their feeling that the glories of the Crow nation and the "good days" occurred in the past, before their subjugation by the United States government. Most Crows chose to take no part in the 1976 national bicentennial celebration, because of past injustices perpetrated upon native Americans by the government.

It is clear that when Crows speak of the beneficence of life before Anglo domination, they are referring to the age of the horse culture on the Plains. For them that brief but influential span of glory stands for the good life and has come to symbolize the ideals of freedom and dignity. Since horses made this former existence possible, and since the Crows were preeminent among Plains tribes for fine horses and skilled horsemanship (Curtis 1909; Denig 1961; Ewers 1955), it is understandable that when they relate to horses and participate in equine activities today, Crow people feel a sense of reverting to something that is uniquely their own.

Horses in the Contemporary Crow Value System

The values of the white man's culture are concepts that the Crows say they still do not understand or share. Many have indicated that they are not yet accustomed to the ideas of money or wealth as viewed by the dominant society. Bank interest, saving today for tomorrow's needs, taxes, and property mortgages continue to perplex them. It still remains generally true for them that "the Indian is not entirely capable of handling a monetary income. His cultural background and present training are such that the Crow has not learned to appreciate the time element of wealth. The present possession of money is more gratifying to him than the vast accumulation of durable wealth over a period of time" (Medicine Crow 1939:8).

As a result, Crows generally like to return, whenever possible, to traditional values, often using horses as symbols of status and prestige, if not actual wealth. Many who do not use or ride them still maintain a horse herd on their land by reason of their long-accustomed role. As a Crow informant explained, "I love horses, and I have a bunch of them at my place. They mean a lot to me. I would have them even if I were broke, as long as there was grass. Horses have status here. The Navajos in Arizona have some horses, but sheep are the mainstay of their lives the way horses are for us." Many natives have said that the sight of horse herds at pasture on the reservation reassures and encourages them. "It's part of our nature to have them," Crows assert. "Like a white man has to have a car, a Crow has to have horses around."

Crows virtually always speak of equine animals in the plural. Usually it is not one particular horse they are attached to but the idea of having, or being surrounded by, many horses. Today a Crow candidate running for political office may promote his campaign by driving conspicuously around town with a two- or three-horse trailer hitched to his pickup truck, even though he may not own any horses. Like his long-ago counterpart, who had to be "handsome on a horse" to attain high rank (Mishkin 1940:36), a contemporary political aspirant must have a solid image as a horseman in order to win public approval.

Numbers of Crow Horses

No exact records are available for indicating the size of the current equine population on the reservation. Since Crow horses are not taxed or required to be immunized, I was told, no one has taken a recent census. Officials such as Bureau of Indian Affairs and Department of Agriculture employees, 4-H Club leaders, teachers of horsemanship, and Crows who were most actively involved in horse-related occupations and activities gave figures with a wide range of variation. Estimates included a conservative "3,500"; "outnumbering the Crow population," which is about 6,500; "ten to a family," which would mean

20,000, since there are "about 2,000 families on the reservation"; "five for every Crow," which would total about 32,500; and up to "about 100,000." Uncounted numbers of mustangs still run wild in the Pryor Mountain area of the reservation, as well. Far more important, however, than figures concerning the horse population is the fact that every person interviewed on the reservation, irrespective of any particular qualifications, unanimously agreed that there are many, many more horses now than at any time since the reservation period began. All say that the number of equine animals is increasing and that horse interest among the Crows has risen steadily in recent years and is now at an all-time high.

Crow Interest in Horses

Evidence of the growing popularity of horses is the recent surge of interest on the part of young people in 4-H Club activities pertaining to horses. Department of Agriculture Extension Service personnel told me that when literature on many topics is distributed to people on the reservation, there is a far greater demand for that dealing with equine care and husbandry, nutrition, and training than for material on the subject of other forms of livestock or agriculture.

"The kids have a great desire to learn about horses," a 4-H official said. "Pamphlets on that subject disappear much faster than those on other animals, and this is increasing all the time. If we ask for youngsters to sign up for a rodeo, horse parade, jockey project, barrel racing practice, or a general horsemanship course, we are swamped with names," I was told.

> Horses are *the* thing in 4-H now; everyone is interested when horses are involved. We're trying to get a cattle project started here, but the Crows like horses better. We get few volunteers for sheep, swine, or poultry programs, and no one wants to learn farming. Nobody on the reservation shows up if we announce a baseball or basketball session. We need the parents' cooperation for success in any 4-H program, and rodeo is the only way to get it. They'll help to plan and run a rodeo and come to see their children compete, whereas they won't participate in other activities nearly as readily.

All who work with Crow young people agree that the "horse movement" is stronger than ever and gaining momentum all the time.

On the adult level, as well, the greater numbers of Crows participating in and attending various horse-related events and activities, with the consequent increase in horses on the reservation, are testament to the overall rise of interest and enthusiasm. In Crow country from early spring to late fall, races, rodeos, mounted parades, and encampments which include horses are held every weekend and are never lacking for participants and spectators. The almost totally horse-centered Crow Fair, which will be discussed in more detail, is eagerly planned for the next year at the close of each annual celebration—an exceptional circumstance among people who claim that they are noted for a lack of scheduling for the future.

The Return of the Crow Horse

The recent comeback of the horse among the Crows can be traced to the time of World War II and is explained at least in part by four identifiable factors in operation during that era. First, at the time of the war, old military customs with regard to warriors were revived for Crows entering the armed sevices. Many of these rites, having originated in the horse culture days, naturally involved the horse and hence refocused attention on the animal. Second, at about the same time, rodeo, an event requiring the use of many horses, became an important national sport, and the Crows, like some other American Indian groups, accepted it readily as their own. After the war, as a third factor, the Crow Fair was revived, having been suspended for the duration of the conflict. Since a part of its purpose was to allow the natives to relive the past and perpetuate old customs, the horse played a primary role, and continues to do so.

The fourth influential factor in the Crow horse revival was the beginning of the annual Custer Battle Reenactment at Crow Agency. This presentation, which was for a time a major Crow tribal project and tourist attraction, had strong appeal for Crows of all ages. It consisted of a restaging of the events leading up to the famous Battle of the Little Big Horn, the classic cavalry-versus-Indians clash, in which the Crows, who in real history were allied with the United States military forces, played the parts of the hostile Sioux and Cheyenne warriors who defeated Custer. The production included a portrayal of the white settlement of the West and the Indian resistance, dramatizing the injustices on both sides that led to war between Plains tribes and whites. Involved in the staging were hundreds of mounted Indians in full regalia, bringing back to life the days of the nomadic horse era. The climax of the performance is the Battle of the Little Big Horn itself, in which Plains warriors of several tribes were victorious over the United States military forces. The recreated battle was fought on territory very near its actual historical location and drew a great deal of interest from spectators.

Additionally, the reenactment fostered a rather rare sense of Crow team spirit (as well as inevitable controversies) and resulted in a great deal of fun and excitement. The "warrior craze," as some tribespeople call it, caught on, and even those without roles in the production were soon playing "cavalry and Indians" on horseback. Many Crow children then begged their parents for, and received, Shetland ponies, and as a result miniature "cavalry" forces continually engaged in mock battles at the reenactment grounds. The appeal of such equestrian games helped to swell the ranks of horse owners and riders, until a common warning heard on the reservation was "It's a dangerous place here, because if you aren't run over by a Honda, you will be trampled by a Shetland pony!" But as the Crows themselves observe, Hondas are no longer popular, and few bicycles are ridden, yet the horses and ponies remain—becoming more numerous than ever.

Horses and Crow Identity and Individuality

"The kids were losing their identity," a Crow teacher of horsemanship pointed out.

> Bicycles and Hondas just don't give them a sense of who they are. The kids are looking for something to make them Indian. Long hair, beads, and floppy hats don't do it. Those things make you a hippie, not an Indian. An Indian is an individual. With the horse, he gets a sense of his own identity and individuality. Individuality was always a part of the Plains Indian; that's what history tells us beat us in battles in the old days, when each warrior fought for individual honors.

As one of the Crow tribal elders put it: "To a Crow, one is not a man unless he does things by himself. Chieftains and warriors were self-made men in the old war days" (Medicine Crow 1939:12).

Horse-related activities on the reservation today are an outlet for the expression of individualism so important in Crow tradition. For example, in the sport of horse racing, man and beast are a unit, and it is "every man for himself" in the struggle for honors. The winner alone reaps the glory and intense pride in owning the fastest horse, which he has probably trained himself. Similarly, in rodeo, ordinarily no contestant is part of a team, but each rides for his own score. The effort is totally individual; the contestant pays his own fees and expenses and is free to make his own schedule for participation. This freedom of choice and independence of action are mentioned again and again by Indian rodeo contestants as being of deep significance.

Crow Indian Rodeo Participation

The great popularity that rodeo has attained among today's Crows, as well as some other American Indian groups, gives indication of the importance that many aspects of the sport have assumed within their life and culture. At first thought it seems incongruous for these people to be so absorbed in a sport alien in nature to their traditional ideology of relating to animals as brothers. The cowboy image and its related complex, however, are pervasive throughout the West, and Plains Indian people such as the Crows of Montana are no exception to the marked effects of its influence. Crow men on the reservation routinely wear cowboy boots and hats, Western-tailored shirts, and Levi's, whether or not they ride horses.

Motivation for the Crows' profound interest in rodeo is not traceable to one source, but rather it is multifaceted. As Ewers wrote of this contemporary phenomenon among a Plains tribe, "Their ready acceptance of the entire rodeo complex may be attributed to their background of skill in handling horses" (1955:321). Horses are used in all standard adult rodeo events except bull riding, and the bronc is the mainstay of the sport. Crows particularly enjoy the rough stock events, in which the object is to stay on a bucking bronc or bull for eight seconds and thus "conquer" the animal. They also like to participate in ranch-oriented events such as calf roping, in which a highly trained horse acts as partner and helper. Interaction with horses, the desire to be around them, handle them, and ride them, does explain a great deal of rodeo's appeal. High valuation of horses and of activities involving the equine species remains a significant element within the Crows' lives and culture.

Other factors, as well, are important in determining the satisfactions derived from rodeo. In the events of this sport, for example, there is not just interaction with animals but a definite representation of

Episode of a Buffalo Hunt by Frederic Remington. Some of the adventure and uncertainty of plains life in the bison-hunting days may be reflected in the excitement of contemporary rodeo events. Courtesy of the Thomas Gilcrease Institute of American History and Art, Tulsa, Oklahoma.

human domination over them. Admittedly, that gives the contestants a feeling of power. It is a particularly appealing sensation for a people who perceive themselves as having been deprived of their own power and autonomy by the dominant culture which they say is engulfing them.

[31]

Though this sense of domination over animals may be foreign to the customary outlook of the past, there are some elements in rodeo which do express old traditional values. For example, Crow rodeo participants describe the winning of a bronc-riding or bull-riding event as the most rewarding moment of their lives.

> There is nothing on earth like the feeling of giving a good ride on a bronc in front of a crowd, with everyone watching. You yourself know it was a good ride, and those in the stands know you gave a good ride. You did it yourself. No one did it for you. It's not like being a member of a basketball team. It's like an old-time warrior in battle who accomplished a brave feat, alone, and received the praise of his people.

Some Crow contestants expressed the feeling about rodeo that "it's a good place to release tensions and show the ability you have. Instead of going to a bar and getting drunk and hitting someone, rodeo is the place to express yourself." Evidently the sport gives vent to an enormous amount of the restless energy characteristic of Crow men on the reservation. As it relieves their frustrations in a culturally acceptable way, it also provides diversion to combat the restrictiveness and monotony which they see as resulting from government interference in their lives. In the thrills and suspense of rodeo, and in the nomadic and unregimented life of following the rodeo circuit "on down the road," there is an atavistic quality reflecting the excitement and uncertainty typical of life in the horse culture days. As one elderly Crow told me, while pointing to a painting on his wall depicting an old-time Plains Indian bison hunt, "We are not so many generations removed from that, and they expect so much of us!"

Writing of his people's history and culture, Medicine Crow gave the following insight: "The style of living among the hunting and roving tribes was active, changing, and eventful. They were not sedentary; likewise their ideas, ideals, and attitudes were not static. They appreciated the spectacular, the novel, and the unusual" (1939:10). Expressing the same concept in modern terms is the testimony of a Crow who had experienced a close association with horses all his life: "I went rodeoing; then I worked for a stock contractor, and I liked it. I started riding bareback horses at thirteen. It was rough, but I liked it. It was the challenge, not knowing what's going to happen, that I liked. It's the opposite of being a worker in an office, eight to five. They sit there all day, and know ahead of time what they'll be doing. I hate to just sit and keep records."

[32]

The spirit of the old Plains Indian custom of counting coup is inescapably present in the rodeo complex. Counting coup was a daring feat performed in battle, in which the body of an enemy was touched by a warrior with a special coup stick. More merit was earned when such an act involved a live, active enemy than a dead one. Thus the higher the risk and the greater the physical danger, the more glory accrued to the perpetrator of this symbolic act. It was central to the ethos of the Plains people, whose culture stressed the value of reckless courage. Rodeo is titled, with good reason, "the suicide circuit," and official programs and announcers generally refer to it as "America's roughest sport." Ambulances wait ominously near the arena throughout all performances, and people remark at the end of the day that it was a fine thing if no rider was seriously hurt. At the championship performance of a recent Crow Fair rodeo, a praise song was sung in the Crow language just prior to the festivities, as a petition to God that no participant be injured or killed that day. Danger is the essential element in rodeo and is a conscious part of the sport sought by participants— just as physical danger was once courted by warriors. It is significant that half of a contestant's score in bucking events is judged on the wildness of his animal adversary. Thus conditions which favor risk and difficulty give the prospect of more glory in the form of a higher marking. The audience applauds a winning performance, giving praise to a courageous rider that is reminiscent of the adulation earned by a brave warrior.

Crow women in great numbers flock to the grandstands on rodeo days to watch admiringly and cheer the contestants on. This important aspect of males "showing off for the girls" or of rodeo as a place to meet women was reported to be very gratifying to participants and relates to the tradition of physical feats as a way of gaining women's approval. Honor for winning is so desirable that I was told about certain men that "just couldn't make it" who bought their own trophy buckles in order to wear this badge of accomplishment even when they could not legitimately earn it. Belt buckles are ostentatiously worn by rodeo champions as Crow men of rank once wore their otter skins or feathers as signs of their attainments.

Modern rodeo participants frequently stress the significance of rivalry in the sport and admit that "we try to outdo each other." In this regard, as well, they are the counterparts of warriors who vied for the honor of the bravest deed. Regarding the cultural roots of rodeo, it is noteworthy that when one young man won the prestigious saddle

[33]

bronc-riding championship at the Crow Fair, his father held a ceremony for changing the name of his son in honor of the occasion. That is what the proud father of a son who had accomplished a brave deed in battle would have done in traditional times (Nabokov 1967).

Horses in Competition

Horse contests of various types, or merely owning or riding better-quality animals, serve as expressions of competitive drives for the Crows. In addition to the rivalry offered in racing or rodeo, an individual may try to win the coveted award given for the finest traditional riding outfit and equestrian accoutrements in the mounted parade, which is the highlight of the Crow Fair. Winning these events takes on added importance in Crow society, for there are few, if any, acceptable or readily available outlets in the sport, business, or professional world for a sense of rivalry. Crow individuals who "excel" in the dominant culture's sense are generally ostracized or brought back to the common level by social pressures.

Other than through their horses, there seems to be no special culturally sanctioned channel for nationalism among the Crows. But like their forebears from the horse era, who always took along their fastest horses to race against their hosts' mounts when visiting other tribes (Curtis 1909), today's Crows like to compete against members of other Indian groups by riding faster, better, longer, or more attractively equipped than their antagonists.

At horse events in which other tribes participate, many Crows would tell visitors that "Crow horses are the best." Or one would point out to me, "That man over there is a championship rider—he's a Crow." Another would say, "A Crow horse won the most important race here today." Crow Fair is officially entitled the "Teepee Capitol of the World," but the focus is on horses. Informants always mentioned that there were more horses in their fair than take part in any other American Indian event. Unanimously they voiced the opinion that "Crow riders are the best in the world." One well-educated Crow feels special pride in his belief that "though the Crows were one of the last tribes to receive the horse, we were the first to develop the horse culture." A prominent Crow horseman stated that his tribe has more feeling for horses than any other Indian tribe. He relates this belief to the fact that the Crow Fair is the best in the country. Having recently

The annual Crow Fair parade provides a modern-day opportunity for expression of the continuing importance of horses in tribal life. Photo by author.

Great skill and artistry are evident in the costumes, riding gear, and horse accoutrements proudly displayed during the Crow Fair parade. Photo by author.

attended the Navajo Fair, he said it was far inferior in every way. A young Crow man, whose buddy quickly nodded agreement, expressed his feeling of Crow superiority over tribes such as the Navajo this way: "There in the South, they have no good grass for horses. They have sheep and goats, and make turquoise!" He added, "My family has always had many horses, and my grandfather told us, 'A horse is the most powerful thing you can own, and the most important thing to give away.'"

Identification with Horses

As in the days of old, so today Crows often have a sense of identification with their horses as extensions of themselves. The fleetness of a man's race horse is a reflection upon the owner and his family. One racing enthusiast took me to see his victorious mount and explained that the power of his own special medicine, as well as communication between rider and animal, was instrumental in the win. The typical history of a winning Crow race horse is that it was bought cheaply by the present owner because it was sick or lame and was laboriously nurtured back to health by "putting a lot of myself into the horse." Identification between horse and man is also evident in the custom on the reservation that if a Crow owns a well-trained roping horse—one who consistently pulls the rope back to just the right degree of tautness when the calf is roped—the animal is called a "professional horse." I was told, "This horse is much in demand, and everyone wants to use it. The *owner* is highly respected for having such a horse."

In the recounting of horse tales such as that of Buckskin Bridle Bit, the famous Crow racer who brought glory to his tribe by his triumphs in spite of the fact that his adversary had all the advantages, there is unmistakable identification with the horse. According to this suspenseful story, Buckskin Bridle Bit, the protagonist, is described as a small, rough-looking, ungroomed, untrained Indian cayuse. He is pitted against a large, sleek, well-trained Kentucky Thoroughbred owned by whites. On the fateful day of the race, held near Sheridan, Wyoming, the "Crow rider of Buckskin Bridle Bit rode bareback, wearing a G-string and moccasins," while the antagonist was ridden by "a hundred-pound jockey in proper apparel and with fancy tack." Whereas "old Buckskin Bridle Bit raced barefoot, his opponent was shod. But old Buckskin Bridle Bit knew something was up, started behind, but late in the race forged ahead. He surprised all the bettors by winning and broke the world's record—he was like Man O'War." One can see here the element of a heroic epic in the guise of a horse story: the identification by the Crows of themselves as poor by white man's standards, and ill-equipped to compete, but as possessing enough fortitude, spirit, pluck, and good fortune to come through and win in the final effort. Indeed, it is the story of their own survival and that of their culture—still enduring in spite of heavy odds.

Horses and Sex Roles

Horse-related spectator sports are still male-dominated, a situation which reinforces the separation of the sexes that is so evident in Crow social life. Even as audience members at sports events, women and children sit separately from men. Women do not ride in horse races, and in standard adult rodeos they are restricted to participation in one contest, the barrel race. Thus sports and even the customary segregation of the audience act to preserve traditional male solidarity and camaraderie.

It is significant, however, that the queen of the Crow Fair rodeo is now required to be an "all-around horsewoman," in addition to possessing beauty and charm. This change reflects a recent trend, in which girls currently have the same opportunities as boys to receive formal riding instruction and animal-husbandry training. The change is largely due to the establishment of 4-H groups on the Crow Reservation. It represents a new freedom for girls, whose group activities since the reservation period began, particularly under the missionaries, have been confined to home arts and child care. It is a contemporary version, perhaps, of the change brought about in women's lives when horses first came to be used for transportation of household goods.

The (male) teacher of riding in the schools at Crow Agency said that he was proud of the progress of his girl students, and admitted that they pay more attention to his instruction than boys, who "think they know everything after the first ride." He related this difference to the fact that "girls never had the chance to learn riding before." Some of the older Crow women expressed great confidence in their horse-handling ability and often spoke of themselves as being more skilled in horsemanship than men. One woman took special pride in her success in handling a team of huge draft horses which always bolted away when a man tried to drive them in harness. "I was able to drive them right through the Big Horn River with no problem," she related. She felt that women have a special affinity for horses and that, in addition to their more gentle way of handling the animals, an important factor was appreciation on the part of women for the elevation in status and the easier life once provided to them by the animals.

Horses and Children

Crow children constantly turn to horses for companionship and recreation. They can easily hop on their backyard mounts to ease loneliness and boredom and to enjoy physical activity. They consider riding part of their nature, and they are aware of the role of the horse in their heritage. Youngsters say that riding is "an Indian thing to do," particularly in the case of Crow Indians. They boast that Crows are, and always have been, expert riders and that Crow children do not fall off horses as frequently as white youngsters do. Whites living on the reservation have a saying that Crow toddlers return home on their horses only to have their diapers changed. The young people's interest in horses is undoubtedly intensified by living on a reservation where there are no swimming pools, Little Leagues, or basketball or tennis courts, and where there are few, if any, concerts, plays, or such programs, which might divert them from the dimensions of pragmatic experience. "It's that kind of world here, a physical world," explained a college-educated Crow who is trying to establish some cultural activities for young people on the reservation. "There are no good reading or music clubs here, so our kids lose out on the abstract stuff."

Horses and Ranching

Of all available work options, ranching is the one most frequently favored by Crow males. Echoing the sentiments of cowboys, they are most willing to do a job "if I can do it horseback." Ranching in the Great Plains has a close connection with rodeo, and every boy dreams of being a combination rodeo star and rancher.

Land on the Crow Reservation is ideal for ranching, and the Crows' traditional outlook, stemming from their background as horse pastoralists, gives them a predilection for stock tending. As Ewers has said of the Plains people, their "preference for livestock raising may be traceable to accumulated cultural experience in horse care and lack of crop growing traditions" (1955:321). Crows feel that their heritage makes ranch work a natural occupation. "My father and grandfather did it, so I want to do it," the men say, and then they ask, "What did your people do?" Life as a cowboy is an existence they consider to be compatible with "the Indian way," which represents to them the antithesis of the work ethic of the dominant society. Though ranching can be hard work, in the Indian view it involves no "nine-to-five" schedules, and each day's duties may be different from those of the one before. It is a physically challenging life and often involves tasks which are accomplished alone or by individual effort. Ranching suits the Crows' needs in providing strenuous outdoor activity involving animals.

Crows have never become close to cattle, however, as they have to horses, and they are not oriented to looking upon animals purely from the vantage point of economic gain. From the beginning of the reservation period, the United States government constantly exhorted the Crow people to exchange their horses for cattle (Bradley 1970), so that they could realize monetary profit from their rich grazing land. But horses symbolized the freedom of past roving days, while cattle came to be associated with the white man's value system. Cattle had never held the important place that horses occupied in exchange, gift giving, and ceremony, nor were they a sign of prestige. Crows told me that some of their tribesmen who go into ranching on the reservation really want to use whatever profit they can make from cattle as a means of supporting more horses. In spite of their general preoccupation with the idea of ranching, very few Crows go into the cattle business as entrepreneurs, as white cattlemen do. Many natives state honestly that cattle ranching is just too great an effort for them. "The matter of raising cattle was too much work for nomads who had just recently become sedentary" (Medicine Crow 1939:21).

Crows who will not adapt to the regular hours demanded by other jobs often accept work as ranch hands. Next to rodeo participation and ranch work, the only popular career aspiration among the young, I learned, is physical-education coaching. Traditional Crows would not in the past, and will not now, willingly engage in work they consider degrading, such as agriculture or factory labor. As mentioned, it is likely that this frame of mind is related to the past, when acquisition of the horse transformed the hunt into an exciting and challenging occupation. It is significant that Crows who are presently employed in industries such as coal mining have generally abandoned traditional ways in other aspects of their lives, as well. Often these workers have been converted to some form of Christianity, have adopted the pattern of living in nuclear families, and speak English almost exclusively.

Although ranching, because it allows them to be with horses, is appealing, few Crows on the reservation ever become "successful" in the white culture's sense of the word. That is partly because of social pressures acting against entrepreneurial ambitions and is also related to lack of financial expertise and opportunity. The policy of local banks dictates that they do not customarily make credit arrangements with Crows, which would furnish the necessary money for capital invest-ment in cattle. Also, much Crow land is owned jointly by clan mem-bers, and it is difficult for an individual or family desiring to stock it with cattle to obtain the required permission from all who are involved. Additionally, a large number of Crows lease their land and live from the income. That is important, for informants say that eighty-five percent of the Crow Reservation is now leased to non-Indians. Taking all these reasons into account, it is not surprising that the majority of Crow men who desire the cowboy life ultimately settle for being ranch hands employed by one of the white lessees.

Horses and Land

For the Crows, "the business of leasing allotments was the thing that eventually warped the progress made" toward prosperity from native use of land on the reservation. By means of this practice, the greater part of the reservation came to be held in leases by white farmers and stockmen. "Leasing of land was indeed big business—for the whites." The profit from leasing his land was impressive to the Crow land owner, and "as usual the Indian had the wrong slant of things." For "in his estimation, as soon as he became a lessor he automatically became a 'rich man,' because someone did his work for him while he was idle and still received an income. He would refer to his lessee as his 'laborer.' White farmers and stockmen were known as so-and-so's 'working man.' It was true that they were working men— but not for the Indians by any means" (Medicine Crow 1939:15–16).

Leasing Indian land at low rates, and with terms favorable to themselves, has become big business for the whites, and many get rich from the profits thus realized. "The Indian himself is at fault, but he should not be blamed for his ignorance of business principles and wrongly construed economic ideas. The tragic thing is . . . that he is now contented to eke out a scant livelihood on his lease income" (Medicine Crow 1939:16). As revealed by both Indians and the white ranchers who lease their land, the situation has not changed. Whites justify their large-scale leasing of Crow land by reasoning that they will make good use of it for profit, whereas in their eyes the natives will not do so. There is a movement on the reservation at present, though, for the Crows to try to regain control of some of their leased land. Many of the natives relate their desire once again to make use of their own land to their involvement with horses, explaining, "When we get back our land we can have more horses." A number of Crows who had leased land to whites lamented that they could no longer own horses, because of having no grazing land available for the animals.

Leasing of their acreage by Anglos and general white encroachment upon Indian land are sources of deep bitterness to Crows, as the size of their reservation has constantly shrunk while their population is increasing. I was told that of the original thirty-eight million acres set aside for the Crow Reservation by the government, there remain now only three million acres. Significantly, horses are a focal point in symbolizing the past injustices in Indian-white land conflicts, because the animals require abundant land for grazing. Montana stockmen say they figure that twenty-four acres per horse are needed during the favorable eight months of grazing, and that considerably more is required in winter. Highly important in the native value system, their horses are still a rallying point for the Crows in their fight against land-hungry Anglos. People from the dominant society continually pressure the Crows to get rid of their horses, animals which they assert are not economically profitable, and urge that they be replaced with marketable cattle. That, as we have seen, the Crows are unwilling to do. Consequently, Indians and whites become polarized by different value orientations which center on horses.

Decimation of Crow Horse Herds

The killing of many Crow horses in the 1920s to make way for white ranching still rankles as the cause of deep anger among the native people. As one Crow man who had been involved in that tragic event in his tribe's history phrased it, "The big cattlemen were grabbing every mouthful of grass on the reservation!" During the early years of the twentieth century, the Crows owned unnumbered thousands of horses, many of them running wild in the hills. This situation made it difficult for white cattlemen to obtain unoccupied grazing land. To stockmen, the presence of horse herds meant that money was being lost on the grass they consumed. So the whites, who measured wealth by land possessed which was being put to economically profitable use, devised a scheme to get rid of the horses that they viewed as useless.

The Crows, still measuring wealth, as well as prestige and satisfaction, in terms of abundance of horses, were not readily convinced to lease their grazing land, with consequent loss of herds. As a result, heated controversy raged between Indians and whites over the issue of horses. It is particularly significant that in the early 1900s, horses, unlike cattle, were evenly distributed among the Crows, being constantly circulated through exchange and giveaway. That was not true of cattle, however, which were concentrated in the ownership of a few Crows. Thus the white value system appears to have been operating for cows, but not for horses (Bradley and Bradley 1976). This difference between the status of horses and cattle in Crow society clearly emphasizes the important symbolic role of horses as redistributable wealth.

The Crows' efforts to retain their horse herds on the range were to no avail, for the opposition involved powerful interests. As Medicine Crow recorded,

> It was the stockman lessee who finally succeeded in decimating the Crow horses. It was for the horses that the Indians refused to lease choice grazing lands to the stockmen, and this was of course a thorn in the path of the stockmen. They went to work and in time induced the government to rid the reservation of wild horses. The government informed the Indians that they must get rid of their horses within a certain length of time; after that the horses would be rounded up and killed.
> [1939:19–20]

The secretary of the interior issued the necessary orders for getting rid of the Crow horses. In 1919 the interior department sent out a circular including a section entitled "Wild or Worthless Horses," announcing that the grass consumed by Indian horses would bring five times as much revenue if consumed by sheep or cattle. The government cited the need of the country for meat and wool as a reason for "ridding the range of these worthless horses" and admitted that it expected to encounter "opposition from some of the older Indians and from non-progressive Indians generally" (Bradley and Bradley 1976). The circular thus clearly reveals that in the minds of both whites and natives, the issue of the horse herd removal involved ethnic values, including the element of traditional Indian identity as represented by the horses.

The government asserted that getting rid of Crow horses would result in more land being made available for Indian use for agricultural purposes and the raising of stock, but these two goals were never realized (Bradley 1970). For "after his horse was gone, the Indian no longer had genuine interest in his ranch life. The idea that he would raise cattle instead of horses did not work out very well. There is no doubt but that the loss of the horse was fatal to the culture of the Crow. He became poorer" (Medicine Crow 1939:21).

After the edict regarding Crow horses was put into effect, the government began rounding up the horses. Those animals with brands were returned to their owners when possible, and many others were sold. The remaining horses were shot, mainly by white gunmen, who were brought in for the job. Traditional Crows would not kill horses, because it was against their religion. Several informants, however, told me about two Crow men who broke with this mandate and were directly involved in slaughtering horses. Both names are still spoken of with horror on the reservation. The two men "died of horse accidents," one Crow told me, while another related that after the killing, both men "drank, beat people, had no luck with their families, and went to early deaths." A Crow who had observed the roundup of the condemned horses as a boy told me that bounties were given to the horse killers by the government for each set of ears cut from the horses they shot. "This caused greedy gunmen to go right into the Crows' barns to kill their horses," he remembered.

Thus, in an event which ever afterward would be linked in the natives' minds with the avarice of the white value system, Crow horse herds were decimated. "The Crows cried," informants recalled. "Killing the horses made the Crow people feel terrible, like killing their family." Many people voiced a feeling that "when the horses disappeared, our culture disappeared." Informants who experienced the horse killing in their boyhood invariably spoke of the stench from rotting carcasses which pervaded the reservation following the carnage. Several described blood from the equine bodies "flowing like a

[43]

stream" from the shooting area. One man vividly recalled a beautiful pinto stallion (a coloration favored among the Crows) as being the last to succumb to the white man's bullets, and described his grief at seeing its death struggle. Another Crow related that when he was a boy he had watched the terrible slaughter. He felt a special grief, he said, because as a youth he was unable to afford a horse, and yet he had to observe animals being destroyed by the hundreds. After discussing the horse slaughter perpetrated by the United States government, one angry native declared, "The Crows were docile then. If such a thing happened now, there would be trouble. A.I.M. would come in to the reservation!"

Writing of the reaction of his people to this bloody event which occurred when he was growing up on the reservation, Medicine Crow stated: "The whole affair was a great shock to the tribesmen, just as much as the previous clearing of the Crow range of buffalo was a sad blow. Other things being equal, the destruction of the horse was one of the basic factors detrimental to the Crows' problem of adjustment, for the Crow culture was based primarily on the horse." Not only was the animal "the most valuable possession" of the Crows, but "the horse was basic to the philanthropic system of the tribe." Thus, "with the loss of the horse, the Indian lost a great deal of his native philanthropy and group responsibility . . . becoming more individualistic, self-gaining, and money seeking, . . . like his pale-faced brothers" (1939:20–21).

For the Crows, who had experienced the disappearance of the bison in the 1880s, the shooting of the horses was a blow that represented the loss of the last symbol of Plains culture. It was no coincidence that a slump in what little Crow agriculture there was occurred at this time. Crow agriculture never returned to its former level after the horse killing. "The Crows, it seemed, had not gone into agriculture for the sake of money, but in part for the love of horses" (Bradley and Bradley 1976). In 1927 the commissioner of the reservation urged the Crow people to stay away from celebrations and tend their farms. This advice, however, was never followed.

Horses and the Crow Fair

According to the official Crow Fair program, this annual celebration, begun in 1904, was undertaken with a threefold purpose. Its goals were: "(1) to uphold Crow traditions and customs, (2) to encourage acceptance of a new way of life of raising farm and garden produce and maintenance of a good farm and clean home, and (3) to provide for exhibits of arts and crafts." Of these stated aims, the first one alone has relevance today. Every summer during fair time, Crows go back to living in teepees, often bringing their horses as well as their families to the campground, and they perform native dances and hold traditional ceremonies as part of the celebration.

The Crow Fair program records that "there used to be many exhibits in which farm produce, garden goods, and arts and crafts were judged in competition. There were also teepee displays, livestock shows, and visitation judging of homes and farms. Rodeos, horse racing, parades, and dancing have always been part of the Crow Fair." Only the last statement, however, prepares the contemporary visitor for what will actually be observed at the Crow Fair, a celebration which the natives call "the greatest in the country." Crows make it plain that they do not put on their fair for the benefit of spectators or white tourists. In contrast to some other American Indian festivals, such as the Intertribal Celebration at Gallup, New Mexico, for example, Crows say that they stage their own events and run them for themselves. Crows do invite members of some other tribes to attend, particularly those interested in horses and racing, such as the Navajo and Osage. And contestants from other tribes regularly participate in the Crow Fair rodeo. The real spirit of the Crow Fair was made clear when a white visitor stopped and inquired what time one of the events was scheduled to begin. "We have no special time to start," answered a Crow official. "We're not trying to entertain anyone here. We're just trying to enjoy ourselves and do things the way we've always done them."

Indeed, one Crow elder told me, "If you stay here on the reservation for the Crow Fair, you won't have to ask any questions about traditional Crow life. It's a reliving of the old way of life of the Plains Indians." Because of the importance of horses in tribal history, it is not surprising that at fair time horses play the primary role for the Crows in the process of enjoying themselves and doing things the way they have always done them. At the fair encampment I saw horses being ridden in every direction around the teepee area all through the day. Tethered beside the canvas lodges or at pasture adjoining the teepee area, there were pintos and buckskins, blacks and grays, sorrels and chestnuts, in

[45]

countless numbers—a scene reminiscent of the old pastoral life on the Plains. Notably, other forms of livestock, as well as farm produce, were not being displayed. Whether as companion mounts, racing steeds, rodeo broncs, or parade horses, the equine species was at the heart of the Crow celebration.

Symbolic Meaning of Crow Horses

Today Crows consider horses uniquely Indian and find them beautiful to see in the pastures of their homeland. Horses have come to stand for the old prereservation life, as well as for the peculiarly Indian present-day enjoyment derived from them. Bad feelings between Crows and white ranchers who lease or own land on or near the reservation still exist. The old grazing controversy remains alive. Testimony from local white rancher informants still focuses on resentment of Crow horses. Ranchmen say Crow horses are not properly cared for— that the Indians let them starve in winter and go without water in dry seasons. Whites claim that the natives do not confine their horses as they should, which results in the animals' trespassing on ranchers' pastures and yards. Cattlemen express concern about Crow horses' overgrazing the land. Above all, the whites continue to complain that Crow horses are not an economically profitable form of livestock. Crows, on the other hand, indicate that they like their horse herds to be abundant and see nothing wrong with the grazing situation, particularly since the reservation belongs to them. Agreeing with Crow Chief Arapooish, they think with good reason that "the Crow country is a good country. The Great Spirit has put it in the right place" (Medicine Crow 1939:vii). In truth, Crow country contains exceptionally fine rangeland, perhaps some of the best in the world. The richness of the grass makes their home territory a source of pride to Crow horsemen— but a potential source of revenue to white stockmen.

Whites claim that Crows' continual involvement with horse activities such as rodeos, races, parades, and encampments, as well as ceremonies that involve the animals, are important factors in preventing the success not only of agriculture but of business on the reservation. Such enterprises as the Crow Agency rug factory and electronics plant, which are now closed, I was told, fail when native workers do not show up regularly. One white informant on the reservation spoke bitterly in attributing the Crows' failure to "get ahead" to their "group narcissism and the fixation on horses and ceremonials." The Indians

[46]

use these, he feels, as a "way of fighting the non-Indian culture." He insists that "if it weren't for horses and horse worship, Crows would be more progressive." Instead of being "obsessed with horses and festivals," he would rather see them "interested in tractors."

Whites say that Crow employees are absent from work for the duration of many ceremonials. A Bureau of Indian Affairs official complained that "one whole floor" of the government office building would be vacated at such a time, since all those working in a certain section were clan relatives, who would attend the same event. At Crow Agency all offices are closed and operations suspended during Crow Fair, as well as throughout the week of preparation for it. At fair time tourists who come to the reservation find no one on duty to cook for them and no laundry or housekeeping tasks attended to in the tribal motel. Virtually all of the native population goes to the campground for the duration of the festivities, taking many of their horses with them. Almost all of this absorbing celebration, as we have seen, is centered upon horse-oriented activities.

Perpetuating the traditional value system which has been described, Crows today still give away horses during events such as naming ceremonies, family adoptions, and rituals associated with the tobacco society. This practice serves well to keep intact the implicit "Indianness" of these important celebrations and to separate them sharply from the festivities of the dominant society. The presence of horses at these times seems to lend an important sense of continuity, the animal becoming a kind of symbolic bridge between the past and the present.

"Among our people, for your brother-in-law to be given a good horse," I was told, "it means your sister is really worthy." Many Crows expressed the idea that "when you truly appreciate somebody, you give them horses." One person qualified this statement by adding: "Of course today, if he doesn't ride you might just as well give him the gift of four new tires. But a horse is the best gift." One man in his early twenties told me that it was sometimes a problem for a Crow of his age to own enough horses that he could give one to each brother-in-law when his sisters married.

Explaining the value of horses in expressing kinship ties, a teen-aged Crow girl described an especially close relationship she had experienced with her late grandfather. Just before his death he had given her a song to sing whenever she was in trouble:

[47]

> Horse will help.
> Horse has a God.

After her grandfather's death, the girl's braids had been cut off and placed over the old man's braids for his burial. He had left his best horse to her, since she was his favorite grandchild. This pinto which had belonged to her beloved relative symbolized for her the strong bond with him and also his belief that the horse could help her in time of need. She vowed that she would never part with this horse.

With some few exceptions, however, Crows generally say that they are not attached to any one horse. Ordinarily they do not seem to regard a certain horse as a special pet. Crows want horses around them in numbers and are grieved by the absence of their herds. People on the reservation are accustomed from childhood to seeing horses pass from one owner to another with frequency. Even the famed Buckskin Bridle Bit had numerous consecutive owners after his unprecedented victory.

The nearest thing I saw to a family argument among Crows occurred when a grandmother announced that the horse her grandchild was riding was to be given away at a forthcoming adoption. "No, it's not that one," said her daughter-in-law. The child heartily agreed, and it was noticeable that the mount he was riding was an exceptionally fine animal—a standout among the six or seven mounts owned by this family. It is still part of Crow custom to give away horses. Just as historically "the horse was the article by means of which wealth was put in constant circulation" (Medicine Crow 1939:20), so today the animal symbolizes the good feeling of relatedness spreading out among a network of different givers and recipients.

Animals as well as people were considered relatives in the traditional Plains Indian world view, and nonhuman forms of life were looked upon as brothers. Much of this ethos continues into contemporary times as part of Crow culture, but there is little opportunity now for people to interact with animals on the reservation. The horse is able to fill the need of many present-day people for kinship with animals. Above all other creatures, the horse had become close, both physically and spiritually, to the Crows' nomadic ancestors on the Plains. Consequently, the presence of the horse reminds Crows of this special relationship in their tribal past, even as their own daily interaction with the animal answers a continuing desire for a bond with nature. Horses are responsive companions, which can divert people from what Crows perceive as a harsh existence on the reservation. And as a form of nature possessing great beauty, horses are a satisfaction to the aesthetic pride which is part of the Crow heritage.

With insight, a native revealed, "Our horses represent an Indian means of fighting the mechanical age." Though the Crows admit that they want to keep the conveniences that stem from contact with the dominant society, and that they have become dependent upon cars and trucks, they still desire to have horses. Crows want the animals not only to ride but to insure that horses appear ubiquitously on the scene in their surroundings, representing the old pastoral image. Significantly, in the light of comparable data from other studies included in this book, Crow people indicate that with this status of the equine animal they associate the spirit of a slower pace. The horse represents values uniquely their own, which set them apart. With the horse, whose rhythm and motion relate them to a past that has deep value and meaning, they find refuge from the hectic pace of the white world, which they still do not completely understand or share.

Historically, those who have strived to acculturate the Indians, to make them conform to the ways of the white world, have often made it known that the natives must first be separated from their horses before they can become integrated. Medicine Crow has noted that "among other things which the tribe has had to discard in the civilization process is the horse. To be sure he did not voluntarily do so, but he was forced" (1939:19). The horse, among its many complex symbolic meanings, has become associated for the Crows with the dilemma of their state of transition. Through the horse, to which they cling in order to retain their own identity and ethnicity, they seem to weigh the whole question of their hesitation about moving forward into new times and alien ways.

Wintering of Crow Horses

The majority of Crow horsemen today like to keep their horses according to the old way, and informants made a special point of this fact when talking about their animals. In virtually all conversations, Crows brought up winter care of their mounts, even when by doing so they abruptly changed the subject. I never had to ask about this aspect

[49]

of horse husbandry in order to receive information about it. Crows stressed it to a degree that reveals the great importance they attach to the wintering of their horses.

Crow horsemen said that they generally leave their horses out with no shelter in the winter and give them no supplementary feeding of hay or grain, just as their ancestors did. Harking back to old values, contemporary horse keepers expressed pride in the hardiness that enables Crow horses to survive the rigors of the Montana winter unaided. Some horse owners indicated that in autumn they would cut down cottonwood trees, leaving them where they fell, to provide winter forage for their mounts. This practice follows an old tradition, mentioned previously, in which cottonwood bark served as winter feed for horses on the northern Plains (Ewers 1955; Curtis 1909). Writing of his observations of Plains Indian life between 1858 and 1862, Henry Boller described native horses as being "kept in good condition all winter" on cottonwood bark, which is "very nourishing, and . . . a horse will fatten on it" (1972:204–205).

Wintering their horses in the old manner not only relates Crow horsemen to their own past, it also draws criticism from their white neighbors. Members of the dominant society complain about "cruel Indians" who, they claim, let their horses starve and freeze. Thus the winter-care issue acts as a powerful force in keeping "the Indian way" separated from, and in contrast to, the dictates of the adjacent white culture.

Some Crows, moreover, insist that "wintered out" horses have been found to be in far better condition in the spring than those which had been sheltered and provided with artificial feed. The intense pride these people feel in their horses' toughness reveals the Crows' sense of identification with the animals, a reminder perhaps of the old unity between warrior and mount. Crows today feel that even though their tribesmen may be losing their former physical strength and endurance by succumbing to a "soft life" on the reservation, at least their horses— as their other selves—are perpetuating the hardiness required for traditional life on the Plains. It is apparent that the Crows' own historic ability to survive, surrounded as they were by powerful enemies, and later to endure white domination with much of their culture still intact, has come to be symbolized by the ruggedness of their horses. This idea is expressed in the story told by a man who in his boyhood had ob-

[50]

served the government killing of Crow horses. He made special reference, again and again, to the fact that *all* the horses had been shot
indiscriminately, not just the weakest or the "locoed" ones (poisoned
by eating loco weed), as the white horse-killers had claimed. Equine
victims of the slaughter included, he stressed, "the ones that could
winter by themselves and survive alone." His words expressed utter
disbelief as he reiterated his feelings about what was to him a prepos-
terous aspect of the horse slaughter. "Many that they killed were hardy,
and needed no care in a harsh winter. Those horses knew what to do.
They could make it themselves, on their own. Even the horses who
were used to the hard winter were killed off with the rest!"

Winter care of equine animals is directly related to Crow religion
in the minds of many informants. Crow elders explained that one of the
reasons supernatural powers had been ascribed to animals in their
traditional belief system was that "they could get along alone, unaided,
without clothing, shelter, and without fire." This remarkable ability
distinguishes nonhuman creatures from mankind, who requires these
artificial things for survival, and helps to explain the animals' roles as
intermediaries with the Great One. "There is power vested in animals,"
Crow traditionalists say, "because they can survive without fire, and
with no contribution from man!"

Treating their horses in a certain way—that is, wintering out—
would from the Crows' point of view, then, be the finest thing to do for
the animals. For this practice evidences admiration for their horses'
endurance and special powers, not callous disregard of their welfare.
Similar treatment on the part of non-Indian horsemen, on the other
hand, might generally be regarded as negligence by white society.
Though one could argue about deep-lying motivations and utilitarian
considerations, nevertheless the important point here is that social
distance is preserved through an aspect of horse care which has assumed ethnic connotations.

Crow Treatment of Horses

Because of the many benefits brought to their people by the acquisition of the horse, which are still remembered and appreciated, Crows
traditionally do not eat horseflesh. Most tribesmen believe, as mentioned, that serious harm or sickness will befall the person who abuses

or kills a horse. On the reservation today, one can still observe that good care and kindness to horses are part of the teachings which grandparents and other clan relatives impart to the young.

A Crow teacher related what he called "the first important teaching role in my people's history" to horses. "When a warrior in the old days owned six or seven horses," he said, "the warrior would instruct his clan nephews how to take care of them for him." Another Crow told of having the lesson of good treatment for horses instilled into him the hard way. "As a young boy I ran my little pinto racer very fast, and was beating everybody," he revealed. One of his elders observed that he was mistreating his horse, commanded the youth to dismount, and shouted sternly, "Now you run the same distance!" The chastened boy had to get home on foot. The man took the horse back and related the event to the boy's grandparents, who further admonished their grandson about bad treatment of animals.

As we have seen, Crows have been noted for good care of horses dating back to the old horse culture times. This custom persists, and it is accompanied by a strong belief about reciprocity of interaction. Crows warn their children, "If you treat a horse well, he will treat you well. If you don't, the horse will take vengeance." Many Crows express the certainty that "cruelty to dumb animals backlashes in your face. If you run horses all the time, you are a dumb kid, and something bad will happen to you sooner or later." One Crow articulated this sense of mutual obligation very clearly: "That's the kind of world it is here; it's like we always feed the river before we swim in it." Several recent drownings in the Little Big Horn River were described by this man, who pointed out that the tragic deaths are ascribed to a violation of proper reciprocal behavior toward the river.

The Horse in Peaceful Adaptation

Crows have a long history of peaceful policy toward whites, and they are perhaps outstanding among Plains tribes for that. In some episodes of military conflict between Plains Indians and their white adversaries, notably in the Battle of the Little Big Horn, Crows, acting as scouts, entered into alliance with United States forces. In general, Crows today are unlike some other Plains groups, who often seek to assert themselves against the dominant society by becoming activists. It is common knowledge on the Crow Reservation, for example, that only two tribesmen have ever joined the American Indian Movement (A.I.M.). Informants feel that horses have been important in keeping their people out of such militant organizations. One Crow who had turned intensely to horses in his own life, and was effectively leading young people in his charge to become involved with the animals, articulated this idea. He turns to equestrian activities, he said, "in order to keep fit, and to avoid the alternative releases of glue, dope, cigarettes, or liquor." He feels "those guys who joined A.I.M. are crazy. Someday they will know God, and get help."

The white stock contractor for the Crow Fair rodeo, who also manages rodeos on other Indian reservations, such as the Gros Ventre, Blackfeet, and Assiniboine, declared that "such an event as the Crows have here in their fair could not take place in those areas. The Indians there are still warriors, and would tear each other apart." During times of upheaval on many Plains Indian reservations, Crows have been noteworthy for remaining peaceful. Though many diverse and complex factors are involved, Crows themselves say that horses are influential in this phenomenon.

From the observations that have been described in this study, it may be concluded that the horse, with its long history of profound influence on Crow life, continues to be a highly significant element in contemporary Crow culture. Beyond its role in providing companionship, diversion, and recreation for people on the reservation, the horse remains as a symbolic expression of pride in tribal identity. The animal stands for the past, relating people to happier times, to the era of freedom before the machine age engulfed them. Through the rhythm and motion that they share with their mounts, time is transformed. Interaction with horses takes them back, even if only briefly, to the days, still vivid in tribal memory, when there was harmony between people and nature on the Great Plains.

Some of the functions served by the horse in the old nomadic life have been perpetuated into the present, even though the animal's paramount roles in the hunt and war were long ago obliterated. In certain aspects, such as its meaning in representing social acclaim and prestige, its importance in gift exchange, and in the spiritual and aesthetic realms, the horse still represents the old values directly. In some other horse-oriented activities, notably the rodeo, roles of the horse which are relatively new to the culture are also related to the past in complex ways.

[53]

Most important, horses, whether used for symbolic expression, competitive sport, or recreation and companionship, have enabled the Crows to combine preservation of the old ways with adaptations to new ways and changing times. This combination of old and new was singularly evident as I watched a street parade of horses at Crow Agency. The parade was accompanied by traditional chanting and singing, the origins of which are lost in antiquity. Yet the performers were seated around their drum in the back of a pickup truck which was equipped with an electrically powered loud-speaker system. Here was a reflection of the fact that one very important trait of the Crows throughout history has been their unusual ability to adapt peacefully to new circumstances. This adaptability, which is expressed today through their varied uses of the horse, has enabled the Crows to survive in the face of adversity, at the same time keeping much of their traditional culture intact. Regarding the recent comeback of the horse, which has been so vital in preventing cultural disintegration, one informant phrased it best in his own idiom: "The Crows came back to their original selves when they got their horses again."

REFERENCES

Alexander, Hartley Burr, ed.
1938 *Sioux Indian Painting: Paintings of the Sioux and Other Tribes of the Great Plains.* Nice, France: Szedzicki.

Alexander, Hartley B.
1939 "The Horse in American Indian Culture." In *So Live the Works of Men,* ed. Donald D. Brand and Fred E. Harvey. Albuquerque: University of New Mexico Press.

Blish, Helen H.
1967 *A Pictographic History of the Oglala Sioux.* Lincoln: University of Nebraska Press.

Boller, Henry A.
1972 *Among the Indians: Four Years on the Upper Missouri, 1858–1862.* Lincoln: University of Nebraska Press.

Bradley, Charles Crane, Jr.
1970 "After the Buffalo Days: Documents on the Crow Indians from the 1880's to the 1920's." Master's thesis, Montana State University.

Bradley, Charles Crane, Jr., and Bradley, Susanna Remple
1976   "From Individualism to Bureaucracy: Documents on the Crow Indians: 1920–1945." Unpublished manuscript.

Bradley, James H.
1896–1923   *The Bradley Manuscript in the Montana Historical Society Library, Helena, Montana.* Helena: Montana Historical Society Contributions, 2, 3, 8, 9.

Burpee, Lawrence J., ed.
1910   *The Journal of F. A. Larocque.* Ottawa: Canadian Archives.
1920   *Pathfinders of the Great Plains: A Chronicle of La Verendrye and His Sons.* Toronto: Champlain Society.
1927   *Journals and Letters of Pierre Gaultier de Verennes, Sieur de la Verendrye and His Sons.* Toronto: Champlain Society.

Coues, E., ed.
1897   *New Light on the Early History of the Greater Northwest, The Manuscript Journal of Alexander Henry.* New York.

Curtis, Edward S.
1909   *The North American Indian,* vol. 4. New York: Johnson.

Denig, Edwin Thompson
1961   *Five Indian Tribes of the Upper Missouri.* Norman: University of Oklahoma Press.

Evans-Pritchard, E. E.
1974   *The Nuer.* New York: Oxford University Press.

Ewers, John C.
1955   *The Horse in Blackfoot Indian Culture, with Comparative Material from Other Western Tribes.* Bureau of American Ethnology Bulletin no. 159. Washington: Smithsonian.
1975   "Intertribal Warfare as the Precursor of Indian-White Warfare on the Northern Great Plains." *Western Historical Quarterly* 6, no. 4:397–410.

Feder, Norman
1965   *American Indian Art.* New York: Abrams.

Garretson, Martin S.
1938   *The American Bison.* New York: New York Zoological Society.

Haines, Francis
1970   *The Buffalo.* New York: Crowell.

Hyde, George E.
1959   *Indians of the High Plains.* Norman: University of Oklahoma Press.

Kroeber, A. L.
1939   *Cultural and Natural Areas of Native North America.* Berkeley: University of California Press.

Le Raye, Charles
1908   *The Journal of Charles Le Raye.* South Dakota Historical Collections 4: 150–80. Sioux Falls: State Historical Society.

Linderman, Frank B.
1930   *American: The Life Story of a Great Indian.* New York: Day.
1932   *Red Mother.* New York: Day.

Lowie, Robert H.
1920   *Primitive Society.* New York: Liveright.
1924   *Minor Ceremonies of the Crow Indians.* Anthropological Papers of the American Museum of Natural History, vol. 21, pt. 5: 329–65.
1935   *The Crow Indians.* New York: Holt, Rinehart & Winston.
1963   *Indians of the Plains.* Garden City, N.Y.: Natural History.

Marquis, Thomas B.
1928   *Memoirs of a White Crow Indian.* New York: Century.

Medicine Crow, Joseph
1939   "The Effects of European Culture Contacts upon the Economic, Social, and Religious Life of the Crow Indians." Master's thesis, University of Southern California.

Mishkin, Bernard
1940   *Rank and Warfare among the Plains Indians.* Monograph of the American Ethnological Society, no. 3. Seattle: University of Washington Press.

Murdock, George Peter
1934   *Our Primitive Contemporaries.* New York: Macmillan.

Nabokov, Peter
1967   *Two Leggings: The Making of a Crow Warrior.* New York: Crowell.

Roe, Frank Gilbert
1955   *The Indian and the Horse.* Norman: University of Oklahoma Press.
1970   *The North American Buffalo.* Toronto: University of Toronto Press.

Warner, John Anson
1975   *The Life and Art of the North American Indian.* New York: Crescent.

Wied-Neuewied, Maximilian Alexander Philip, Prinz von
1906   "Travels in the Interior of North America." In *Early Western Travels,* ed. Reuben Gold Thwaites, vols. 22–24. Cleveland.

Wilson, H. Clyde
1963   "An Inquiry into the Nature of Plains Indian Cultural Development." *American Anthropologist* 65:355–69.

Wissler, Clark
1914   "The Influence of the Horse in the Development of Plains Culture." *American Anthropologist* 16:1–25.

Yellowtail, Robert
1937   "Fine Horses: Pride of the Crows." *Indians at Work* 4:37–39.

The White Mustang of the Prairies

2

One of the most vivid and symbolically expressive legends in the annals of the American West is that of the White Mustang. Inhabiting the vast reaches of the Western plains, the stallion was said to have "paced from the mesas of Mexico to the Badlands of the Dakotas and even beyond, from the Brazos bottoms of eastern Texas to parks in the Rocky Mountains," during an interval extending from about 1825 to 1889 (Dobie 1952:144, 170). Alternately known as the "White Steed of the Prairies," the "Pacing White Stallion," the "Phantom White Horse," and the "Ghost Horse of the Plains," his story occurs again and again in sources dealing with the frontier.

In *A Tour of the Prairies*, a record of his 1832 excursion into the plains of what is now the state of Oklahoma, Washington Irving described the White Steed as he had heard about him one evening around the campfire. In his journal entry for that day, Irving related that his party had been eagerly anticipating a buffalo hunt. There had been keen excitement among the hunters when a faraway object was sighted and believed to be a buffalo. At closer range, however, the animal was found to be a wild horse (1971:116). The manner in which this event is described gives the reader the sensation of first visualizing the unidentified object off in the distance and makes one aware of the overwhelming vistas of the Western plains as they appeared to an easterner. As the narrative reveals the object to be a horse, there is the sensation of a telescope suddenly bringing the image into close range and sharp focus. In describing how the horse was initially mistaken for

[57]

something else, the narrator adds a sense of mystery, a feeling of remoteness from his subject, making it seem unapproachable, a thing apart. This sighting of an ordinary wild mustang during the day, Irving wrote, prompted evening campfire stories of the superb White Steed who had been frequenting the area for six or seven years. The basic characteristics of the White Mustang are then set forth: his sex, color, bodily proportions, and beauty and grace, his wildness and solitariness, and the pacing gait which gives him such great swiftness that he has never been caught.

George Wilkins Kendall's *Narrative of the Texan Santa Fe Expedition,* resulting from his 1841 journey into the Staked Plains of Texas, also contains a description of observing "one day at sundown a drove of mustangs." Again, seeing them dimly at twilight imparts an aura of romance and mystery; they are not seen sharply, clearly, or close at hand. Once more the horses are first mistaken for other objects—in this case, mounted Indians. Thus suspense is introduced, a moment of wonder and a sense of the unexpected. Kendall, like Irving, describes the campfire setting as the backdrop for the stories told "by some of the old hunters, of a large white horse that had often been seen in the vicinity of Cross Timbers and near the Red River." Although he expresses the opinion that some of the stories "told by gossiping campaigners were either apocryphal or marvelously garnished," still he finds "no reason to disbelieve." Kendall notes that the "White Steed of the Prairies" is "well-known to trappers and hunters by that name" (1929:107, 109)—a rather poetic title, I think, for such men to have used in common speech, and thus an indication of his evocative power over their imaginations.

A significant aspect of the White Mustang tale is this element of its circulation by mountain men, hunters, and trappers. Of course, these were the men whose occupations took them to the wild country where the horse might be seen. A deeper meaning, however, seems to lie in the fact that such men lived intimately with nature and were often imputed to have a particularly keen understanding of the natural world not possessed by people more removed from wilderness. Such men might have a special feeling of kinship with the White Mustang, making his story peculiarly expressive of their ethos and way of life.

The White Steed is again described in Josiah Gregg's *Commerce of the Prairies,* published in 1844. The author states that he has heard "marvelous tales" of a "medium-sized stallion of perfect symmetry, milk-white, save a pair of black ears—a natural 'pacer,' and so fleet, it has been said, as to leave far behind every horse that had been tried in pursuit of him, without breaking his 'pace.'" Gregg goes on to relate that "the trapper celebrates him in the vicinity of the northern Rocky Mountains; the hunter, on the Arkansas, or in the midst of the Plains" (1966, vol. 2:207–208).

Many times during the period of his fame on the frontier in the nineteenth century, the story of the White Steed of the Prairies was repeated. Robert M. Denhardt asserts that all the early travelers on the plains heard of this fabulous horse, and news of his whereabouts was avidly sought. "For fifty years it was every youth's dream to capture and tame the 'White Steed' for his own." The mustangers, wild horse traders, he writes, tried every way they knew to catch him, including snaring him, creasing him, roping him, running him down, penning him, cornering him in a canyon, and keeping him from water, but all in vain (1975:117). One particularly impressive story tells of a hundred men on their best mounts trapping him in a circular arroyo. They chased him around the circle by turns until each of the hundred horses was exhausted; then the White Mustang *paced* up an unscalable cliff and went his way (Stong 1946:195).

But even in legend the magnificent stallion could not live forever; in tales dating from about 1881 to 1889, and in areas ranging from the Rio Grande in Texas to Phoenix, Arizona, the heroic horse meets death at last. J. Frank Dobie, in *Mustangs and Cow Horses,* gives a vivid and detailed account of the death of the White Steed, which was purported to have taken place around 1881. Since it was every frontiersman's dream to subdue him, and because "a small fortune" had been offered for his capture, the White Stallion was tracked relentlessly. Still he eluded his pursuers, pacing all the while and heading toward the Rio Grande River. When he reached the sparsely watered country of Texas, between the Nueces and the Rio Grande, he was gaunt from thirst, "evidently jaded," and yet he maintained "an alertness in ears, eyes, and nostrils." There he was trapped by a vaquero at a "boxed waterhole"—the only source of water for many miles around. Although the still-superb Steed put up a noble struggle, his endurance was worn down, and he was finally subdued by a trio of vaqueros, each roping him at the same time. They staked him out on the grassland with a sawed-off barrel of water within reach, but he never once ate a mouthful of grass or drank a swallow of water, and after ten days the magnificent creature lay down and died, unwilling to live without his freedom (1940:175–79).

It is evident that a pattern of repetition of the main thematic details concerning the White Steed of the Prairies has emerged, with remarkable similarities in all versions of the tale. The figure of the Mustang that has been handed down represents the crystallization of certain key traits which have come to distinguish him. He is always a fine stallion, whose color is white or, rarely, some variant of white, such as gray in Irving's description (1971:116), or white with black ears in Gregg's account (1966:207). The Steed invariably paces, and his gait makes him the epitome of swiftness. His endurance is legendary; no horse has ever been able to outdistance him. He is intelligent and wary, his ingenuity often being a factor in eluding his pursuers. He is noble in spirit and a paragon of equine beauty and grace, with a long and flowing mane and tail. The Stallion is often seen in lonely splendor, without the company of other horses. Above all, he is wild and free, never having been caught and subdued by man until his capture in the final cycle of tales. In all versions of those stories he dies of his own volition, preferring death to a life of subjugation.

These striking characteristics have created a powerful image of the Steed which is an appropriate and compelling subject for the lore of the American Western plains, and one that is in many ways peculiarly expressive of the frontier ethos. I would like to explore the dilemma posed by the figure of the White Mustang as to its underlying significance and timeless appeal. By analyzing the symbolic messages conveyed by each of his key characteristics, I will develop some of the meanings that are articulated through the Mustang's story. Within such an interpretive analysis, several meanings exist at various levels simultaneously; thus no single explanation has to stand as the one final answer. Different and even contradictory meanings may be evoked by the same image, and these are not necessarily reconcilable on a logically consistent level. Certainly symbolic connotations, because they are products of human thought, may reflect the ambivalence that is so often characteristic of that thought.

The Mustang as Hero and the Horse as Symbol

At the outset it is most appropriate for a horse to be a heroic figure within the context of the frontier West, as it can be said that the prairies once truly belonged to the horseman. The horse was the essential instrument by which penetration into the wilderness and settlement there were made possible. The frontiersman's livelihood, as well as his very life and safety, depended upon his mount. And beyond the utilitarian ends that it served, the horse was a responsive living creature. Particularly under the often solitary conditions of frontier life, it was natural that the horse would become more than a man's servant. Often it was a trusted partner and friend, his closest companion. Horses possessed beauty and power, but to make them useful for human purposes they had to be tamed—first subdued and then trained to do man's bidding. That meant that they had to leave the realm of the wild and enter the sphere of the domesticated. Although the process was necessary, it could be tinged with empathetic regret.

A well-trained horse became a source of great pride to a rider, for by transference the rider could make the power of the animal his own. A man could take unto himself the strength and swiftness that he harnessed with the mastery of the horse. A process of identification with the animal often took place, making each person yearn to own the strongest and fastest. The White Steed was the embodiment of all that was desirable in a mount; to use one writer's expression, he represented a "cowboy's wishful thinking" (Stong 1946:195).

Another apparent impetus for the creation and perpetuation of the stories about the White Mustang is related to the idea of the horse as a powerful symbol for man's conquering force. Conquering was a central theme in the American westward movement: overcoming all types of hardships and obstacles—the harsh climate, the Indians, the vast distances—and above all, conquering the land, coming to grips with nature itself and forcing it to yield, transforming the wilderness into civilization by the imposition of human will. I propose that this process of conquest may be conceptualized as an embodiment of the culture-nature dichotomy, a pervasive theme in the ordering of human thought that may also be expressed as the oppositions of tame-wild or human-animal.* The frontier is often defined as the place where civilization (culture) confronts savagery (nature); "taming the raw land" is a phrase frequently quoted to describe the winning of the West. What better

---

*Though I do not draw upon it directly here, the work of Claude Lévi-Strauss should be cited in connection with the nature-culture theme. See especially *The Elementary Structures of Kinship* (Boston: Beacon, 1969) and *The Raw and the Cooked* (New York: Harper, 1975). Very useful in elucidating the way in which the terms *nature* and *culture* are used is Sherry B. Ortner, "Is Female to Male as Nature Is to Culture?" in *Woman, Culture, and Society*, ed. Michelle Z. Rosaldo and Louise Lamphere (Stanford: Stanford University Press, 1974), pp. 72–73.

way to symbolize this process and the ambivalence and conflicting images it evokes than by a beautiful wild horse who is so resistant to taming? The White Steed is a particularly appropriate representation of nature in this context, for, riderless, he is the product of the free, open rangeland, a creature far superior in every way to the domesticated horses that have been produced by selective breeding. He is of the land, he belongs to it, and no man is his master.

Two of the earliest writers who gave accounts of the White Steed of the Prairies included in their journals some perceptive observations about the transformations of the taming process. Gregg noted that "the wild horses are generally well formed, with trim and clean limbs; still their elegance has been much exaggerated by travellers, because they have seen them at large, abandoned to their wild and natural gaiety. Then, it is true, they appear superb indeed; but when caught and tamed, they generally dwindle down to ordinary ponies" (1966:208). The author then goes on to describe the reverse process—that is, the change from tame to wild: "It is a singular fact, that the gentlest wagon horse (even though quite fagged with travel), once among a drove of mustangs, will often acquire in a few hours all the intractable wildness of his untamed companions" (1966:208). Anthony Amaral, writing on the natural history of the wild stallion, agrees, stating that "animals capable of domestication are known to be wilder . . . when they have gone wild." He quotes a stockman who observed that in a roundup "the hardest one to 'cut out,' the leader of them all in a mad race across the prairie, is the old, gentle, well-broken saddle or work horse, once he gets a taste of freedom" (1969:38).

Rufus Steele expressed the same concept, adding the man-horse identification theme to his colorful comment on the range-born mustang that reverts to the wild after a period of captivity:

> You can talk about your Patrick Henrys and your George Washingtons; you can warble about your country "'tis of thee," the Star Spangled Banner and our own red, white and blue; but the upright tail of a mustang that wore cinches for years and then got back to the great unfenced will continue to fan the atmosphere as the true banner of freedom that never does come down. [1941:188]

According to such evidence, then, a feral animal (a formerly domesticated species now gone wild), such as a mustang like the White Steed, would appear to be a more precise symbol of freedom and intractability

[62]

than a true native wild animal of the plains. Although the horse once evolved in the American grasslands, the native equine species became extinct here sometime after the last Ice Age. The mustangs are considered to be the descendants of domesticated stock, reintroduced by the Spanish, which had escaped and reverted to the wild. Thus the Steed, though he himself has never been vanquished, is descended from those who have been and bears within him the inherent capacity of his kind for both extremes in the duality of wild and tame. The paradox of his belonging to the species most typically in bondage to man yet being entirely free himself, lends emphasis to these oppositions.

Irving, like Gregg, also found himself drawn into contemplation involving this wild-tame duality, and gives evidence of the human tendency toward identification with a mustang just captured:

> I could not but look with compassion upon this fine young animal, whose whole course of existence had been so suddenly reversed. From being a denizen of these vast pastures, ranging at will from plain to plain and mead to mead, cropping of every herb and flower, and drinking of every stream, he was suddenly reduced to perpetual and painful servitude, to pass his life under the harness and the curb, amid, perhaps, the din and dust and drudgery of cities. The transition in his lot was such as sometimes takes place in human affairs, and in the fortunes of towering individuals;—one day, a prince of the prairies—the next day, a pack horse! [1971:122]

Here the free mustang is depicted as a privileged dweller in the Western wilds, untainted by the ills of civilization, which include industrialization. The writer is giving voice to a view that would become a persistent and romantic conception of the American West as a primeval paradise—a notion later referred to as "the Myth of the Garden."*

The story of the White Mustang expresses the freedom-captivity or savagery-civilization dichotomy that is intimately tied to the Western frontier mystique and seems to take on the universality of the nature-culture dilemma in a wider sense. For at the same time that the White Steed was greatly admired, and no doubt envied, for his freedom and wild spirit, the very people who extolled these traits wished to

---

*For a discussion of "the Myth of the Garden," see Henry Nash Smith, *Virgin Land: The American West as Symbol and Myth* (Cambridge: Harvard University Press, 1971), and Leo Marx, *The Machine in the Garden: Technology and the Pastoral Ideal in America* (New York: Oxford University Press, 1976).

deprive him of them. Countless attempts were made, time after time, to capture him, and in the several versions of the tale in which he prefers death by starvation to loss of liberty, there is no record of any thought of setting him free to save his life. His captors, like the one in the Will James version, simply let him die "of a broken heart"; it is clear they wanted him to live only under their conditions (Wyman 1965:313). They are never motivated by sheer aesthetic joy in the stallion's beauty and grace but rather are willing to destroy what they cannot subdue and possess. The White Steed, as an object of beauty, a thing apart, unsuited to a pragmatic world, must inevitably be sacrificed, and thereby attains universal significance.

Thus the Mustang seems to embody the duality intrinsic to the westward movement. Emigrants were attracted to the new land's wild splendor and vastness, yet at the same time these qualities frightened and repelled them. They wanted to settle it, tame it, and civilize it. Often they strove to create something that resembled their place of origin, even though they were destroying in the process those very qualities that had appealed to them in the new land.

The sense of mastery that was paramount in the conquering of the West found expression in the tale of the White Mustang, and in this respect it conforms to a pattern in which horses are commonly associated with conquest. The Steed of the Prairies, never vanquished in spirit, can represent the frontiersman's ambivalence about conquering—he wants to dominate, yet he admires indomitability, freedom, and wildness. This dilemma is partly resolved in the tale by the manner in which the White Stallion ultimately wills his own end rather than having death inflicted directly by man.

Traditional stories of historical mounted conquerors make explicit the close relationship that existed between their horses and their accomplishment of military feats. According to Plutarch, for example, the famed war horse Bucephalus was completely intractable until tamed by Alexander the Great (1949:3–4). Then horse and rider agreed that "together we'll conquer the world," and, true to their pact, they were partners in conquest until the horse's death (Klimo 1974:34). This classic tale illustrates the point that the figure of a horseman implies that a rider is already the conqueror of his mount, and his dominance symbolically sets the stage for further conquest. Power and might have traditionally accrued to the mounted man, whether he be among the plundering hordes of Genghis Khan or the feared Comanche raiders of

[64]

the New World Plains. In the American Western frontier culture, one's status and manhood came to depend upon being mounted; a common adage declared that a man afoot was no man at all.

The eventual capture of the White Steed was accompanied in the tales by explicit violence—more than would be the case with an ordinary wild mustang, because of the Steed's great power and endurance and his spirit of determined resistance. After the first vaquero had roped him, it required the strength and skill of not one but three men to subdue and throw him. Working together, the trio tied ropes on him, "fixed a clog on one of his forefeet, and staked him" (Dobie, Boatright, and Ransom 1940:178). Such details seem to be the expression of what Richard Slotkin has termed "regeneration through violence," a concept he applies to events on the American frontier (1973). The explanation offered by Slotkin's theory helps to elucidate the central dilemma posed by the story of the White Steed: Why, if something is valued for its beauty and freedom, does man set out to conquer and destroy it? The proposed answer is that a process of regeneration takes place in the conquering through the absorption of energy from the conquered. Thus one gains more power and energy by taming the fiercest spirit, through controlling something that was once the epitome of freedom. The greater the struggle, the greater is the resultant invigoration from the process. This idea may be somewhat akin to the motivation underlying blood sacrifice, possibly having the same conceptual roots. Such a practice, as described by anthropologist Marcel Griaule among the Dogon, for example, is based upon the notion that in ritually killing the animal, an individual could share his victim's "life force" (1975:131).

Though he is sometimes called the Deathless White Stallion, it is a paradox that in the tales death is inevitable for the heroic horse. He becomes a kind of sacrifice to liberty itself, to the values of individual freedom and mobility that he personifies. It is his thirst, in the setting of an arid land, that ultimately brings him toward his doom, and even the wind is in his captor's favor (Dobie, Boatright, and Ransom 1940:177). I find a striking parallel in the recent Western film *Tom Horn,* in which the hero, who does not refute the charges against him at his trial, also symbolically dies for his freedom. When Tom is hanged, no one is willing to take the responsibility of executioner, so a special gallows is designed in which water is used to spring the trap. Thus, as with the White Mustang, it is apparent that the very forces of nature conspired with man in the killing. It is clear that the stallion wills his own death by thirst and starvation in order to avoid enslavement. His sacrificial act heightens the power of the opposition between the tame and the wild—or the new order and the old, civilization versus savagery—and he is cast in the role of a victim who is trapped between the incompatible forces of culture and nature as they clashed on the frontier.

The Mustang's Masculinity

By choosing death over a life of captivity, the legendary White Stallion has enacted the "code of the West," which, reflecting the chivalric ideal, places honor above life. It, of course, is a masculine code, and the Mustang's identity is always male. His sexuality is expressed in the muscular power of his body and symbolized by his long, flowing mane and tail, which are emphasized in every version of the story. The White Stallion is usually described as being alone, as befits a creature superior to his own kind, or, less commonly, in the company of the band of mares that he protects. His aloneness and aloofness may represent not only his status as the paragon of all horses but also the high valuation placed upon the quality of individualism that is so deeply entrenched as part of the Western frontier complex. Ultimately, the lone White Steed must pit himself against a human force, and it is appropriate that as a classic animal antagonist he should be the strongest and fittest male of his species. Just as the westward experience was a masculine conquering, so the White Stallion will be vanquished by males. The human struggle against nature is often symbolized by a man-stallion battle that becomes a test of manhood. The American West provides a fitting backdrop for such a contest, as illustrated, for example, by Arthur Miller's film *The Misfits*. Here the hero is more than a cowboy roping a wild horse, for his defeat of the stallion takes on the wider dimension of man's conquest of nature.

The Mustang's Strength, Intelligence, and Nobility

Until men can vanquish him, the White Mustang appears to reign unchallenged as lord of the Western plains. Admired for his unsurpassed endurance and extraordinary intelligence, he is also depicted as generous and gallant, the noble steed. His anthropomorphization reaches its epitome in the "Little Gretchen" story as recounted by J. Frank Dobie in *On the Open Range*. The event was said to have taken place around 1848, when some German colonists were settling Texas. A little girl, riding an old mare to whose back she had been tied for safety, became lost when the mare strayed away from the wagon train in search of grass. The White Mustang suddenly appeared and led the old mare, with the girl, back to his own band of mares. The stallion, now as a tender and chivalrous patriarch, responded to Gretchen's cries by biting the ropes that bound her and lifting her up by the collar of her dress in the manner of a mother cat. The first time he picked her up and removed her from her mare, and the second time, after she had rested, he put her back on her mount and told the mare to take her back to her family's camp. So the child was rescued by the marvelous White Stallion, which she described as "arching his neck and pacing with all the fire of a mustang emperor" and as having "something about him" that prevented her from being "in the least frightened" (1940:103–109).

Similar stories center on horses who perform heroic deeds on behalf of humans, and often the horse, like the White Steed in the Gretchen tale, assumes a protective role involving supernatural power. One such legend relates that Saint Anthony, an Egyptian Christian who later became the patron saint of horses, was saved from a martyr's death at the hands of the Egyptian king by the actions of the monarch's own mount. As the story goes, this noble beast, who in the past had always been remarkably quiet, suddenly threw his rider and then fatally bit him, in order to prevent him from killing Anthony (Howey 1958:184). This legend and the Gretchen story share the dramatic theme of nature's intervention in human affairs through the agency of a horse. The impact of these two tales stems from a reversal of the usual order of the human-dominant-over-the-animal or culture-dominant-over-nature theme. For here, by means of actions that produce tangible results, an animal is able to extend itself into the human or cultural sphere through its own special wisdom and power.

The Mustang's Gait

The White Steed of the Prairies invariably paces, and to me that is the most intriguing of his characteristics for symbolic analysis. This gait is quite different from that of an ordinary wild mustang. With some exceptions, a pace is an unnatural gait that a horse may acquire through training. In a true pace the horse uses the legs on the same side of his body in unison, rather than those on opposite sides, as in the trot. Though there are some natural pacers, most animals must be schooled for this gait. It is relevant that Washington Irving wrote of the White Steed: "They say he can pace and rack (or amble) faster than the fleetest horse can run," thus mentioning two other unusual gaits for a range horse (1971:116). Five-gaited American Saddle Horses are trained to perform two unnatural gaits that somewhat resemble the pace—the slow-gait and the rack, in which only one foot is said to touch the ground at a time. Both are exceedingly smooth for the rider. In these gaits the exaggerated leg action of the mount coupled with the lack of movement in the rest of the animal's body produces a spectacular aesthetic effect: it almost seems that the horse is floating. Tennessee Walking Horses, another American breed, must also be trained to use the "walking" gait, or amble, for which they are known, though breeders say the horses are born with a propensity for it. Ordinarily, all these unnatural gaits must be taught, and often such horses need to be continually reconditioned to execute them.

Descriptions of the White Steed always emphasize his unusual pacing gait with its great smoothness and speed, a grace of motion that is awe-inspiring to the beholder. Indeed he seems to glide over the earth, and his pace sets him apart from all other creatures. I suggest that implicit in this trait is the idea that something of "culture" may in a certain mysterious way be part of the extraordinary makeup of the Pacing Mustang, setting him apart from other wild horses. Also, I see the pace as a device to attribute to him a unique power of movement, making him the swiftest and most graceful of all horses, and giving him the nearest earthly substitute for the wings of Pegasus. Thus, not only through the "cultural" association of his special gait might he span the worlds of man and nature, but with the inherent power of his pace to carry him beyond all worldly horses, he also seems to traverse a path that links the natural with the supernatural.

The only horse I have found to rival the White Steed for symbolic expressiveness with regard to its gait is the mount of Sitting Bull. Again, this horse's unusual pace is imbued with meaning. It was a gray, a trained circus horse that had been presented to the celebrated Sioux leader as a token of esteem by his friend Buffalo Bill Cody at the conclusion of Sitting Bull's season of participation in Cody's Wild

West show. According to the tragically ironic story, the rifle shots that killed his Indian master were heard by the nearby horse and taken as cues, causing him to go through his paces once more, as he had in the show (Vestal 1932:308). The same theme appears in the satiric 1976 Robert Altman film *Buffalo Bill and the Indians, or Sitting Bull's History Lesson*. Regarding Sitting Bull's role in his Wild West show, Buffalo Bill is informed that "Sitting Bull has decided that he will do the only thing that he had seen here that he would want to show his people." When Cody asks, "What's that?" he is told that "Sitting Bull will make the gray horse dance." Later, when presenting the horse to the Indian, Buffalo Bill tells him, "Chief, I'm gonna make you a gift of that dancin' gray. You two deserve each other. Shoot a gun and you . . . dance." Still later, when news comes of Sitting Bull's death back on the reservation, the Wild West performers are told, "They say the horse danced when they shot the chief" (Rudolph and Altman 1976:118, 141, 148).

As Sitting Bull's biographer described this event, the Indian police who had shot the Sioux leader were frightened by the horse's "putting on his stunts" at his master's death, and they viewed this strange phenomenon as "worse than the guns of their enemies." They thought that the spirit of the dead chief had entered into the performing horse. Here again is the concept of a human influence or "cultural" quality represented by the animal's gait. Also like the Mustang, the circus horse appeared invulnerable, for he was unaffected by the flying bullets and "came through without a scratch." Those who were present said that "he sat down gravely in the middle of all that carnage, and raised his hoof" (Vestal 1932:308). Or, as the poet John Neihardt describes it,

> Haughtily he raised
> A hoof, saluting, as a horse should do.
>
> [1935:87]

In this story I see not only the bond that linked an animal to its dead master but an equine figure whose special gait, like that of the Pacing White Steed, symbolizes his role as an intermediary between nature and man. The artificiality of the learned "circus tricks," or dance steps, exhibited by this horse is part of the human "cultural" world, part of the taming process that had been imposed upon the beast as "nature," linked with the same complex of domination that had conquered land, Indian, and animal alike.

[69]

The Mustang's Color

Whiteness is the most prominent attribute of the Steed in almost all versions of the tale. In a few accounts he is gray. Some gray horses are white at certain stages of their lives; the Lipizzan stallions, for example, are gray throughout their early years and attain creamy whiteness only at about age ten (Weeks 1978:1). Grays, then, are almost as close to white animals in the world of nature as they seem to be in symbolism. The Mustang's whiteness is the most complex and mysterious of his qualities and is subject to many interpretations, not all of which are consistent with each other.

Whiteness may represent the essence of the Stallion's wildness; in my own professional experience with stockmen, I have frequently encountered their firm belief that the whiter an animal is, the wilder it will be. Whiteness could also represent the Steed's universality, his composite nature, since white is technically the reflection of all colors. Or it may symbolize his spirituality, the supernatural aura with which many of the tales endow him—for gods are often clothed in white. Whiteness may be the expression of his goodness, his purity in the face of evil that surrounds him and always threatens to snare him. In this interpretation whiteness sets him apart as nature undefiled, primeval. White may stand for coldness, the antithesis of the passionate element of life; but a contradiction is inherent in that image, for "white heat" is the opposite extreme. Herman Melville expressed this duality when he wrote of the White Steed galloping "with warm nostrils reddening through his cool milkiness" (1930:276).

On a more mundane level, his color may be thought to stand for the white race. Such a meaning is imputed to the Saxon Horse, a British emblem of the conquering people (Howey 1958:168). The frontier experience of the American West has been conceptualized largely as a white Anglo-Saxon male endeavor, and only recently has there been appreciable interest in the part played by blacks, Mexicans, and other (dark) minority groups (Webb 1975). Indeed the concept of the Anglo-Saxon as the one people ideally suited to carry out the conquest of the American West has been set forth with conviction by Owen Wister (1972:77–96). It was not only the Anglo-Saxon's special traits, Wister asserts, but also the destiny that brought the man of this stock into partnership with a particular kind of horse, the mustang, as "foster-brother" and "ally," which resulted in the development of the New World cavalier who determined the course of history on the American continent (1972:81). It is possible, then, that some frontiersmen could have seen a reflection of themselves in the proud and superior white creature who appeared as lord of the plains. I find it significant that it is vaqueros who are ultimately responsible for the Mustang's capture. Symbolically, that has the effect of removing guilt from Anglo-Americans and placing it instead on persons of Mexican or mestizo descent. From this point of view, the idea of the dark foreigner as villain, not "one of us," assumes importance in identifying the destroyer of the freedom of the beautiful White Steed.

White animals have often been regarded as essentially different from those of other colors, in many cases as embodying the supernatural. The Plains Indians, for example, considered the rare white buffalo sacred and had many taboos about its use, particularly the hide, which was given to the Great Spirit (Roe 1970:715–28). White elephants are said to be sacred in India, as white asses are in Persia (Howey 1958:185). Though many white animals occur in literature, I have encountered no more memorable creatures than the two spotless and specially blessed white mules, Contento and Angelica, ridden by the padres in Willa Cather's *Death Comes for the Archbishop.* "They are as good as their names," their owner noted. "It seems God has given them intelligence. When I talk to them they look up at me like Christians; they are very companionable. They are always ridden together and have a great affection for each other" (1942:69).

Nor can one forget that the mythical unicorn was pure white. Melville's *Moby Dick,* with all its complex symbolism, however, is no doubt the best known of all white animals. In his discussion of the quality of whiteness, Melville includes a glowing account of the White Mustang:

> Most famous in our Western annals and Indian traditions is that of the White Steed of the Prairies; a magnificent milk-white charger. . . . Nor can it be questioned from what stands on legendary record of this noble horse, that it was his spiritual whiteness chiefly, which so clothed him with divineness; and that this divineness had that in it which, though commanding worship, at the same time enforced a certain nameless terror. [1930:275–76]

Here reflected are the ambivalence and mystery represented by whiteness, simultaneously inspiring both fear and a sense of holiness.

In the same passage Melville indicates that "always to the bravest Indians he was the object of trembling reverence and awe." Some

The Last of the Buffalo by Albert Bierstadt (1888). In
this spectacular scene an Indian riding a white horse is the
momentary conqueror of an animal whose species is soon to
be doomed by civilization. The rearing white horse appears
to endow the hunter with special power. Collection of the
Corcoran Gallery of Art, Gift of Mrs. Albert Bierstadt.

tribes of Indians had their own legends about the Phantom White Mustang, which probably antedated those of the white settlers. The
Kiowas, for example, believed that this horse could not be harmed by
arrows or rifle balls and could run unscathed through a prairie fire. The
Blackfeet considered him as possessing the potency to sire war horses
that made their riders invulnerable in battle (Denhardt 1975:119).
Navajos have a high regard for white horses, and their mythology
describes the sun and moon deities as riding on elegant milk-white
steeds. White is the color that Navajos associate with dawn, since the
early morning light banishes the shadows and mysteries of the night.
Because of this association, a Navajo who owns a white horse considers himself fortunate and believes that no bad luck will befall him
when he rides it (Clark 1966:22).

Throughout the world there has been a preference for white horses
as the mounts of the gods. Vishnu, the Hindu deity, is said to have
ridden a white (and winged) horse (Howey 1958:29). In Saint John's
vision of Christ in heaven as warrior and King of Kings, he was seated
upon a white horse (Revelation 19:11–16). Joan of Arc, later a saint,
rode a spotless white steed on her holy mission. Correlated with their

role as mounts for sacred heroes is the strong tradition identifying white horses as steeds of conquest. Of the Four Horses of the Apocalypse, each one a different color, the white steed is so designated, for "he that sat upon him had a bow; and a crown was given unto him: and he went forth conquering, and to conquer" (Revelation 6:2). Each of the Four Horses, according to the Book of Revelation, will bring a source of destruction to the earth, but it is notably the white horse who represents the force of conquest itself.

Worldly conquerors also have a strong predilection for white mounts, and many famous military leaders have chosen them as war horses. The pure-white steed Marengo carried Napoleon Bonaparte, Tor was Charlemagne's huge white stallion, and Old Whitey bore Zachary Taylor to battle under four different flags. Portraits of George Washington as a military hero usually show him astride a white charger, and it is difficult to separate the warrior image of Robert E. Lee from that of his gray horse, Traveler. Stephen Vincent Benet describes them both as "iron gray," noting that

> He and his horse are matches for the strong
> Grace of proportion that inhabits both.

[1955:170–71]

More recently, General George Patton was instrumental in saving the famed Lipizzan horses of Vienna from destruction by the Nazis during World War II. Thus he preserved for posterity the world's most highly schooled horses, trained to execute almost incredible feats of precision—all pure-white stallions.

Buffalo Bill, whose popular image is that of conqueror and despoiler of the West, is always pictured riding a magnificent white horse in his Wild West show. A poster once used in advertising the performance depicts two men on white chargers, one Cody and the other Napoleon (Sell and Weybright 1955:226). Rosa Bonheur's widely reproduced portrait of the triumphant showman astride his white stallion contributed greatly to his fame, and the poet e. e. cummings has celebrated Buffalo Bill as the one

> who used to
> ride a watersmooth-silver
>   stallion.

[1978:7]

Colonel William F. Cody by Rosa Bonheur (1889). In his public appearances "Buffalo Bill" Cody frequently rode a splendid white horse. This celebrated painting contributed to his image in the popular mind as a heroic conqueror and despoiler of the West. Courtesy of the Buffalo Bill Historical Center, Cody, Wyoming.

Buffalo Bill's favorite mount, Brigham, plays an important symbolic role in the Altman film *Buffalo Bill and the Indians*, in which he is referred to as "a magnificent white stallion," who has clearly contributed to Cody's "heroic image." As pointed out in the script, "When Bill's dressed for a ride and mounted on that high-steppin' stallion o' his, any doubts concernin' his legends are soon forgot." Buffalo Bill's haughty figure on his white charger contrasts ironically with that of the humble Sitting Bull, portrayed as a small man riding a small pinto. Later, when Sitting Bull finally acquires the tall circus horse from Cody, the Indian's status has been somewhat improved, yet the animal turns out to be a mare. When Sitting Bull rides into the show arena on this gray mare and is pointed out as "just a little old man," the response is "Well, maybe the horse is too large" (Rudolph and Altman 1976:47–126).

Black Elk, the famed holy man of the Oglala Sioux, though not destined to become a warrior, was granted in his early youth a supernatural vision to show him how to lead his people. In this vision many splendid horses appeared, and of these, twelve were white, with "manes flowing like a blizzard wind." White color in Sioux sacred ceremony stood for the north, "whence comes the great white cleansing wind." Thus, like the White Steed of the Prairies, these horses could symbolize strength and endurance, the ability to survive in the face of adversity, as well as purity and beauty. Describing the white horses of his dream, Black Elk revealed that "all about them white geese soared and circled" (Neihardt 1961:2, 23). These birds might represent winged spirits that attend the white horses; they also suggest an analogy between Black Elk's visionary steeds and the god-horse Pegasus, with his wings and white color, as well as his general depiction as riderless. True to a common thematic pattern, the white horses are specially set apart in the narrative by unusual characteristics.

Unlike Pegasus, however, the Pacing White Stallion was mortal. Though he lived in legend on the plains for many years, it was inevitable that he would die. For the kind of unbounded freedom that he represented ended when the frontier was closed, making his uncompromising spirit of liberty an anachronism. The new pragmatic order of the civilized world that was closing in on him demanded that he be usefully subjugated or else destroyed. Like the bison and others who would follow, he could not be left to exist for his own sake. But as people still yearn with nostalgia for the lost wilderness, so they remember the White Mustang who once paced across its limitless expanses in freedom, an image expressing the very essence of the untamed frontier.

REFERENCES

Amaral, Anthony
    1969   "The Wild Stallion: Comments on His Natural History." In *Brand Book no. 13*. Los Angeles: Westerners.

Benet, Stephen Vincent
    1955   *John Brown's Body*. New York: Rinehart.

Cather, Willa
    1942   *Death Comes for the Archbishop*. New York: Knopf.

Clark, La Verne Harrell
    1966   *They Sang for Horses: The Impact of the Horse on Navajo and Apache Folklore*. Tucson: University of Arizona Press.

cummings, e. e.
    1978   *100 Selected Poems*. New York: Grove.

Denhardt, Robert M.
    1975   *The Horse of the Americas*. Norman: University of Oklahoma Press.

Dobie, J. Frank
    1940   *On the Open Range*. Dallas: Banks Upshaw.
    1952   *The Mustangs*. Boston: Little, Brown.

Dobie, J. Frank; Boatright, Mody C.; and Ransom, Harry H., eds.
    1940   *Mustangs and Cow Horses*. Austin: Texas Folk-Lore Society.

Gregg, Josiah
    1966   *Commerce of the Prairies*. 2 vols. New York: Readex.

Griaule, Marcel
    1975   *Conversations with Ogotemmeli*. London: Oxford University Press.

Holy Bible, The (King James Version)
    n.d. London: Cambridge University Press.

Howey, M. Oldfield
    1958   *The Horse in Magic and Myth*. New York: Castle.

Irving, Washington
    1971   *A Tour on the Prairies*. Norman: University of Oklahoma Press.

Kendall, George Wilkins
    1929   *Narrative of the Texan Santa Fe Expedition*. Chicago: Lakeside.

Klimo, Kate
    1974   *Heroic Horses and Their Riders*. New York: Platt and Munk.

Melville, Herman
    1930   *Moby Dick.* New York: Modern Library.

Neihardt, John G.
    1935   *The Song of the Messiah.* New York: Macmillan.
    1961   *Black Elk Speaks.* Lincoln: University of Nebraska Press.

Plutarch
    1949   "Alexander the Great and Bucephalus." In *The Great Horse Omnibus,* ed. Thuston Macauley. New York: Ziff-Davis.

Roe, Frank Gilbert
    1970   *The North American Buffalo.* Toronto: University of Ontario Press.

Rudolph, Alan, and Altman, Robert
    1976   *Buffalo Bill and the Indians, or Sitting Bull's History Lesson.* New York: Bantam.

Sell, Henry Blackman, and Weybright, Victor
    1955   *Buffalo Bill and the Wild West.* New York: Oxford University Press.

Slotkin, Richard
    1973   *Regeneration through Violence: The Mythology of the American Frontier, 1600–1860.* Middletown: Wesleyan University Press.

Steele, Rufus
    1941   *Mustangs of the Mesas.* Hollywood: Murray and Gee.

Stong, Phil
    1946   *Horses and Americans.* New York: Garden City.

Vestal, Stanley
    1932   *Sitting Bull: Champion of the Sioux.* Boston: Houghton Mifflin.

Webb, Walter Prescott
    1975   *The Great Frontier.* Austin: University of Texas Press.

Weeks, Morris, Jr.
    1978   "Home Turf of Those Great White Horses." *New York Times,* 2 April, p. 1.

Wister, Owen
    1972   "The Evolution of the Cow-Puncher." In *My Dear Wister: The Frederic Remington-Owen Wister Letters,* ed. Ben M. Vorpahl. Palo Alto, California: American West.

Wyman, Walker D.
    1965   *The Wild Horse of the West.* Lincoln: University of Nebraska Press.

Rodeo Horses

THE WILD AND THE TAME

3

> The hero is a man with a horse and the horse is his direct tie to the freedom of the wilderness, for it embodies his ability to move freely across it and to dominate and control its spirit. Through the intensity of his relationship to his horse, the cowboy excites that human fantasy of unity with natural creatures—the same fantasy seen in such figures as the centaurs of Greek mythology.
> —John Cawelti, *The Six-Gun Mystique*

The New World cowboy gained his prominent place in the consciousness of Americans—indeed in that of the world—not by virtue of being a cattle tender but rather as a mounted figure driving unnumbered herds of longhorns over vast stretches of previously untouched land. Without the horse, the cowboy's particular form of work and his unique adaptation to it would not have evolved. It is understandable that his horse—his partner and essential helper in all his tasks—became the focus in his way of life, and often the object of his greatest concern.

It was the cattle herder's relationship with the horse that determined many of the traits characteristic of cowboys. These include his contempt for ordinary labor, especially farming, expressed in a willingness to carry out a task only "if I can do it horseback"; the possession of confidence, sometimes extending to aggressiveness, which shaped his self-image as a conqueror; and probably his adherence to a chivalric code often found among mounted people. There was about him, too, a closeness to animals, to natural rhythms, an undefined merging of himself with the beasts which so intimately shared his life and work, and with the land of which he became master.

The sport of rodeo as we know it today is a legacy from the trail and range cowboy, kept alive by his descendants, the modern cowboys and cattlemen of the ranching population. Rodeo is extremely popular throughout the contemporary American West. It is a particularly important part of the traditional way of life for people in the Great Plains, where there is historical continuity between the cattle frontier, ranching, and the "cowboy sport" which developed from it. The origins of rodeo can be traced to the Wild West show, as well as to the sports and contests that were first held by early-day working cowboys for their own amusement (see Lawrence 1982:44–82). Rivalry between cowhands as to who could ride the wildest bronc for the longest time or rope the liveliest calf or biggest steer led to riding and roping matches. Ultimately these became popular with spectators and developed into full-scale rodeo, in which the utilitarian skills of cowboys became intensified as the sport of cattle country, comprising both performance and contest.

Rodeo, in its particular social and cultural context, serves as an important ritual event, participated in and sponsored by the ranching population—and those who share that ethos—which serves to express, reaffirm, and perpetuate its values, attitudes, and way of life. Rodeo picks up the main themes from the life of the cowboy, identifies and magnifies them, and makes them explicit through patterned performances, almost all of which involve and display various types of horse-human interactions.

Like his counterpart, of whom it has been said "Unhorse a cowboy and you unman him" (Westermeier 1976:89), the rodeo contestant finds his identity through interaction with livestock, which are still essential to his way of life. Among rodeo animals, horses are foremost; they are involved in virtually all standard professional events, with the exception of bull riding. Horses are the rodeo participants' antagonists in bronc-riding contests and their helpers in the various mounted contests referred to as "timed" events, in which cattle are the quarry.

At the very heart of rodeo is the bucking horse, central symbol of its spirit, which has come to stand for the West itself. Born out of the needs of ranching, and exaggerated for the sport of rodeo, the contest of riding a bucking horse, in my view, serves to express man's basic concern with the phenomenon of subduing that which is free, taming that which is wild, and measuring his own part in it. Rodeo people say of their classic saddle bronc event that it "shows the process of making a bronc into a partner."

Of all animals, I find that the horse is uniquely suited to represent, and demonstrate through constant recapitulation, the conquest of the wild—the extension of culture into nature. For the horse embodies, and is able to exhibit, the polarities of wild/tame, and within one species it encompasses the varying degrees between them. The equine animal in America includes many gradations along a continuum which I see as existing between wild and tame. Near the wild pole are the feral animals descended from the original Spanish mustangs, a few of which still remain in the West, and which presumably have never been handled by man. Next in progression are broncs, which can usually be handled to some degree, and may be halter-broken, but cannot be easily ridden. Near the tame pole in this conceptual scheme are the trained saddle horses—dependable, safe, and obedient to the rider. Then there are the horses that go further, to learn the skills of calf roping and steer roping, which require still more cooperation between mount and man. Advancing even closer to tame, and in the direction away from nature toward culture, are the highly trained animals such as dressage horses who perform intricate feats for their riders. In rodeo, novelty acts involving clowns and their trained horses are in this category. Still further along in this direction are various high-schooled horses which can perform tricks and sequences under the tutelage of a trainer without a rider on their backs. Some of the maneuvers of calf roping are in this category, since the horse must carry them out after the rider has dismounted.

Thus I am asserting that the horse, with its many forms running from wild to tame, serves as a symbolic bridge between nature and culture. Since the species partakes of both realms, an individual horse has within it the potentialities for many of the stages in domestication which the species may exemplify. One who deals with horses becomes aware of the ease of transformation which they frequently make evident. My own mare, who is well trained and quite obedient during a ride, when turned out into pasture afterward may kick and buck wildly, momentarily resembling an untamed range bronc. She will swerve sharply at such a time and gallop away at a pace little resembling the modulated canter that she had just performed under saddle. If I tried to catch her at that moment it would be impossible, yet a short time later she will come to the gate as docile as a pet. The facility with which the spheres of wild and tame are apparently entered and reentered by the equine spirit is a remarkable quality of this animal.

It is this very quality of horses that a former saddle bronc champion who is now a rodeo manager and director of a rodeo bronc-breeding farm recognized when we talked about preserving wilderness. Elucidating the saddle horse's affinity for the wild, which paradoxically exists simultaneously with its tameness, he said, "My idea is to keep cars and motorbikes out of a wild area. But a horse is different; a horse is almost a wild animal, and one should be able to ride him into it."

This dual nature, I think, has particularly fascinated people, though generally not on a conscious level, and accounts for the very special position of the horse as a symbol in traversing the pathways between the wild and the tame. Other animals, of course, possess this quality to some degree, but the horse, through its various well-defined roles within the fabric of human society, particularly in the West, exemplifies it to a much greater extent and displays it more obviously.

To be useful for human purposes, a horse must be transformed from wild to tame, even though the species is a domesticated one. Generally, the tradition in the East is to train a horse very gradually, starting even from the day of its birth, when as a foal it is first handled by people. Thus it grows up familiar with human contact; it is halter-broken at a few months of age, is often trained to commands on a lunge line when a yearling, and is perhaps broken to harness by two years. When it is old enough to bear the weight of a rider, the animal is already accustomed to the idea of human control, though it can still be fractious. On the Western range, by contrast, a colt may come to his first day of training with very little, if any, past experience with people and no concept of being subject to their domination. Thus an entirely different situation exists, in which there is an immediate and intense human-animal contest; it is often interpreted as a "battle of wills," in which a person opposes the brute strength of the horse with his own type of weapons—whip, spur, and bit, the instruments of culture—because he is inferior to the animal in muscular strength and power. There results a dramatic process, characteristically abrupt and violent, which has become universally symbolic for the act of conquering itself, the process of extending culture over nature.

Working cowboys were by necessity intimately concerned with this process, because the maintenance of their way of life depended upon the possession of riding mounts trained for absolute obedience. Most cowboys probably broke their own horses as part of their job, though there were on the early range "bronco-busters," men whose special business it was to travel around and perform this service for a fee. A usable "broke" horse was then, as it is now, not just a dependable work partner but also a source of satisfaction to a cowboy, ranchman, or rodeo hand.

Within the context of rodeo, as we shall see, the wild-to-tame transformation is dramatized and explored. The capacity of the equine species to embody varying degrees of wild and tame is represented by the many different categories of horses which occupy particular roles in the various events included in the cowboy sport.

Wild Horses

From the earliest days on the American frontier, wild horses have held a fascination for travelers who were fortunate enough to see them. The transformations of the taming process often arrested the attention of perceptive chroniclers such as Washington Irving and Josiah Gregg, whose accounts are described in connection with the White Mustang of the Prairies (see pp. 62–63), and who expressed empathetic identification with the freedom-to-slavery transition. Fully trained and obedient mounts, however, can revert to the feral state, as once did the Spanish mustangs who gained their freedom on the New World Plains. Still enduring, the one thing that the wild mustang represents in the human imagination is freedom. Hope Ryden emphasized this point when she wrote:

> The wild horse in America has a romantic history that dates back nearly four centuries. His domestic ancestors carried the Conquistadors through the unexplored territory, transformed the Indians' style of life, and gave inspiration to such artists as Remington and Russell. The age of exploration might better have been called the Age of the Spanish Horse, for without this particular type of horse, the New World would have been almost impenetrable. But the most interesting thing this horse ever did in America he did for himself when he took his freedom. [Serven 1972:17]

In the conquering of the mustangs, frontiersmen found expression for the same sense of mastery which was paramount in the conquest of the West. But, as expressed in the tale of the White Stallion, there was (and often still is) a contradiction, for at the same time that men wished to conquer the mustangs, they also admired their wildness and indomitability. It is this very quality of ambivalence which I see strongly emphasized as a theme in rodeo.

Ranch/rodeo people express the need to recapitulate the taming of the wild in a ritual glorification of the process, which they have struc-

[82]

tured into a sport. They long to be the conqueror, the winner, the one who can ride the unridable, who can defeat the rankest animal. They say there is no feeling on earth so good as the satisfaction that comes from knowing you have done it, you have made a good ride. Yet at the same time they want the wildness of the animal preserved, so that they may continue to pit themselves against it. Significantly, broncs are never demonstrably changed by the events of modern rodeo; they are not "broken" in the arena, and they still appear wild when they leave it after each performance. (In very early rodeo, horse and rider were turned loose, and the contest was continued until the horse stopped bucking or the rider was thrown off.) Today, the eight-second buzzer abruptly halts the contest, and the broncs are not literally "conquered" (though the word is used) by the contestants in the same sense that, say, the bull in a Spanish bullfight is ultimately vanquished by the matador. It is indeed remarkable the way that this contradiction has been made a basic element of rodeo. For in the scoring procedure, the marking for the horse—based on its "wildness," those qualities which have made it the most difficult to ride—counts just as much toward the contestant's final score as the rider's demonstration of skill and control. This preordained and structured counterbalance between the forces of rider and horse, tame and wild, dominance and resistance, represents the essence of the sport. The spirit of these oppositions is reflected by the oft-repeated rodeo verse

> There isn't a bronc
> That can't be rode;
> There isn't a cowboy
> That can't be throwed.

The wild horse remains as a symbol of the wildness of the Old West, and of the excitement of taming it. The exhilaration born of the gigantic struggle between man and nature on the frontier came to an end, and its loss is mourned. Nostalgia makes people look backward to the challenge. Cattlemen from the beginning have glorified the early days of their historic struggle, and they continue to look back with longing toward a vanishing way of life. They often dwell on the advantages of the old days, and consciously or unconsciously they try to recreate the past. Ranch/rodeo people tend to cling to traditional values and a way of life that do not always fit the context of modern times. They still place horses at the center of existence, and through interaction with these animals they feel that the pace of life is in tune with the spirit of the cattle frontier. Rodeo is a major factor in perpetuating this mystique, and in keeping alive the essence of the wild-to-tame transformation which has come to have such deep meaning in the value system of the people involved.

The Mustangs

At the wildest end of the spectrum are the few remaining mustang herds which still run free in certain areas of Western rangeland. These feral animals are presumed to be descendants of the domesticated Spanish horses that were brought to the New World and have reverted to the wild state. Their continued existence is precarious, because of dwindling land and the controversy which rages about their status and value. Those who want the mustangs destroyed say that they compete with cattle and domestic horses for grass, and that they use land which should be reserved for game animals. Since mustangs are feral and not native wild animals, their detractors claim that they upset the natural balance of the ecosystem. Defenders look upon the wild horses as living symbols of the historic and pioneer spirit of the West. They also point out that even though native wild horses became extinct in North America as a result of some undetermined cause operating just after the last Ice Age, they had previously evolved as a species on the plains of this continent and therefore would still be compatible with prairie ecology.

Even when their own ranches are located far from the regions where feral equines could be a threat, cattlemen as a whole show much preoccupation with the subject of mustangs. The editor of the ranch-rodeo magazine *Hoof and Horn* describes the difficulties which beset the cattle industry. He complains that "in some areas, because of a foolish law, half-starved and worthless wild horses and burros roam the lands the ranchers pay to lease, competing for the sparse grass with the cattle" (Searle 1977:3).

Beyond their economic interests, which in some cases are a very real concern, stockmen on a deeper level generally emphasize the role of "the wild" in opposing their interests and tend to view it as "the enemy" to a degree that often goes beyond practicality. Ranchers speak with disdain of the mustangs, asserting that "they take too much room, too much grass. They serve no useful purpose. This country

[84]

isn't rich enough to afford the land to keep them. People's needs should come first." Rodeo participants often have a somewhat different perspective, showing a certain ambivalence toward what to them represents the wild realm. A champion saddle bronc rider who is one of the few without a ranch background thought "we should keep some wild horses; after all, they've been there from the year one." The manager of a very large rodeo, a rancher and former saddle bronc champion, believes that "wild horses should get some protection, but it should be limited"—an attitude that sums up the majority of rodeo participants' opinions. Most feel that to set aside "large areas" is impractical, because of the increasing human population in the country. One man, a rodeo manager and rodeo school operator with long experience in the sport, gave me particularly interesting insights. Regarding the issue of saving the wild horses, he said, "I would hate to see them all gone, but I sympathize with the people who are bothered by them. I have been too busy making a living to get into it, but I would hate for my grandkids not to see them like I have. But then, these kids will be able to go to another planet and see it there, which I can never do. So it's what's important while you're here."

A saddle bronc rider with a ranch background, who is also an official of the Professional Rodeo Cowboys Association, had given much thought to the issue. In discussing the subject of wild horses, he indicated perceptions which are especially pertinent. "Wild horses are not good for anything. If you catch them, their mentality is so low you couldn't ride them. They are just scrub animals. There's no use for them, and we should get rid of them. They are inbred, unintelligent, and their body conformation is not good. Inbreeding has a lot to do with it; some breeds are less intelligent, harder to train." Another rodeo man said, "As they multiply, the wild horses get smaller and weaker." In these men's attitudes I see a prime example of the use of the nature/culture opposition: they were expressing the belief that without the influence of man—that is, of culture—exerted upon it, the wild horse became totally useless. Left to itself—that is, purely to nature—the animal degenerated physically and mentally. The whole complex of domestication comes into play here—the intervention of man through selective breeding to "improve" livestock, to alter the animals' characteristics in order to make them more useful for human needs. In these informants' views, the imposition of culture over the natural animal not only molds the species to human need but, as a

[85]

concomitant of the process, leads to increased intelligence and vigor. According to biologists, however, that is not necessarily true; a wild species can possess more intelligence and vigor than its domesticated counterpart, and often does. In his study of mustangs, J. Frank Dobie asserts: "the common idea that wild horses gradually degenerated through uncontrolled breeding is contrary to fact. Only the fittest stallions had a chance to breed. . . . Until the white man interfered, mustang stock did not degenerate any more than deer, antelopes, buffaloes and other wild species left to themselves degenerate" (1952:139). But the reason I find these rodeo men's perceptions, which embody a contrary principle, so significant is their assertion of the idea that what is domesticated through the imposition of the will of man is in so many ways improved. They are the reflections of an ethos which generally places man, and all that results from human manipulatory power, on a level of greater value than that which is natural, or wild.

The Wild Horse Race of Rodeo

The wild horse race of rodeo is an event which attempts to reenact the process which occurs when wild horses are broken. When this performance is included, it is always the last feature of the program, and is referred to as "the grand finale." The horses used for it are supposed to be animals which have been handled little, if at all, and are not halter-broken. Everything is done to make them appear wilder— particularly shouting and gunfire. To a sensitive observer, the horses seem to be a study in fear; every motion of their bodies expresses terror at the unnatural situation into which they have been so abruptly thrust. The announcer at Cheyenne Frontier Days, though, where the event is an old tradition, drew the spectators' attention to "the stored-up cussedness of these wild, vicious, and defiant mustangs." I found it a violent and confused panorama, consisting of a melee of plunging hooves and rearing bodies, dust, and the sounds of shouts and whinnying. Groups of men pulling and straining on ropes attached to the horses' halters appeared to oppose the balking animals with brute force. Yet they were waiting to subdue the beasts with the accoutrements of culture, for the horses must be saddled and ridden. The event, described as "a rodeo unto itself"—a meaningful title, since it represents the spirit of the sport and its origin—has great audience appeal, and ranchers especially enjoy it. One older Montana ranchman said

[86]

RODEO HORSES: THE WILD AND THE TAME

I won the wild horse race at Whitehall in 1938. I liked doing it; it was no different than what I had done all my life as a cowboy. We rode horses that way all our lives. At that time the country was black with horses. I still train my own horses and wouldn't let nobody break a horse for me yet. Maybe I will at seventy. We break 'em as three or four year olds, and they're wild till that time. We don't raise 'em like in the East, around a barn and in a small pasture. It's a different life for a horse.

Anticipation of the wild horse race builds up throughout a rodeo performance, and announcers take advantage of it to stress the coming excitement. Periodically during two rodeos I attended in the rain, announcers made such remarks about the contestants as "Sealey says he's worried about holding these horses today; their ears are getting wet," and there was continual banter about the practice of "earing a bronc"—grabbing and biting the horse's ear in order to restrain it. Spectators commented long in advance of the event, "The wild horse race will really be something in this mud."

The ear biting was uppermost in the minds of both audience and participants, and though some of its appeal is no doubt due to sensationalism, I feel there are other factors involved. The mouth contact suggests a kind of close intimacy between man and animal, a feeling that they are in one moment simultaneously conjoined in wildness and bestiality. In the human biting of the animal there is expressed a combination of revulsion and attraction—a ritual in which one is impelled to bite, to hurt the animal, and yet by doing so to identify with it, to become one with it. By man's inflicting pain on the horse in such an elemental way—without whip or spur or prod as extensions of culture, but rather with a part of his own body, as nature—I see a welding of the two in wildness, a merging of the two in nature. Though informants said of the tradition of "earing" that "it's the best way to hold a bronc," there are undoubtedly other ways of doing it. At Cheyenne, for example, the ear biting is not allowed because of a local ruling, and the ear is only twisted or pinched, yet the event proceeds similarly in other respects.

The Broncs of Rodeo

Rodeo broncs are different from wild horses. As one informant aptly phrased it, "They have the wild edge taken off them." They can be handled to some degree, are accustomed to human contact, and are usually halter-broken. It is mainly when one attempts to ride them that they demonstrate the qualities that designate them as rodeo rough stock. Real wild horses, I was told, such as the mustangs, do not make good bucking horses; "they are too scared. They would fall down, run into fences with you and break their necks; they wouldn't buck too much. Wild horses try to get away, but bucking horses are not afraid of anything, they just concentrate on bucking you off." It is clear, then, that in transition from wild horse to bucking bronc, there has been an intrusion of a certain amount of culture. Broncs can be handled enough to allow their hooves to be trimmed, for example, and are routinely shipped by truck. With their status a balance is struck between the extremes of a feral horse, at one pole, and the "broke" or trained horse, at the other. In the case of the broncs, a small amount of human input, or culture, has moved them farther along the continuum away from pure "nature." This balance is the thing that, I contend, makes the bronc the essence of rodeo and the foremost symbol of what it is that the sport, at its deepest level, is expressing.

Rodeo, in its structuring and ordering of events, manipulates the amount of culture exerted upon the broncs in various significant ways. The bareback bronc, for instance, wears no halter or rein, and its free head gives it more control over the rider, while affording the rider less control over the horse. As one bareback contestant said, "The rider must show controlled wildness." By that he was also referring to the required spurring action of the rider in this event. The bareback rigging consists of only the barest essentials—a leather strap with a hand-hold—allowing the rider to be in direct contact with the horse's back. Interestingly, the leather glove and the leather handhold into which the hand is inserted are viewed by the bareback rider as extensions of his body, and many rituals are attached to these items. For endless hours during his apprenticeship and between rodeos, the contestant works on his glove and his grip, until he comes to feel more natural with his gloved hand in the handhold than in its normal state and feels "it's just like part of my body." Artificial aids such as stirrups are of course lacking to the bareback rider, so that he is more confined to nature during his event than is the saddle bronc contestant, and exerts less control.

It is rodeo tradition that the bareback event occurs first on the program, the saddle bronc event somewhere near the middle, and the bull riding at the end, unless a wild horse race is included as the finale.

[88]

Viewed as wild and rebellious "outlaws," bucking broncs are the cowboys' antagonists in the man/horse contests of rodeo. In the bareback riding event no saddle, halter, or reins are used. Photo by Dusty Allison.

Thus it is significant that rodeo begins and ends with the "wildest" events—those in which the human control element is minimized. I view the program as neatly framed by a keynote and a finale in which there is comparatively more of nature and less of culture than is true of intervening events. These wilder events encompass and contain the other events, in which the balance of control swings more in the direction of the element of human control. These are the timed events (to be discussed later) and the classic saddle bronc event.

Superficially, the saddle bronc event seems much like the bareback. But in a symbolic way it is quite different. Here the horse wears a halter, and the attached rein gives the rider some measure of control of his mount's head. A saddle with stirrups provides more apparatus to signify control, and the event becomes more highly suggestive of the overcoming of the wild through the imposition of these

[89]

objects representing culture. The close contact between the man's body and the horse's has been eliminated in the saddle bronc event, and the total effect of all the regulations is to swing the balance more heavily in favor of the culture end of the scale. It is noteworthy that points are deducted for losing one's stirrups—signifying failure to maintain control—as well as for touching the animal or equipment with the free hand—indicating too much control. Thus the rider is judged on the amount of force exerted over the animal, and the horse is evaluated on the degree of wildness exhibited in opposing the contestant. Degrees of human control (culture) versus varying amounts of resistance (nature) allowed to the horse are being regulated in order to produce the differently balanced contests that make up the sport of rodeo.

Perceptions of Broncs

Since informants' perceptions of broncs give much insight into the horse-human interactions which are the object of this study, I spent a great deal of time eliciting these from many different rodeo and ranch people under various conditions. One word was most closely associated with broncs in all minds, and that was *outlaw*. Officials, contestants, spectators, ranchers, and anyone speaking of rodeo categorized the bronc, as the Lame Deer, Montana rodeo announcer did, as "mavericks and outlaws who delight in tossing the cowboy to the ground." As one rodeo man summed it up, "Broncs are crazy, they need some outlaw in them; the best ones have meanness, toughness, and buck bred into them." A saddle bronc rider gave the illuminating insight that "bucking horses are outlaws; they are not really wild, but they don't want to cooperate with society. You couldn't use them on a ranch for nothing, they would keep bucking." One stock contractor likened them to "families of people who rebel against society." A rodeo manager called them "unbroke stock horses." He said, "Some were, or are, broke, but they don't want anybody to ride them." Another saddle bronc rider, also a rancher, thinks "horses are just like people [it is significant that many prefaced their remarks with this statement], some are okay. But these rodeo broncs are outlaws, criminals."

Another belief is:

> It's got to be in him to buck; only about one out of a thousand that are
> tried will keep it up. The famous bronc Midnight was gentle in other

ways but great for bucking. Broncs are ornery in general, and they've got to have a fighting heart. They are like a prize fighter. You couldn't make these guys [the rodeo contestants] into prize fighters, because they haven't got what it takes. All horses will buck once or twice when they are wild, but then they quit. These broncs, the buckers, will keep it up.

Another summed up the essence of a bronc this way: "The horse who will buck is like a barroom brawler. When you walk into a bar there is one man who will brawl. He is like the rodeo horse—his point of resistance is close to the top. If you back him into a corner, the barroom brawler comes out fast. But the passive person, like the horse who doesn't buck, will stay there in the corner all day." Put another way, "A good bucker will resist you, and that resistance will come out in the form of a pure, honest buck. This is the bronc's way of saying 'I will not be pushed.'" It is frequently stated that "the bronc has an inbred resentment for man." An information sheet distributed for publicity purposes by the International Rodeo Association calls attention to the fact that "power, violence, and rebellion" are "terms of pride" when applied to bucking horses, and stresses that violence and rebellion are "natural traits of that one-in-a-hundred horse."

A rodeo manager and former contestant assured me

that if a horse wants to buck, there is no way to stop him unless you kill him. Similarly, there is no way to make him buck if he doesn't want to. A bronc is a horse you are never able to trust or put someone on. He is like a man who was sent to jail for killing three or four people, and they say later he is rehabilitated. But you can never trust him in your heart again, at least I wouldn't.

Broncs are often perceived as "bad," as when an announcer at a collegiate rodeo in Nebraska explained, "That's how the game of rodeo began—with cowboys getting together to ride bad horses."

Broncs are thus viewed as rebels against society, who cannot be relied upon for the useful jobs that are meant to be done by horses. Their image is essentially one of unpredictability, a quality generally stressed. Announcers frequently remind the audience that "there is no such thing as a trained bucking horse; you never know what they will do next." Or, "Bucking broncs are not trained, just mean, and you can never tell what one will do." Rodeo people assert that "broncs can change their minds just like humans; they are unpredictable." They want it to be known that "it is not possible to teach a horse the bucking motion; there is no way to train and cue a bucking horse."

A few rodeo people impute a conscious thought process to the broncs. As an illustration, one stock contractor said that "when a bareback bronc finds he cannot buck off his rider [due to use of a new and tighter handhold], the horse suffers brain damage [frustration]. They become discouraged this way, and are damaged for a long time." The announcer at Lincoln, Nebraska attributed premeditated cunning to the equine animal, explaining that "the horse lays a trap for you; he goes easy at first, and waits 'til the cowboy's guard is down, and then lays it onto him." Here, the bronc is imbued with a sense of purposeful malice and enmity of nature as it opposes man.

With few exceptions, I found that whatever factors informants feel are responsible for making a good bucking horse, they are considered to be inherent, innate in that particular animal. That is an extremely important point, for it makes clear that in their minds it is always nature, not culture, that produces the buck. The contest could then be considered an uncomplicated example of culture (human) versus nature (animal). The process of making the bronc wild by the routine use of spurs, prodding, noise, and tightening of the flank strap around its body does not seem to enter into the concepts of broncs which rodeo people express. Horses do stop bucking when the flank strap is released immediately following their event in the arena, though they may still remain "wild" in the sense of unmanageable.

The widespread belief that broncs are wild solely because of innate predisposition has practical implications for the sport. For now that good broncs are much in demand because of the increasing popularity of rodeo, attempts are being made to produce them on special farms, where they are selectively bred for the characteristic of bucking. The most notable example is the Calgary Stampede Ranch, where geneticists and veterinarians under the leadership of the Stampede manager are working with a large herd of horses to produce stock for this gigantic rodeo. The director told me of the plan to use embryo transplants in order to produce the greatest number of the best bucking stock possible. A fascinating point that I would like to emphasize here is that in essence such efforts are an attempt to reverse the techniques which have over centuries been directed toward breeding the buck out of the horse. Historically, through the ages, mankind's progress has been associated with the production of a tame horse, obedient to the rider's will. Now, in order to insure the continuance of rodeo and to preserve the spirit of the frontier past which the sport exemplifies, people are conversely trying to breed the buck back into the horse. The hopeful director of one such project says, "So long as we produce horses with the will to resist by bucking, we'll continue to have rodeo." The efforts being made are, I think, remarkable testament to the strength of the frontier ethos, and to the importance that is attached to keeping it alive by the ranch/rodeo people to whose world it continues to give order and meaning.

Stressing the inborn nature of broncs, one rodeo official and saddle bronc rider told me

> A bronc has a personality like people do. Every individual has a different personality. For example, out of a family of kids, two may turn out to be professional people—a doctor or lawyer—some white-collar and some blue-collar workers, and a couple will be completely outlaws. What is the thing that makes them go in different directions? A lot of it is in the genes, and this can be related to bucking horse-breeding programs.

The degree to which rodeo people attribute the trait of bucking to genetics is especially significant when one considers the prevalence today of the opposite notion, that environmental conditions are in large measure responsible for behavior. No informant ever attributed the outlaw quality of a bronc to a condition of its early life, in the way, for example, that one hears that a dog bites someone because it was beaten as a puppy, or a man embezzles money because of the trauma of a deprived childhood. As genetic traits, then, bronc resistance and "orneriness" are viewed as inextricably part of nature.

In the outlaw imagery so consistently used by rodeo informants, I find that though the contestants think of themselves as conquerors, they also have a contradictory sense of identification with the creatures they consider to be outside the bounds of conventional society. They express it by their pride in their own lack of conformity to the code of the greater population. They reveal it in song, where lyrics place cowboys at the farthest pole from "doctors and lawyers and such"— symbols of society's acceptance. Once, when I was introduced to a

[93]

bronc rider described as "flaked out," the rodeo participant who wanted me to meet his fellow contestant did not criticize the rider's bizarre actions. Rather, he indicated his own feelings about nonconformity: "That guy is the most free you can be, doing his own thing. They tell him what to do, where to hold the rein, but he does it his own way. Nobody can be totally free, but he is near it."

Over and over again, rodeo people stress that the greatest percentage of bucking horses are "spoiled saddle horses" or "kids' horses or riding mounts that go sour." Such animals are believed to be the commonest sources of broncs, since breeding farms as suppliers are still in the future. It is said that a riding horse "goes bad" or "turns sour," starts bucking riders off, learns he can do it, and is henceforth unsafe to ride. No special event or cause brings this propensity about; the bucking trait is just "in" this particular animal and presumably has been previously held in check. The dichotomy of wild/tame is exemplified here, as it exists in the horse's dual nature. The animal has the capacity to be in either realm; it can shuck off the restraints of culture that have been imposed on it by man's training and revert to the wild—its true nature in the case of a bronc. The belief that "the best broncs" are obtained in this way is indicative of the concept that a former state of domesticity means an increased degree of wildness in an animal. Relevant here is the story a bronc rider told me about a pack horse in Glacier National Park who started bucking off his packs. The animal was, of course, sold because of this habit, and eventually it became one of rodeo's star broncs. Known as "Descent," this horse won the bucking horse of the year award six or seven times.

Rodeo stories support the notion, frequently encountered in frontier reminiscences, and described in the chapter about the White Mustang, that horses can go in either direction between wild and tame and often do. A Montana rancher told me, "I once got a horse from a bucking string and it was one of the best saddle horses I ever had. I had to educate it a bit. It didn't buck very often; it only piled me a couple of times. After I treated him gentle, he quit this. He was always a one-man horse, though; I was the only one who could ride him. A stranger might make him buck." Thus he indicated that a conversion between wild and tame was made, but it was a fragile and quickly reversible one and did not essentially change the horse; the animal was transformed only in relation to a particular person. These data again demonstrate the basic duality of the horse, which enables it to act as a symbolic intermediary between man and nature, in both directions.

With one accord, rodeo people indicate that the flank strap tightened around the bronc's body just before its release from the chute into the arena does not make the horse buck. They are adamant on this point and enraged at the myths commonly promulgated among Easterners and humane societies that the strap is lined with tacks and burrs, or that it is applied to a stallion's genital organs to cause pain. Ranch/rodeo people do conceive of the sport as violent and dangerous but not as deliberately cruel. An articulate informant who manages a rodeo school said that the flank strap "only changes the style of bucking on a horse that will do it anyway. Without it he would rear up in front rather than in the hindquarters. Horses bucked differently in the old days, when the cinch was the only foreign object that touched the horse's body." Others agree that the strap only "increases bucking potential" and does not in itself cause the bucking, though a few admitted that "it annoys them, as the flank is a sensitive spot." All opinions thus confirmed the notion that it is not something attributable to culture that causes bucking but an element intrinsic to the animal.

One Wyoming collegiate rodeo contender, who "would rather go down the road on the rodeo circuit than go to college, because it's the most romantic of all sports," said he feels horses "enjoy bucking." He seemed to feel a sense of identification with the bronc, associating bucking motion with play. The idea of play is important to rodeo people, but it merges with work, for their play *is* their work, and they seldom, if ever, turn elsewhere for recreation. Another interesting notion I (rarely) encountered is that bucking is atavistic, representing an old pattern of equine reaction to attack by a predator. Rodeo's concern with bucking might be theoretically related in this way to the stockman's hatred of predator species and a feeling of unity with horses against a common enemy.

As we have seen, there may be a sense of identification with the bronc on the one hand because it is looked upon as free of the constraints of society, but on the other hand there is the predominating idea that the bronc is a wild element that must be conquered. In ranch/rodeo tradition, riding a bronc is perceived as a totally masculine pursuit. Women have their own rodeo circuit, in which they may compete in bareback riding, but they cannot enter bucking events in standard

[95]

professional rodeos. Female bronc riders are subject to social approbation in ranch/rodeo society and are generally ridiculed or ignored by male bronc riders.

Perceptions of women and broncs are often implicitly revealed in the context of rodeo. A sign often encountered at rodeos and which I observed glued to a bronc rider's saddle on several occasions reads "Put something exciting between your legs." There is more than an attempt at "punography" here. For indeed I found that rodeo people, like cattlemen, very often categorize women with horses. Both, they say, "need to know who's boss"; both are "unpredictable," "wild until a man tames them," "good for only one thing," and so forth. The slogan frequently seen on rodeo participants' trucks—"Cowgirls like to horse around"—expresses this likeness. Bumper stickers proclaim "I'm a liar, a drinker, and a wild filly rider," "Cowboys stay on longer," or "Bronc riders do it with rhythm."

One bronc rider, associated with rodeo all his life, believes

> horses and women are the same: they don't know if you treat them good or bad. If you treat them bad they don't know it, and if you treat them good they might divorce you. If you treat a horse good, it might kick you in the leg and break it. Women are like horses—you can't depend on them. You treat a woman nice and she might be running around. You treat a horse good, turn it out to pasture, and it may run away on you.

What he was getting at here is a concept which I could identify as a common thread running through many similar conversations, and a theme uppermost in the thinking of rodeo men. It is the notion of *predictability,* an attribute which they see as existing in varying degrees as a characteristic of various types of horses along the continuum from wild to tame. Predictability is associated with tameness, with being conquerable, with being in the realm of culture; unpredictability is associated with wildness, with being less easily conquered, with being a part of nature. The unpredictability which rodeo men attribute to women is also a key quality of broncs, and both seem closer to nature than to culture. Unpredictability expresses the essence of the spirit of the sport, and as announcers often repeat, "Anything can happen in rodeo, and usually does," or "No two performances are ever the same." The bronc's trait of unpredictability fits in with the animal's (and the woman's) designation as a part of nature over which the more stable, masculine conquering force of culture should prevail.

Horses of the Timed Events of Rodeo

In contrast to the unpredictable bronc, who occupies a position near the wild extreme of the wild/tame dichotomy, is the timed-event horse, who appears far along toward the sphere of the tame. Unlike the bronc, the enemy of society whom men admire yet strive to defeat, the roping or steer wrestler's horse is the counterpart of the cowboy's mount, his indispensable servant and companion. If, as a newspaper reporter was told at Cheyenne Frontier Days, the rough stock (bucking) events constitute the "macho" part of rodeo and the timed events the "muscle" portion, then muscle power must include that of the horse as the contestant's helper.

The Calf Roper's Horse

Within the context of the standard rodeo program (exclusive of novelty acts), I view the calf roper's horse as the nearest to the tame polarity. It is interesting to observe how this concept is structured into the sport. If a rodeo logo or motif includes a second equine figure, it is always that of a calf-roping horse—his motionless, subdued, and controlled pose contrasting sharply to the leaping, kicking, bucking bronco.

Calf roping is called by rodeo officials "the horseman's sport," the clearest example of cooperation between horse and man. Announcers point out that a large share of the success in this event depends upon the horse. Ropers told me that not every horse has the potential to become a calf horse. "If the horse doesn't fit you, you get rid of it." A champion calf roper gave insights about this event when he told me, "You can't baby a calf horse; he must listen and respond like a child. They have to fear you a little. You can't make a calf roper out of a horse if it is against their nature to do it. You have to stop then, and get another horse to try with. You go through dozens and ruin them. You ruin several before you know how to do it." Here, as with the broncs, it is noteworthy that, in spite of the great amount of training given to a

[97]

Calf roping, a rodeo event involving ranching skills, depends on a close working relationship between man and
mount. The horse, as a highly trained and obedient partner,
is essential to the contestant's success. Photo by Dusty Allison.

calf horse, there is still something innate within the individual, a capacity or potential, which is a prime requisite. With the calf horse it is its
ability to accept—not resist as the bronc would—the superimposition
of culture (in the form of training) over its animal instincts (nature).

All contestants in this event agree with the champion roper at Big
Timber, Montana who claimed, "There is more to calf roping and training a calf horse than is true of any other rodeo event." He went on to
identify the characteristics of the horse's training. "The things they do
are against nature. They have to move backwards, pull back against
the rope, and they have to stand firm without moving. What the calf
roping horse does is completely against nature. The rider is not on him
while he pulls back against the calf rope; he has to do it on his own."
There was a preoccupation in the roper's mind with the horse moving
backward. The calf roper stressed this point: "Did you ever see a horse

grazing backwards in a pasture? It never happens, and yet the calf roping horse has to go backwards. This is not natural for a horse, and it takes a lot to train him for it." So it seems that the role of culture in subduing nature was again the uppermost concept in the contestant's mind, and moving backward represented for him the force of schooling that can, with difficulty, overcome natural instincts.

Calf-roping horses stand at the epitome among rodeo animals for doing the bidding of man, and they perhaps best represent the fulfillment of what society views as the proper role of a horse. Interestingly, ropers' horses are not usually categorized with women, as are the broncs. Perhaps that is because the closeness to nature, the unpredictability, and the exciting and sexually suggestive elements which rodeo men attribute to bucking horses are lacking. Calf horses, in contrast, are more likely to be classed with one's children. Ropers feel that their horses must behave toward them like obedient offspring. A rodeo official, taking every opportunity to emphasize the good care given to rodeo stock, framed his expression in these terms: "The roper's horse gets better care than his children; it's his bread and butter." Within this context, the horse is an underling, a dependent subject to "parental" authority.

Such categorizations are not definitive, and the roper's horse moves back and forth between the "child" classification and that of a partner. Calf roping has also been called "the marriage of horse and man." The partner image is stressed by announcers and described in rodeo programs. As the event is in progress, comments are made: "In this contest a lot depends upon the horse," or "Horses deserve a lot of credit in this event." Mounts are described as "usually Quarter Horses, with the speed plus the know-how to get back off the rope. It's up to the horse to hold the calf on the ground by backing up on the rope." The image of the calf horse as a working animal committed to its task is demonstrated in such announcements as "If a horse does his job in this event, he faces the calf." At Cheyenne, where horse races were taking place outside the arena simultaneously with calf roping, the announcer praised one roper's horse: "He didn't even look at the race horses going by him. That horse knows what he is supposed to do." Such observations indicate that the ability to concentrate, a human value, has been imposed upon the animal—a high degree of culture extending over nature. Similarly, at the Little Britches (children's) rodeo, a youngster, lacking expertise, looped his rope over his horse's legs.

When the horse stood quietly in spite of this predicament, the announcer pointed out, "That's a well-trained horse; he is to be congratulated for not coming unglued and causing a wreck." The implication is that his animal nature has been overcome and he is in a realm of super-domestication—predictable. That is especially so since it is in a horse's nature to "spook," or shy, a characteristic that has never been successfully bred out of domestic horses.

Conversely, I was struck by the evident lack of patience with the roping horses' mistakes. One contestant at Calgary, in a rage because his horse failed to pull back on the calf, threw dirt at the horse. Such public displays are frowned upon, but it is clear that perfection is demanded of the animals. It is noteworthy that the sympathy of audiences never appears to be with the roping horse. My observations among spectators indicate that they view this type of horse more as a kind of machine rather than empathize with any lapses in skill of performance. For example, once when the horse dragged the calf away from the roper instead of holding it still for the roper to tie, spectators shouted, "The poor guy" and "Get a two-by-four for that horse!" They identified completely with the man in this recapitulation of ranch life, calling out such expressions as "It's a bummer" and "Get rid of that horse" when the animal failed to perform properly for the contestant. Thus culture is seen as having been exerted over animal nature to a far greater extent with the roper's horse than with the bronc. The image of the bronc as essentially unpredictable and closer to nature is now reversed, for dependability is the paramount quality of the roping horse. It is constantly emphasized that to do well in this event, man and horse must "know what the other is going to do, know what is expected of one another." Great advantage is said to accrue to the man whose horse gives a consistent performance from one rodeo to the next.

Ropers are quick to point out that horses must never become "pets." Speaking of calf horses, a roper told me, "You can't treat a rodeo horse like a dog. If you pet him he will not work well in the arena. You don't have to abuse him, but he must have discipline to perform." There is a precedent among working cowboys, who felt that "the meanest, most unreliable object in cattle country was a 'pet horse'" (Rollins 1973:268). Analyzing this concern, it is obvious that a pet horse would not have the machinelike precision required of a calf horse and would expect to have an input of its own—an intolerable condition for a roper's mount, who must be constrained at all times by his rider's will.

The most significant thing about the horse's role in the calf-roping operation is that he performs his most essential function while he is not being directly controlled by the contestant. For the horse is not mounted during the critical time of the tying of the calf. That places him near the extreme tame end of the spectrum. His status is dramatically emphasized: being free from the physical domination of a rider, he could bolt and run away, or refuse to pull the rope, but he very rarely does.

Horses in Other Timed Events

In other timed events, the horse does not work in a riderless state, but nevertheless a considerable amount of training is required. The steer-roping event, in which the contestant ropes, knocks down, and ties a large bovine animal, is sometimes called "the thinking man's part of rodeo," because it requires great skill. The horse shares in this image. With its intricate maneuvers and the great weight of the steer, contestants admit that "it's very demanding on the horse; there's a lot to learn." They feel horses have to be "level-headed" and have a "steady disposition" to qualify. One participant said of this event, "These horses are like race horses, they have to practice every day. You need to go slow teaching horses this event." To the spectator, however, the rider's skill appears paramount in the arena, and the horse seems only instrumental to it.

In team roping, the factor of two horses and two riders working in conjunction adds a dimension of camaraderie between the men and demands an extra measure of cooperation from the two horses. Each mount must maneuver his rider into position according to whether he is the header (who ropes the head of the steer) or the heeler (who ropes the hind leg or legs). Both horses must face the animal once it is roped. Their riders remain in the saddle throughout.

In the steer-wrestling event, the contestant leaps from his horse and throws the steer to the ground. Even though the steer wrestler is on foot for the major accomplishment in this event, his horse plays a significant part in the contestant's success. The mount must be carefully trained to gallop up next to the running steer, enabling the rider to jump at just the right time and place.

Thus in the timed events of rodeo, man-horse relationships show important differences from those in bronc riding. Roping animals, in particular, are far along on the tame end of the continuum from wild to tame. They act as servants of man, and they are manipulated to show off the contestants' skills. Each is an adjunct to the rider, never occupying "center stage."

Rodeo Horses as Counterparts of Cowboys' Mounts

Appearing in the arena during much of the rodeo performance are two other classes of equines—the stock contractor's horse and the pickup men's horses. The stock contractor's mount is a quiet, responsive, and tireless animal, in which he places a great deal of confidence; he rides it continually while directing the operation of the rodeo. The horse used by the pickup man, whose task is to rescue the bronc riders as soon as their rides are over, has to be fearless, willing, and dependable, for it must come in close contact with wildly bucking and kicking broncs. It should be agile enough to avoid the hooves of the broncs and at the same time stay near enough to allow a contestant to jump off the still-plunging animal and onto its back behind the pickup man. It must also allow its rider to release the flank strap of the bronc at the end of the ride. These two types of horses, both significantly characterized by the quality of predictability, are categorized as friends, totally dependable partners. It is possible for them to share the symbolic, as well as the physical, realm of their riders. The stock contractor's and the pickup man's horses occupy a position at the contrasting pole from that of broncs. Going beyond merely carrying out their riders' wills, they seem, through close communication and interaction, to have been accepted into the human circle of domestication. In a sense, the horse has become part of its rider's cultural sphere, and the man, in turn, has extended something of himself into the animal by close contact and mutual dependence.

The seeming paradox in which the oppositions of partnership and dominance are at once part of the man-horse relationship is explored by Paul Bouissac with reference to

western film narrative, in which the domination of a man over a horse is highly stressed; a cowboy, as a rodeo performer, is a mythical breaker of horses as well as an excellent rider. His horse is simply an aspect of his power and prestige; and when the horse contributes to the cowboy's survival, it is as an instrument the perfect functioning of which is credited to the owner. In some early westerns the horse played the role of the owner's best friend; that does not contradict my hypothesis, because the horse can be viewed as a psychological extension of the cowboy's domination (which humanizes his mount). [1976:147]

The same ambivalence was noted by a chronicler of range life, who wrote that "the highly trained ponies that he personally rode" were adopted by a cowboy "into his family, and they took him into theirs. Nevertheless he at times might enthusiastically quirt them, and assuredly they frequently deserved the treatment" (Rollins 1973:55).

A cowboy's horse was a trusted friend, but also his servant. The old range adage that the West was hell on horses (and women) is no doubt true; for hard use and long hours of toil under adverse conditions were the cow pony's lot. Mastery was paramount in a cowhand's relationship to his mount. He typically boasted that he could "ride anything that has hair" (Seidman 1973:178), and he placed great emphasis on his own ability to make the horse do his bidding. A cowboy's ego was closely bound up with horsemanship as his dominant skill (McMurtry 1968).

A good cowboy, of course, took as good care of his mount as the circumstances of his own harsh life allowed. Often it was the only living thing he cared for, and cowboy writings contain references to deep feelings for horses. Charlie Siringo's devotion to "Whiskey-peet," from whom "he couldn't even bear the thought of parting," is revealed in his autobiography (1950:113). Andy Adams revealed that "on the trail an affection springs up between man and mount which is almost human. And on this drive, covering nearly three-thousand miles, all the ties which can exist between man and beast had . . . become cemented" (1903:382).

Tales of heroic horses' bringing cowboys home through blizzards or risking their lives for them in other ways are still commonly told in ranch country. In addition to a horse's "cow sense"—the quality that makes a mount a skilled partner in the cattle-herding operation and is reflected in rodeo's roping events—the most important quality of a range horse is dependability. It is these attributes which characterize the roper's and the steer wrestler's horses, as well as the stock contractor's and pickup men's mounts, rodeo's analogues of the working cow-boy's horse.

Based on his lifetime of experience with contemporary cowboys, Larry McMurtry points out that

> the tradition of the shy cowboy who is more comfortable with his horse or with his comrades than with his women is not bogus. Cowboys express themselves most naturally, and indeed, most beautifully, through their work; when horseback they perform many extraordinarily difficult acts with ease and precision and grace. As the years pass they form very deep bonds with the men and the horses they work with. [1968:72]

McMurtry refers to these friendships as "mateships" and writes of "the sacramental relationships of man and horse" (1968:27).

The Sacrificial Role of the Horse in Rodeo

If the horse-human relationship is sacramental, then I suggest it may also be sacrificial. Much of the cowboy's equipment, derived from the Spanish, is punishing to the horse. His stock saddle is heavy beyond utilitarian purpose, his spurs are designed with elaborately pronged rowels, and the curb bit on his bridle is of a type that has been described as an instrument of latent torture.

Though it does not deal specifically with the cowboy complex, except, significantly, as a symbol of freedom from parental authority, the idea of the horse as a sacrificial animal was explored in the play *Equus* (Shaffer 1974). In this work the horse takes on aspects that cast him in the role of victim of the sadistic cruelty and display of power associated with the crucifixion. Equus is referred to as "my only begotten son" (1974:50), "in chains for the sins of the world" (1974:65), and as taking a lump of sugar for his "last supper," eating it "for my sake" (1974:70). The hero in the play replaces his picture of the tortured Christ with the likeness of a horse, and the two are transformed into one symbol. The horse's bit becomes synonymous with pain and man's domination. The archetypal horse, Equus, is "the God-slave, Faithful and True," and "into my hands he commends himself" (Shaffer 1974:71). I find it particularly relevant for this study that it is the singular nature of the equine that makes it ideally suited for the sacrificial

[104]

role. The term "God-slave" expresses the paradox of the horse's submissiveness, its strange willingness to do man's bidding and bear the pain he inflicts, in spite of the possession of physical power and strength far in excess of that of its human masters. Relating this observation to the nature/culture theme, it seems that because of the extent to which man's cultural realm has been exerted over the horse's nature in dominating so large and beautiful a creature, the equine animal becomes a peculiarly appropriate and tragic sacrifice.

The association of the horse with the crucifixion is not original with *Equus*. There is the tradition, of course, that "Christians of an earlier age seem to have considered the horse as a blessed animal, since our Savior was born in a manger" (Howey 1958:192). And in legend the greatest possible honor was paid to the horse of an emperor when the mother of the ruler obtained the sacred nails of the cross on which Christ was crucified. Not knowing how best to preserve the holy relics, she was advised by the bishop to "take these precious nails for thy son the emperor. Make of them ring for his horse's bridle. Victory shall always go with them" (Howey 1958:193). So, as will again be mentioned in connection with the legend that a Gypsy smith forged the nails of the crucifixion, the horse has been linked to Christ through their common pain.

Oddly enough, one of the early rodeo books refers to "that *passion play* of the West, the Round-up held at Pendleton, in eastern Oregon about which country so much of the history of the Northwest is wrapped" (Furlong 1921:xii). I found the sacrificial motif running like a thin thread throughout the deeper level of rodeo. Observing a bronc in the chutes who was missing one eye, I felt a symbolic connection with *Equus,* in which the horses, as sacrificial gods, had their eyes put out by the protagonist. Often I noticed that rodeo men spit on the sides of the horses in the chutes, a strange act which brings to mind the treatment of Christ by the high priests before His sacrifice (Matthew 26:67). On many broncs bloody marks were visible over their forequarters, where spurs had gouged the flesh. And to encourage a bronc rider to spur harder, I heard announcers urge, "Show the pony a lot of iron!" "Knife him out" is a rodeo term for spurring a bronc into the arena to begin a ride. Sometimes, before letting them out of the chutes, broncs are hit with a leather strap. (This practice is specifically allowed in the rule book.) Horses are often prodded, pinched, or punched while in the chutes. Rodeo people would be quick to claim that these acts are not evidence of cruelty, and would assert that they are meant to "wake them up" in an effort to increase the animals' bucking potential. Yet it could be questioned whether these procedures are efficacious in making a horse buck harder, especially since they are generally done so far ahead of time. I feel they are ritualistic expressions, sacrificial in the sense that they are believed to evoke the resisting power of the animal, only to have that power more fully oppose the rider in the arena. Through a heightening of the animal force, I suggest that man expects to gain a more potent victory in subduing it. In a sense, then, the horse's increased power would be taken as the rider's own, and would constitute a sacrifice to it.

A saddle bronc rider who ranches in Wyoming reflected the sacrificial strain in horse-human interactions when he told his fellow contestants about his technique for training a horse. The mare in question, he said, had a habit of "raring up" when ridden, and he had been asked to break her of this dangerous behavior. He described his procedure of deliberately making the mare rear up by jerking on the bit and then repeatedly hitting her over the head, first with a piece of pipe and then with a baseball bat, "with all my strength." The choice of words in his narrative and his use of detail not necessary to convey its surface meaning were remarkable. He laughed as he related, "The blood flowed everywhere. She was a yellow buckskin mare, and she ended up covered with blood. I have never seen so much blood. The mare had started out a yellow color, but you wouldn't have known this after she was covered with red blood." I felt in the relating of this episode that the horse had taken on the role of an expiatory animal, a scapegoat. In the huge muscular form of the narrator there was the overweening spirit of power that can make martyrs of the submissive. The rebellious yellow mare, at the mercy of his bit and weapon, became that sacrifice because of her bleeding head, the loss of blood denoting the ebbing of her strength to resist.

Horses possess powers which man generally lacks but admires— especially great strength, grace of motion, and speed. Blood, however, may be conceived of as something they share in common. Indeed, blood is often mentioned in rodeo and, as one looks about, is frequently in evidence. I sometimes noticed blood dripping from the mouths of bitted horses ridden in the arena. Broncs often exhibit open wounds and fresh brands. Many contestants leave the arena bleeding, and their condition seems to be taken in stride. Stock contractors, rodeo managers and helpers, and pickup men are subject to bloody wounds and kicks and commonly display them. When a contestant is bucked off and appears to be slightly hurt, the rodeo clown often asks, "What color is blood?" The announcer answers, "Red." Then the clown calls out, "Okay. He's okay, then," as he inspects the man on the ground. Another typical quip is for the announcer to tell the clown to "be sure to get a good seat for the rodeo, so you can see it in living color—blood red."

Horses in the Special Acts of Rodeo

From a discussion of the rodeo horse as a sacrificial animal, I will now turn to the horse as it is portrayed in the sport as a humanized animal. In this form it occupies a position even further along the continuum from wild to tame, from nature to culture, than is the case with mounts such as calf-roping and pickup horses. I am referring here to horses which appear in special acts and individual exhibitions and provide a contrast to the standard events. Horses in these contexts may be viewed as defying the traditional role that society assigns to this species, as another way in which the sport of rodeo further explores and comments upon the dilemma of horse-human relationships. The themes expounded in these acts sometimes contrast to rodeo's overall message concerning the human domination of nature and the conception of nature as a force inimical to man. The acts seem to belong to an ethos alien to rodeo; they are real, but temporary, counterpoints to it.

True performing horses, such as those typical of early circus and the English hippodrome, for example, are rarely seen in standard rodeo. In A. H. Saxon's study of the hippodrome, it is pointed out that spectators viewed the equine actors in these productions as "sagacious," and were inclined to feel more sympathy for them than for the human actors in the dramas. Such audiences are described in terms unthinkable for rodeo enthusiasts, as having "an attitude toward animals that is quite foreign to the present century. At the time of the appearance of these plays Romanticism was in full bloom. Darwinism and the theory of the indifferent universe was still some fifty years in the future; nature was viewed, with childlike simplicity, as being sympathetic to man" (1968:8).

Almost all the specially trained horses in rodeo appear in novelty acts with clowns. As the classic figure of ineptitude, the clown serves as a foil for the horse with which he is paired, making the animal appear smarter. Often this status is portrayed by means of a routine in which the blundering harlequin tries unsuccessfully to put a saddle blanket and saddle on the horse. Not only is the horse shown to be superior in intelligence by outwitting the man in this act, but it has also defied the traditional role of equine subservience by refusing to accept the symbols of human dominance. Of course, in rodeo this routine evokes much laughter; the general belief holds that such a situation can occur only in a mythic universe—the carnival world momentarily created by buffoonery. It is soon over; the broncs are in the chutes, the roping horse is ready to aid its master in tying up the calf; things will return to normal.

There are several typical varieties of clown-horse acts, and the animal does not always end up in a position of control, though it may reach that position at one time in the sequence. Sometimes a scene is staged in which the horse brings the clown home safely after he gets drunk on Saturday night. In this act, the horse will push the clown out of the arena with its nose, as he staggers forward. Or the horse may come up behind the clown, lower its head between his legs, and cleverly appear to put the man on its back, carrying him from the arena in a mounted position. Here there is a temporary reversal of roles—the horse is wiser, and is the "keeper" of the man. Nature is thus seen to triumph over culture, especially when "culture" has included getting drunk. It is significant that at some point during a typical clown-horse performance, the horse usually rolls over on its back, and the clown will sit on its recumbent body, reemphasizing human control and dominance. Then the animal will rise and again become the "superior" of the clown. Needless to say, such an act is the product of arduous training and mastery over the horse, but it is made to appear otherwise to the spectator. Cues are disguised by comic gestures and are seldom evident to the amused audience.

Frequently at the end of such a repertoire, the horse is "dressed" by putting a hat and a large pair of glasses on the animal and placing a pipe in its mouth. Here I find the ultimate extreme in representing culture over nature—the horse is humanized to the furthest extent possible. As a finale, the announcer typically gives a name to the caricatured horse—saying, "There you have it, folks, that is Hubert

Elton" (some well-known figure who is disliked). Rodeo parades, as an integral part of the bigger celebrations, also display the prominent themes of the sport. Near the beginning of the Cheyenne Frontier Days parade, for example, this motif of culture over nature was keynoted. A famous rodeo clown walked beside his faithful companion, a horse dressed in a pair of pants—undeniable evidence of the humanization of the equine species.

An interesting rodeo variation on the theme of performing horses was an act which was heralded by trumpet fanfare and a proclamation by the announcer that the audience would now be treated to a display of the equine brilliance of the world-famous Lipizzan stallions. "Here, direct from Austria, you will see high-schooled horses perform difficult feats like the capriole." At this point, having built up the audience's anticipation, he is interrupted by the entrance of a clown who rides two mules "Roman style"—in a standing position with one foot on the back of each. With mock seriousness, the announcer calls for a "reverse," and each mule goes in the opposite direction, confounding the clown. Here, the lowly and ungainly mules provide an ironic contrast to the vision conjured up in the minds of observers of the precise and intricate maneuvers exhibited by the Lipizzans. For the celebrated horses are paragons of equine expertise and as such, I suggest, symbolize the highest degree of human culture being extended over the natural realm. The Lipizzans, of course, would be as out of place at a rodeo as a cowboy in a tuxedo. The message in the act just described is that such sophisticated performances are all right for cities and Easterners, but as for the West, give me the simple life! Let us cling to rural values, lowly creatures, and down-to-earth attitudes. The antiintellectual, anti-aesthetic strain of the frontier is clearly framed in the language ranch/rodeo people best understand—through the use of horses.

Another example is relevant here, an equestrian act which I saw at an Eastern rodeo (Rhode Island), and which typically would not be observed as part of a standard rodeo in the Great Plains. A distinct contrast to Western rodeo acts was an exhibition of classic equestrian skills and dressage. The rider was a young woman, and as she guided her mount through its paces, her cues to the horse were carefully concealed. A performance like this one would be out of keeping with the Great Plains ranch/rodeo spirit, in which emphasis generally is placed not on what the horse can do but rather on what the rider can make the horse do. An equestrian display like the one included in the

Eastern rodeo tends to focus attention on the skill of the horse. Horse shows also provide a contrast to rodeos in this way, for the rider participating in them is specifically designated as the "exhibitor" of the horse, and the animal is afforded paramount emphasis (except in equitation classes, where riding skill alone is judged). In a horse show, accordingly, it is recognized that it is the horse who wins the ribbon which is always fastened to the animal's bridle. Rodeo, on the other hand, makes it evident that human input is of central importance, and it is the rider who receives the trophy award—a buckle to be worn by him and not the horse.

A further factor of significance is that in an equestrian performance such as the one just described, the horse and rider appear "center stage"—alone in the arena. Such solo presentations contrast sharply with the mounted displays that typically occur within the Western rodeo context. In these a horseman's drill team with headquarters in some nearby town often puts on an exhibition at the beginning of the program. These are group affairs, demonstrating the collective skill of riders working in unison. They consist of various movements such as quadrilles, modified square dance routines, figure eights, criss-cross formations, and concentric circles, symbolically stressing conformity. Speed is a conspicuous part of the displays when some of the routines are executed at a gallop. Unity of motion is the overall effect, since individual riders are submerged in the visual pattern created. Riders are generally all male or all female. Men's groups adopt a title such as "Cheyenne Sheriff's Posse," and they often wear uniforms with star-shaped badges and holsters with revolvers. Women's groups, such as the "Casper Dandies" or the "Foxy Ladies," wear matching pastel or gaudily colored Western-tailored suits. One announcer drew attention to the uniformity in apparel of a ladies' drill team, telling the audience that the riders were "all wearing Tony Lama boots" and "underneath it all—Vanity Fair."

These displays of mounted teamwork in rodeo suggest the collective power and force implicit in the conquest of the West, depict the isolation of the sexes into separate spheres of life, and also represent the role of the traditional social order in controlling behavior. By stressing conformity, they provide a striking contrast to the individualism which is constantly extolled as being one of the most important of frontier traits, the one which the sport of rodeo generally emphasizes and which ranch/rodeo people value highly and wish to perpetuate. A similar example is represented by the liberty horses, who in the classic circus act are manipulated in specifically meaningful ways, through which they express a paradoxical message. Being "harnessed like domestic animals," but "unmounted and unhitched, like wild animals," they are "simultaneously controlled and free." Thus the decoded message of the act, symbolized by these combinations, represents the conflicting cultural values in the order "Conform and be yourself!" This paradox is felt to be "at the root of moral education in Western cultures" (Bouissac 1976: 134, 136). Within the context of the cowboy sport, the ranch/rodeo society expresses through horse-human interactions both its emphasis on individualism—as with the lone bronc rider or roper—and its regard for cultural conformity through group displays.

The Horse in the Bar

One more outstanding example is relevant to the topic of culture being extended over nature through the agency of increasingly "humanized" horses. This example is the act of riding a horse into a building, almost always a barroom. It is a commonly occurring motif in the folklore of the American West, in which a cowboy coming off the range nonchalantly enters a saloon with his horse and orders a drink for each of them. I found that this event was often in the minds of ranch/rodeo people, and that a rodeo version of it has become traditional. While it may not be carried out frequently, because of practical limitations, the possibility of doing it is constantly considered, joked about, and discussed. Informants took delight in telling about riding a horse into the Mayflower Bar during Cheyenne Frontier Days, and they indicated that some rodeo cowboy usually manages the stunt during the annual rodeos at Denver, Fort Worth, and North Platte, as well. Fascinated by this idea as it relates to my theme of the horse as an intermediary between nature and culture, I wanted to be in the right place at the right time to experience it firsthand. Failing to do so, I talked whenever possible to men who had accomplished the feat, and to bartenders who were undecided as to whether they dreaded or welcomed the equine intrusion into their domain.

The general procedure is that rodeo hands who are "whooping it up"—often on a dare—will "steal a pickup horse and ride it into a bar."

Significantly, participants assured me that "a pickup horse will go anywhere." Thus, according to my interpretation, this versatile horse is
made to seem at home in both worlds—the animal and the human. It
then becomes an agent which transcends its usual role in society, vio-
lates order and propriety, and extends itself into a "higher" realm. In
their concern with this act, rodeo participants are imposing culture
upon the horse to a degree that seems like the ultimate possibility—
taking the animal into a strictly human sphere. The whiskey-drinking
horse of the old Western folk narratives and tall tales does not only
express the cowboy's philosophy of "what's good enough for me is
good enough for my horse." For, in addition, by partaking of liquor, the
equine animal shares in the consumption of an unnatural substance
which has undergone a "raw to cooked" (Lévi-Strauss 1975) or nature-
to-culture transition, a substance which has power to affect the mind.
This act thrusts the horse further into an artificial and incongruous
realm.

A bar in the Old West served as the center of social activity, a
gathering place for men from outlying areas to exchange news and
share conviviality, and was symbolic of the existing order of the group.
It was a male world, with the exception of "bad" women who may have
been accepted there. "Decent" women were, of course, excluded. Bars
in today's ranch society have retained some of the same functions and
often serve as places of business for men of the cattle trade. By bringing his horse into this setting, in reality or in a tale, the cowboy was
making the ultimate statement about this animal's inclusion in the
deeper aspects of his life. The horse can be accepted into the male
camaraderie mystique, which finds the most fervent expression of its
intimacy in the atmosphere of the bar. Today's rodeo hand, with a
strong sense of identification with his cowboy predecessor, is
motivated to recreate this scene with his equine partner under the guise
of a prank.

Summary of Horse-Human Relationships in Rodeo

There are many ways in which the sport of rodeo manipulates and
dramatizes various categories of horses to give concrete expression to
relationships existing between people and the equine species in the
ranch/rodeo culture of the Great Plains. These range from the wild

(feral) horse, through the bronc, to the roping horse, pickup man's horse, trick horse, and "humanized" horse. I have proposed that these types of horses demonstrate progressive degrees of man's control and dominance over them, and that they represent various stages in the transformation of wild to tame, nature to culture. The horse is remarkable in its capacity for participation in both poles of these dichotomies. Bridging the realms of nature and culture, the horse becomes a symbolic representative of the conquest of the "Wild West."

A certain ambivalence often characterizes ranch/rodeo interactions with horses. There is an apparent paradox, for example, in a man's feeling of close partnership with his horse at the same time that he experiences dominance over the animal. There can also be a sense of personal identification with the power and freedom represented by the horse, even as the attempt is made to master it. In addition, the horse may take on the role of a sacrificial animal, victimized by pain and domination in the ranch/rodeo setting. This process is related to the phenomenon of power accruing to the forces of culture through the conquest of nature, suggesting that a sense of renewal emanates from the struggle between man and nature which took place on the American frontier.

The oppositional contests between man and horse in rodeo are structured so that the performance of the bronc—that is, the degree of its rebelliousness toward man—is counted equally with the rider's skill in scoring the event. Through use of varying amounts of equipment representing extensions of culture, as well as in the ordering of events on the program according to amounts of "wildness" exhibited, rodeo explores the balance between wild and tame.

The wildness of rodeo broncs and their resentfulness of man are considered to be inborn, and at the wild polarity horses are perceived as unpredictable and undependable. Rodeo men sometimes categorize women with broncs, since females are said to share these qualities. At the opposite, or tame, end of the spectrum, horses such as those used for calf roping and steer roping are characterized as predictable and trustworthy, suitable as partners for cowboys and ranchers. At the furthest degree toward the polarity of tame, a horse may be trained for special routines of complex and highly symbolic interaction with a person, or may be "dressed" or ridden into a barroom. Thus the equine animal can be "humanized" enough to temporarily enter man's own domesticated sphere.

The bucking bronc remains as the key animal and central symbol of rodeo, and at present effort is being expended to "breed the buck back" into these animals, thus reversing the centuries-old process of genetic selection for more docile mounts. This phenomenon illustrates the strong appeal of the Western frontier ethos and the importance attributed to keeping alive its wildness of spirit and continued challenge for conquest.

REFERENCES

Adams, Andy
    1903   *The Log of a Cowboy.* Boston: Houghton Mifflin.

Bouissac, Paul
    1976   *Circus and Culture: A Semiotic Approach.* Bloomington: Indiana University Press.

Cawelti, John
    n.d.   *The Six-Gun Mystique.* Bowling Green: Bowling Green University Popular Press.

Dobie, J. Frank
    1952   *The Mustangs.* Boston: Little, Brown.

Furlong, Charles Wellington
    1921   *Let 'er Buck: A Story of the Passing of the Old West.* New York: Putnam.

Holy Bible, The (King James Version)
    n.d.   London: Oxford University Press.

Howey, M. Oldfield
    1958   *The Horse in Magic and Myth.* New York: Castle.

Lawrence, Elizabeth Atwood
    1982   *Rodeo: An Anthropologist Looks at the Wild and the Tame.* Knoxville: University of Tennessee Press.

Lévi-Strauss, Claude
    1975   *The Raw and the Cooked.* New York: Harper.

McMurtry, Larry
    1968   *In A Narrow Grave.* New York: Simon and Schuster.

Rollins, Philip Ashton
    1973   *The Cowboy: An Unconventional History of Civilization on the Old-Time Cattle Range.* New York: Ballantine.

Saxon, A. H.
    1968   *Enter Foot and Horse: A History of Hippodrama in England and France.* New Haven: Yale University Press.

Searle, Walt
 1977 "Hoofbeats: Hats Off to the Cattleman." *Hoof and Horn: The Magazine of Ranch and Rodeo* 47, no. 3:3.

Seidman, Laurence Ivan
 1973 *Once in the Saddle: The Cowboy's Frontier, 1866–1896*. New York: Knopf.

Serven, James
 1972 "Horses of the West." *Arizona Highways* 48: 14–39.

Shaffer, Peter
 1974 *Equus*. New York: Atheneum.

Siringo, Charles A.
 1950 *A Texas Cowboy, or Fifteen Years on the Hurricane Deck of a Spanish Pony*. New York: Umbedenstock.

Westermeier, Clifford P.
 1976 "The Cowboy and Sex." In *The Cowboy: Six-Shooters, Songs, and Sex*, ed. Charles W. Harris and Buck Rainey, p. 85–106. Norman: University of Oklahoma Press.

Mounted Police

A SYMBOLIC STUDY OF URBAN HORSES

4

"How do you like being a city horse?" a passerby asks of a policeman's mount, extending a hand in an overture of friendliness, which is translated into a pat on the neck or nose. Certainly one of the most frequently asked of the many queries directed to police horses, it is one which strikes the heart of a perceived notion about the role of the horse and its place in society. Accustomed to thinking of horses in terms of rural settings and wide open spaces and as largely endemic to the Western states, many people are surprised when equine animals turn up in the city and fill a definite role there. But the mounted policeman, patrolling in a congested urban area, is a phenomenon which is becoming more and more common for those who currently live in or visit cities. Increasing numbers of metropolitan police departments, many of them in the East, are finding that horse and rider units excel in such functions as crowd control, traffic regulation, and deterring street crime, and thus are effective and beneficial agents of law enforcement.

Under conditions of the complete mechanization of modern times, however, many observers are struck by the incongruity of a man on horseback appearing in the context of the busiest cities, and regard it as somewhat of an anachronism. For this reason alone (additional reasons will be discussed), the mounted policeman commands attention. A standout amongst the trappings of civilization—buildings, cars, trucks, and buses, elevated railways, blowing paper, screeching sirens, and the shouts and tramping of the masses of people whose realm the city is—his very conspicuousness is strongly related to his effectiveness.

MOUNTED POLICE: A STUDY OF URBAN HORSES

A study of the horse in this urban setting provides many insights into the extraordinarily complex and often contradictory symbolic meaning with which the horse in our society has become imbued. It was with the intent of shedding light on some of the deep-lying meaning inherent in the horse-human relationship that I undertook this study of the mounted police. The fact that I concentrate on the imagery and symbolism involved, of course, does not mean that the mounted force on a pragmatic level is not doing a superb job at fulfilling its very important function. Quite the contrary—it is my point that this job *is* performed with efficiency in large part *because* of the profound meaning the horse has in the human consciousness. As Firth expressed it, "Symbols have work to do. They are not just static expressions of social relationships or ideas about the meaning of the world; they are instruments in an on-going process of social action" (1975:261).

The social action in this case—that is, the function of any police in society—is to maintain order. The central question to ask, then, is how does the horse contribute to this function? How is the horse/rider unit different from a policeman on foot, in a squad car, or on a motorcycle? For clearly the horse is interacting with the policeman who is astride him and powerfully affects the actions of that officer of the law, as well as influences the ways in which the officer is perceived and treated. That is true even though, as all mounted policemen are quick to point out, "we're police officers first and mounted officers second." Indeed, all members of the mounted force are required to have spent time "on the street" in other departments between their graduation from the police academy and their induction into the mounted unit.

As for efficiency as a law enforcement agency, it has been proven to the satisfaction of those in charge of many metropolitan police forces that just by virtue of being there, a mounted policeman is instrumental in greatly reducing the incidence of crime in crowded areas. Thus in police parlance, the horse/rider unit is said to possess high *visibility*—the most important and most frequently cited advantage of the mounted force. "Visibility is the key," one sergeant who was retiring after thirty-five years on the mounted force told me. "Our presence deters crime. A policeman on a horse is ten feet tall, and people see him from quite a distance." It is known that from this special vantage point he can spot suspicious people and control unruly crowds. The impact of the mounted police officer's conspicuousness, of course, is felt both by the would-be criminal who is contemplating a street crime and is deterred by his presence, and by the masses of people whom the

An important advantage for urban crime prevention is the increased "visibility" possessed by the mounted policeman. From his higher vantage point astride the horse, the mounted man can see, and be seen from, a greater distance than his fellow officer riding a motorcycle, on foot, or sitting in a squad car. Photo by author.

law seeks to protect. Informants from the ranks of the latter group reveal that they find a definite sense of security and comfort through the proximity of the mounted officer. Both the potential offender and the public at large are profoundly affected by the sight of the horse/rider unit—an image whose mere presence has a strong impact, becoming an example of what Firth calls "public symbols." These powerful collective symbols can become "bases for or expressions of common action; the element of communication of meaning is dependent upon the possibility of shared understanding" (1975:208). A function of such symbols is that of "facilitating social interaction and co-operation" (1975:90).

The Horse as a Reflection of the Social Order

Appropriately, everything about this particular horse in the city, the policeman's partner in law enforcement, gives evidence of orderliness. Far from the pastures and ranges where he would move in unfettered freedom, his image here is one of restraint and control. Tame and quiet, calm in the face of city situations which would ordinarily terrify unconditioned members of his species, his neck is arched under the influence of a regulation bit and bridle. He may also be fitted with a martingale to further curb his actions. Riding him in a McClellan-type saddle is a blue-uniformed officer, booted, spurred, and helmeted—a study in dark blue and black leather, accented by metal. Appropriate weapons complete the rider's ensemble. Beyond any possible doubt, the horse has been conquered, subjected to the restraints of civilization, which are blatantly symbolized by gear, accoutrements, and uniformed rider wearing badges and insignia. Authority, with generations of war and conquering behind it, springs from horse to rider, and again from rider to horse. A dynamic dimension from human history, laden with the charges of a thousand cavalries, adds to the aura and image of conquest and control which are transmitted to the viewer.

Describing city policemen (not mounted) in his detailed ethnography, Rubinstein notes that "the policeman's principal tool is his body," which is "a piece of equipment" essential to his trade (1980:267). His gun and nightstick, Rubinstein reveals, are not simply weapons but extensions of the policeman himself, used to do his work. But "unlike anyone else whose body is the tool of his trade, the policeman uses his to control other people" (1980:268). "Every aspect of a policeman's appearance has been calculated to assure that there can be no mistake about his social identity" (1980:268). His uniform makes him visible and proclaims that he is not a private person but a cop. His weapons are extensions of himself and symbols of force and authority (1980:277, 290). "Whether he wishes it or not," a policeman "is used as a symbol of authority and discipline" (1980:436). To carry this idea further, certainly the horse adds a powerful and richly significant dimension to the armament—both symbolic and actual—of the mounted patrolman. This dimension, as mentioned, rises partly out of the conquest which is implicit in the horse/rider relationship. In addition, however, the very nature of the horse itself makes this animal particularly appropriate for its special role in the maintenance of order and preservation of authority in human society. It is noteworthy that for artist George Stubbs, generally considered to be the best painter of equine subjects who ever lived, "the horse was his chief image of social harmony: order on four legs" (Hughes 1984:132–33).

Appeal to the human sense of touch is a significant factor in the popularity of city police horses. Photo by author.

The horse, most particularly the city horse—ridden, checked, and
reined—generally carries out with apparent acquiescence that which
society decrees to be its proper role. Meeting human expectations, it
can usually be counted upon to be obedient, orderly, and nonaggressive. Under normal conditions, then, it can be thought of as a kind of
gauge of the existing state of order. If all goes well, it behaves and
completes its expected rounds without serious interruption. It is this
strange capacity to reflect the moral order which Shakespeare attributed to horses in *Macbeth*. For in that play, these animals become the
central symbol for the unnaturalness of Macbeth's crime, a murder
which not only has violated the human social code but has offended the
very order of nature itself. One of the characters, Ross, reveals that,
responding to calamity with drastically altered behavior,

> Duncan's horses—a thing most strange and certain—
> Beauteous and swift, the minions of their race,
> Turn'd wild in nature, broke their stalls, flung out,
> Contending 'gainst obedience, as they would make
> War with mankind.

An Old Man adds:

'Tis said they eat each other.

And Ross replies:

They did so, to th' amazement of mine eyes,
That look'd upon it.

[1972:73–75]

The images of tame horses, sedate and disciplined, going wild and of once-gentle herbivores tearing into and devouring each other's flesh are events so out of keeping with nature that they have been drawn upon to dramatize the enormity of the effect of so heinous a crime as the murder which has just been committed.

It is this capacity for reversion to the wild state, even after years of restraint, which makes the horse uniquely suitable as an image of the balance that exists between civilization and chaos. Beneath the surface of reliable and expected behavior, there is always the chance, though it may be minimal, that the animals will throw off the accustomed yoke of subservience and demonstrate wild and "uncivilized" behavior. "What horses tend to remind us of," as one author phrased it, "is the instinctual life which flows forever below the layers of restraint laid down by the millennia of civilization" (Baskett 1980:8). In the police horse, virtually all evidence of the natural wildness which is characteristic of the equine species has been pushed far beneath the surface. The indication that this wildness is completely under control is largely responsible for symbolically imparting to city people the sense of security and the feeling that all is well with their existing order. It is the perception of the horse as a stable and dependable indicator of the social order itself (at opposite poles from the "outlaw" bronc) that forms a vital part of the police-horse image.

The regularity of the mounted patrolman's appointed daily rounds underscores the cyclic recurrence of his aura of beneficent protection and dependability. Each officer's "beat" remains generally predictable, and city people anticipate the good feelings and sense of relief engendered by his presence in their area. As a result, "whenever there's a cutback in the city budget, and the horse is gone from their district, merchants call headquarters and say they want it back," many officers told me. City officials are constantly besieged with complaints when horses are removed because of lack of funding; "people say they do not feel safe anymore without the horse." "With the horse back on the street, people tell us they can get outdoors." Again and again city dwellers speak of the comfort they derive, especially at night, from knowing the mounted patrol is on duty through hearing the sounds of the horses' hooves on the pavement. That is a subject to which we shall return for further discussion.

Questions Asked of the Mounted Officer

Two questions stand out as those most frequently asked of the mounted policeman while he is patrolling the city streets. First, virtually all people who stop beside his horse ask the officer, "What's his name?" Indeed, this simple question is so often asked of the officers that, at the end of a trying day, the men revealed that they are hard put to keep their patience. But they always manage to do just that—and answer one more time, and then again—before their daily tour of duty ends. People on the street evidence a real curiosity, a genuine need to find out the name of the horse, and seem to derive a sense of satisfaction from having this information. Upon reflection, the significance of this basic question is clear, for the answer establishes the position of the police horse in our society not only relative to people but relative to other animals, to whose status the police horse is often compared. (Parents showing the police horse to their children will often say, for example, "He's a lot different from the dog we have at home, isn't he?" or make a similar remark showing a comparison between the present animal and another species of domestic animal.)

As Sahlins has pointed out in his study of contemporary culture, "Dogs and horses participate in American society in the capacity of subjects. They have proper personal names, and indeed we are in the habit of conversing with them as we do not talk to pigs and cattle" (1976:174). Animals thus named and spoken to are, of course, generally perceived as close to mankind. (As a corollary, they are considered inedible by our society, with dog meat being strictly tabu and horsemeat certainly viewed with disdain if not with horror by the residents of most American cities. See Sahlins 1976:172–75.) Lévi-Strauss's discussion of race horse names in France is pertinent to reflect on here, for, as he observes, race horses "do not form part of human society either as subjects or objects." Rather, "they are products of human industry and they are born and live as isolated individuals juxtaposed in stud farms devised for their sake." Thus "they constitute the desocialized condition of existence of a private society" (1966:206). Race horses, as almost everyone is aware, have names which are generally unfamiliar in human usage and whose meanings are no doubt clear only to those intimately involved with the horses in the race world.

Differing from race horses, who are ordinarily separated from human society, a high percentage of police horses have human names—as opposed, for example, to descriptive ones defining their color or characteristics, such as "Blackie" or "Spitfire," metaphoric names such as "Genuine Risk," or those taken from other domains, such as "Man O'War." The rule for a policeman's equine partner is to be given a name such as "Jack" or "Kevin," or one commemorating a cowboy hero, such as "Hopalong Cassidy," or a song hero, such as "Mr. Bo-Jangles." In the small number of cases in which police horses do have descriptive names, it is noteworthy that these relate to the rider and not the horse. Hence "Irish" expresses one rider's pride in his ethnicity, "Whiskey" another rider's fondness for strong drink, and so forth. Such names act to draw the horses into a closer relationship with their human partners.

These naming practices serve to give immediate notice that the police horse stands as an agent who is to a certain extent *within* human society. It does not always connote an equal relationship as partners, however, as many officers (reminiscent of rodeo contestants in roping events) refer to their mount as more in the nature of a "son" or a "big kid," who must be disciplined and controlled through measures resembling parental authority. Some even speak indulgently of their horses as "babies," the objects of "baby-sitting." But overall, an officer's mount is regarded as a kind of subordinate, not as a creature of an alien order but rather as one who partakes of the human social realm on city streets. This quality, in fact, is an important component of the force and authority generated by the police horse/rider unit. For through such partial humanization, the horse becomes more potent as an element to be reckoned with, not a mere objectified tool in the sense of a motorcycle policeman's "bike" or the squad car. While retaining equine characteristics, the horse is yet drawn into human social affairs, representing a transformation of nature into the human cultural sphere. Hence the animal can serve as a powerful symbolic element from nature which now belongs to and partakes of the most "civilized" of all human realms—the city.

Whereas the first question, involving the animal's name, serves to effectively delineate the position of the horse with regard to its context, the second most commonly posed query relates to the questioner's own location within the complex structure of the city. This question, or category of questions, directed to the mounted policeman as he stands among the crowds on the streets or rides over his beat, concerns directions to some specified place or area within the city. Those unfamiliar with the city who search for a destination unknown to them find it convenient to take their bearings from the mounted figure which looms as authority. The asker's objective may be, for example, a school, church, store, business office, restaurant, or particular street. The mounted officer in an urban area is expected to be familiar with them all, and usually he is. Once again, this function, facilitated by the accessibility which comes from being astride the horse, fits his role as a keeper of order. Out of the chaos and confusion of a downtown district, people turn to a figure perceived as having a vast knowledge of the city's layout. Then, at least momentarily, the patrolman makes order for them, as he patiently and clearly guides them to their destination. People turn to the horseman for this service most frequently, they say, in preference to the foot patrolman, who may be nearby yet not be visible, and to the motorcycle man, who may be going too fast, and to the policeman in a car, who may pass through the area too quickly or who is less accessible, set apart and enclosed, as he is, in his vehicle.

Communication and Public Relations

This feature of *approachability* distinguishes the mounted patrolman from all other types of policemen in the minds of informants. Beyond the pragmatic factors of visibility and availability, however, there are deeper elements which draw people to the police horse. Pedestrians interviewed in downtown areas indicated the strong attraction they feel for the horse. If a cruiser and a horse are together on the street, by far the greater majority always go to the horse. Many verbalize their feeling of pleasure at relating, however briefly, to something "nonmechanical," something "alive and natural" to be found in the industrialized sphere of the city. As one man expressed the deep-lying concept that many seemed to share, "You get more support as a unit, man and horse, then when police are mechanized. The human-animal combination carries more weight emotionally; they are more personable." The city populace's general perception of the horse as inherently good, and particularly as a "noble animal," a beautiful and willing coworker, adds a unique aspect to the mounted branch of the municipal police, sharply differentiating it from other departments.

In essence, the presence of the equine animal in close association with the policeman removes hostility and acts to make the confrontation between citizen and law officer far less threatening and formidable than it would otherwise be. Police administrators call this interaction "good PR" and are quick to credit their mounted unit with the highest achievement in this area, categorizing it with crowd control and crime prevention through visibility as its three vital functions.

Observing people of all ages and types crowding around the horse and rider on a city street, one has no doubt about this dynamic effect. Many urbanites go out of their way daily to bring packages of carrots, lumps of sugar, peppermints, candy bars, or apples for their favorite police horse. In field work, I encountered one woman in particular who regularly spends her lunch hour buying a plateful of greens at a salad bar and feeding it, bit by bit, to the horse in her district. Broad, spontaneous smiles, seldom observed in congested marketplaces, light up the faces of many citizens as they catch sight of the horse and rider and spread to a broad grin as they walk over to stand admiringly beside the pair. Many people talk to the horse, saying things such as "You're so beautiful," "I hope they never take you away from here," and "I love your eyes." Others say wistfully, "I'd like to ride you across the park, but it's not allowed," or "You're a city horse, one of the last of your kind." An admirer claimed, "These horses have more personality than most people." One said, "I love those horses. They are so innocent; I think they will inherit the earth, don't you?"

Almost all those who stop beside the horse reach out to touch the animal, patting it most usually on the head, neck, or nose. Their feeling of satisfaction is clearly evident as they relax and enjoy the benefits of their sense of touch, an experience so generally denied to people in contemporary society. According to an authority on the human tactile modality, one of the negative achievements of Western civilization has been the repression of the pleasures of touching (Montagu 1978:249). The indulgence of our tactile sense is one of the benefits of association with horses, and city people find police horses one of the few available recipients of patting and caressing. Artists have traditionally emphasized the aesthetic appeal of horses' coats and have taken delight in painting them sleek and shiny. This texture is especially apparent, for

[125]

Otho, with John Larkin up by George Stubbs. For the celebrated English painter of horses, George Stubbs (1724–1806), the equine form whose image he perfected became a symbol of order, representing social harmony. Courtesy of the Tate Gallery, London.

example, in what is perhaps the most celebrated of all horse paintings, George Stubbs's *Whistlejacket* (see Baskett 1980:36). Many people remark about the well-groomed coats of police mounts, and few are content to look without touching. As Kroeber observed, "What is seen and touched is always made part of ourselves more intensely and more meaningfully than what is only seen" (1970:267).

Communication is no doubt the key to the special quality of success that characterizes the mounted force. "The mounted policeman communicates with the general public more because he is exposed; he has no shield, and people come to him more readily for services," observed one veteran sergeant. Looking beneath the surface, it is the implicit communication between horse and rider that sets the stage for the free flow of communication which exists between people on the street and the mounted officer. Observation of mounted patrolmen interacting with their horses and conversation with the men about horses and horsemanship reveal that communication with their horses is very much a priority. As one man explained it, "The horse communicates closely with the officer on his back through body movements and expressions of his eyes. In turn, the officer communicates with the horse through voice, touch, leg aids, hands, reins, blunt spurs, and the shifting balance of his body." Another assured me, "Police horses are responsive to you." Many agreed that "the horse knows what you want him to do. If you're chasing someone, the horse senses it and tries harder to go after them." "The horse gets to know what you want to do; he will even push a drunk away." Not only does the rider communicate with his mount, but, as many patrolmen told me, the relationship is reciprocal. "You become like one with the horse, and know what will scare him. You can anticipate what is going to make him skittish, how he is going to react, so that you can prepare yourself." As another officer expressed it, "You get used to being on your horse. You talk to him; you ask his opinion." One sergeant admitted he was embarassed when he bumped his horse's head with his own head and instinctively said, "Excuse me!"

Because of his relationship to his horse, people view the mounted officer as "patient." Some say a man who is good to his horse must be a good man. He is seen as "agreeable and at peace with himself and the world when riding his horse." Because the mounted patrolmen like horses, people feel, "they seem to be at peace." People on the street want to communicate with the mounted men. "This is not the way it is in cruisers." Many noted that "mounted men are friendly. They are communicating with a live animal, not something mechanized." One spoke of them as "two live entities, the rider being one with the horse." Many commented on the relationship between friendliness and the horse: "Everyone loves horses, and mounted policemen become friendly to people because of the horse."

Mounted policemen themselves are well aware of the effect of their equine partners on their own image and on the image of policemen in general. As one said, "With the horse, you can communicate with the public to a much greater extent than other policemen. You can break the barrier. At first, people are scared of you, but because of the horse, they will talk to you. Then they want to buy candy or an apple for the horse. Soon they aren't afraid any more, and then they admit 'I've never talked to a policeman before.'" The men are proud that

[127]

"mounted police are important in public relations. A child may pat the horse while his mother talks to the patrolman. The child may have never seen a horse before, and the experience is an exciting one." A mounted officer told me, "People are comfortable patting my horse. I can give them information, whereas if they were talking with a policeman in a car, they would be suspicious."

Mounted officers who have recently worked in a squad car compare the experience and their effect on the public. "When I was in a cruiser, I was not involved with anyone. No one speaks to you. On a horse, thousands of people speak to you. You bullshit with them, you kid and joke. I like it. The horse job is good for that, whereas the cruiser is not." Many were frank in admitting they liked the attention which a mounted officer attracts. "As a mounted policeman, people like you better. If they see you at nine in the morning off the horse, they go right by you. But later, when the same person sees you on the horse, he does notice you. On the horse, you are in the limelight." The effects of their equine coworkers were clear in many officers' minds. "Because people in general have a good feeling about horses, they look at us as a nice person instead of as a person who is going to hurt someone." Quite a few men admitted that their horses got much more attention than they did, and that if it weren't for the horse, they would be totally ignored. "People sympathize with the animal, ask if he has enough water, if the rain bothers him, or if the sun is too hot for him. They are very concerned. If the horse sweats, they always think you ran him too hard. People don't give me that kind of attention."

The low status of police in society, the men think, is improved by the mounted unit. Policemen on horses are often referred to in the media as "Blue Knights," with a heroic image. "The horse changes the bad image of the police. They see that we are courteous and we are not all killers." "People treat policemen on a horse with a lot more friendliness. Those who scream profanity at men in a cruiser are the same ones who want to pat the horse and feed it apples and cookies." One officer who had grown up in a "tough neighborhood" said, "The horse does away with the fear people have of communicating with policemen. When I was a young boy with a gang of kids on the street and a cruiser pulled up, we knew one of us was going to get hassled. But when the horse walks up, it breaks the ice. No one says, 'This guy is here to hassle us.' It breaks the ice, totally." This same idea was expressed by another mounted officer, who told me, "One of the main purposes of our being out here is communicating with people so we are not stereotyped as cops liking to knock heads around. Horses come between us and the general public, and we are part of the department that breaks the ice."

The fact that "reactions to the horse are always positive" was felt by mounted patrolmen to be extremely important. "Everyone loves the horse. The horse is a majestic animal. I never met a person who didn't like horses. Some people don't like cops, but they pat the horse, and then they say cops aren't all that bad. Their opinion changes. They don't relate this way at all to a motorcycle or a car." Many are especially gratified by their effect on younger citizens. "People get to know you on a horse, especially the kids. Kids are important in community relations. People are amazed to find that in a short period of time, we get control over kids. Those who formerly drank and harassed police on bikes were impressed when we chased them on horses." City kids, the officers say, look forward to the appearance of the mounted policeman in their area.

> Kids on street corners at night are generally bad actors. They have no place to go, and nothing to do, so they take drugs. They are antagonistic to police in cruisers. But they talk to me every night and pat my horse. Later they ask, "Why take drugs?" The horse makes the kids friendly. They all love the horse. One boy whose brother had been shot by a regular policeman said to me, "You cops on horses treat us like human beings." I became friendly with this boy through the horse.

It is a source of pride that

> with mounted policemen, even gangs are friendly. They get to know the horse's name and its color. It works. Those kids will do everything for you. Before I went to this area of street gangs, people told me I would be stoned. Instead, they became friendly. They looked forward to the horse coming. They did whatever I asked. Often these kids know where the problem areas are, and they make your work easier when you have their confidence. Once I asked one of them to hold the horse while I went into a restaurant for coffee. He did it, and I was able to trust him enough to relax.

Several mounted men described the experience of a quick reversal in attitude of a hostile crowd. "In hostile crowds, people are angry, shouting and threatening. But after the crowd is dispersed by mounted officers, members who had been demonstrating will come over and pat the horse a few minutes later. They are no longer angry, and they can relate to the horse." It was often remarked "no one pats a cruiser!" "People even thank you for being out on the street on the horse. You never get this in a cruiser."

Duality in the Perception of the Horse

What is it in the nature of the horse or the way in which it is perceived that makes possible these interactions and transformations involving the police and the people of the city? As one mounted officer explained it, "There is an image of mildness, a 'mystique' which surrounds the police horse. People in these congested areas say they look upon the horse as 'nonaggressive.'" Indeed, people in the city told me that it is important that "horses do not bite, claw, or attack." People generally look upon the equine animal as "peaceful," one who by nature "wants to be left alone, and whose survival in the wild depended upon fleeing, not fighting." Many point out that "the horse, unlike a dog, will not attack a person." This peaceful and nonviolent image often merged with a sense of justice or fair play for parents who stopped beside the police horse and told their children, "He won't hurt you unless you hurt him."

At the same time that the horse is regarded as a mild and gentle herbivore, however, it also inspires the contradictory element of fear as part of its image. As one person said, "There is something about the horse—it commands fear, yet the horse wouldn't really hurt you." As expressed by the characters in *Macbeth,* people are aware that horses have a dual nature and that, though they are routinely gentle, paradoxically they have the ability to evoke fear in certain situations. It is this quality of engendering fear that enables police horses to control unruly crowds and restore order. That crowds fear and respond to horses in a uniquely effective way is a well-known fact. Police records document the successful work of mounted officers in this regard, and patrolmen vividly recount experiences of participation in activities in the line of duty during which crowds were broken up and riots put down. The efficacy of "a couple of mounted men to do the work of many foot or bike men" is a constant source of pride to the mounted patrol. "One horse," some say, "is equal to one hundred men on foot in crowd control, especially if the crowd is hostile." "People instinctively back up and give ground for a horse, whereas they will not do so for police-

The man/horse unit of the mounted police is acknowledged to be unsurpassed for efficiency in crowd control on
city streets. Vic DeLucia/NYT Pictures.

men on foot, on a bike, or in a car. Less people get hurt when horses
are used, yet there is something about the horse that makes people
retreat." People in crowds are known to "take one step back from a
motorcycle, but thirty steps back from a horse."

The common explanation of this reaction is that being stepped on
by the horse is what people fear. "Being stepped on is the psychological
factor," officers say. "Crowds will push over a police motorcycle, but
never a police horse." "You have control; a guy can't knock you over
on a horse." It is felt that

> in hostile, adversary demonstrations, people know that the police
> won't drive a motorcycle or a cruiser into the crowd, because of in-
> juries which might result. Mounted police won't be criticized by the
> media or other agency if they physically push the crowd back. If some-
> one is stepped on, that's unfortunate, but it's fair game. Police in this
> region of the country can't use fire hoses or charge in with dogs as they
> do in the South. These measures are not accepted here, nor is use of the
> cattle prod. But if we utilize the horse as an extension of the police, this
> is accepted.

One officer said, "The horse is an asset, a resource for our primary job. The horse is an extension, a bond. When you move, the horse is going to move with you."

It has been frequently observed that unruly members of a gang or criminals who are being chased by a mounted policeman have a great fear of being stepped on by the horse. After being chased by mounted officers in a city park, two suspects revealed that their dominating fear was that "the horses would trample us." The commonest response from the suspect when the officers make an arrest is "Don't let that horse come near me!" One is on record as saying to the patrolman, "What are you, crazy? Don't let him step on me." Pursued suspects often voice their fears: "Are you going to run me down?" Trying to move a suspect out of a congested shopping area, a mounted officer was told, "You don't have to have the horse *that* close to me!" Arrested criminals often say, "I'm afraid of horses. I don't care what you do with me, but just keep that horse away." Suspects shriek, "What are you doing this [coming close to them on the horse] for? I give up!" One patrolman, described as a "better than average rider," cornered a suspect in an alley by "putting the horse's nose right up to the guy's face." The suspect screamed, "Don't come any closer. I'll go in a car. Don't take me with the horse. Get him away from me and let me go peacefully in a car." Because of the fear the horse inspires at certain times and in some individuals, officers feel that being mounted is a strong advantage in apprehending wrongdoers on city streets. "Many suspects figure the horse is coming at them, and they want to retreat. Not too many of them will come at you, because of this fear they have." The mounted men note a pattern in their law enforcement experiences: "Once a person has committed a crime, a paranoia grows in the criminal's mind, and he thinks the horse will attack like a dog." One officer thinks, "If a person is guilty, the horse can stare them down."

Mounted officers do, in fact, utilize people's perceptions of the complex and contradictory nature of the horse—the wild versus the tame—to increase the effectiveness with which they carry out their work. An officer may willingly allow or encourage the horse to go out of control, or rather to give the impression of being out of control, in order to make use of people's reactions to this wilder, fear-inducing element of the horse's nature. Breaking out of his usual stance of controlled and disciplined horsemanship in order to control people or get them to do his bidding more quickly, a mounted officer will shout,

"Watch out! I can't control this horse!" Explaining his actions, one man told me:

> I try to instill in the people the idea that the horse has its own brain, so they will have more fear of it. Even though I actually *could* control the horse, I tell them, "This horse may act up if you don't pull over!" I keep telling them, "Watch out for the horse! Watch out for the horse!" The horse may not really do what I say; it may stand, step in place, and I wonder if it will spin or rear up. I shout, "Watch out! This horse may go up in the air," and this really helps to control people.

Another way in which the potential wildness of a police horse may be used is exemplified by an instance in which a mounted officer was attempting to get an unlicensed musician who was begging for money out of the downtown area. "She was very obstinate and just would not leave. I was angry," he admitted. "I hoped the horse would take a big dump near her. I put my horse in front of her, so the horse blocked her from the audience, and no one could see her or get between her and the horse. Then she finally went away. I would have been legally right if I had broken her instrument," the officer asserted. "I would have said that I couldn't control the horse."

Drawing powerfully upon the complexity in the repertoire of equine behavioral elements and the public's perception of them, the police horse becomes a symbol which can operate selectively according to varied conditions which affect social demeanor. Municipal police reported, for example, that in one large city park that had been set aside for "family recreation—picnicking, camping, and the like"—a serious problem arose, in which "undesirables began invading the area. They were drug users and drank heavily; assaults occurred, and families could no longer feel safe there. When mounted policemen were dispatched to patrol the area, however, the horses accomplished what previous efforts by police had been unable to do: the wild people left for good. They didn't like the idea of troopers on horseback. Now the families have returned." The same tactics were tried again at another park, and "when the horses arrived, the undesirables left." Implicit in the recounting of this incident and similar events is a concept which seems to pervade the operation of the mounted police force: the guilty, choosing the wilder image, generally fear the horse, while those who are innocent by virtue of being within the bounds of the social order view the horse in its milder light. Thus it is this very

[133]

quality of duality itself in the image of the horse, which at first seems so paradoxical, that gives power to the man/horse unit in enforcing order.

Characteristics of Police Horses

What are the particular characteristics of police horses, and how are they chosen? A review of the requirements as to size, conformation, color, sex, temperament, age, and breed which must be met in order for a horse to become a permanent part of the mounted police force reveals much about the ways in which the man/horse image is created and maintained within the force.

Size and Conformation   It is generally specified in mounted police force requirements that horses be "at least 15.2 hands" in height (a hand is equal to four inches, and the number following the period refers to inches; the measurement is taken at the withers), with 15.3 or 16 hands preferred. That means that police horses, for the most part, are bigger than average riding horses. Size of mounts is constantly mentioned both by the public in describing their views of the force and by the officers themselves in discussing their role. "Performing your job while controlling an animal of that size" takes a great deal of ability and is a skill the men are proud of. "A big horse is an important resource in this job," officers believe. One patrolman whose horse measures 15.3 hands in height told me, "I wish the horse were 16 hands. I would feel better about him; we could do a better job." Even though what was being discussed was literally only one inch, it was of great importance to this man to be able to refer to his horse as 16 hands high.

Virtually all police horses are "strongly built," as the men say, and are big-boned, possessing what is called "substance." Requirements for police mounts state that they should weigh at least eleven hundred pounds; many are far heavier. People in the street nearly always remark about the large size of the police horse, saying they admire the rider's control over such a big animal. Mounted patrolmen know that and admit, "People are impressed with something bigger; it makes us look bigger, and we are more powerful." Officers revealed that "our horses must be 15.3 or higher; on a big horse you are taller. You feel 'I am a superman.' You feel far superior on a big horse compared to being in a cruiser." "It's really great to have fifteen hundred pounds under you." "Police horses are big and blocky; any criminal in the city would be scared, having seventeen hundred pounds running after him." People in the street must always, in the literal sense, "look up" to the man/ horse unit, and the difference between a man on a small horse and one on a large horse is perceived to be considerable. Some police horses must carry heavy riders, of course, though many are paired with trim and light officers. Regular policemen's equipment, too, must be carried, but the total weight carried by a police horse is generally much less, for example, than that borne by a Western ranch horse, who is typically much shorter in stature yet wiry and deemed to be well able to bear considerable weight, including the ponderous stock saddle.

In contrast, however, a big horse is an inextricable part of the mounted officer's image. Large horses are felt to be "more intimidating and impressive," an important advantage in controlling people, especially crowds, in quelling riots, and in being visible on the streets. Perceived strength and power for duties involved in law enforcement are uniformly felt to be magnified in the case of taller horses. An officer explained, "Being up high, you have more power. You are god in a crowd; you can move anything you want to." Even the hooves, which are conspicuously eyed by almost every observer in the street, add to the image of tallness. Most of the horses, neatly shod, are maintained with relatively long hooves, and protective pads which are placed between the hoof and the shoe may add still more height.

"Good conformation" is listed as a requirement for a police horse, and this specification is generally borne out by the mounts seen on city streets. One rarely finds an unattractive horse ridden by a patrolman. Occasionally a mount may have a fault of conformation, such as a "Roman nose," for example, a feature often found in horses of Standardbred breeding. Without exception in such cases, however, the overall appearance of the police horse is attractive. Horses chosen in spite of having some kind of individual fault are nevertheless well proportioned and commanding in their bearing. A particularly impressive manner of moving or an alertness of spirit gives these horses an ambience that makes conformation faults inconspicuous.

Color   The coat color of the chosen horses is one of the most predictable and meaning-laden characteristics of police horses. Requirements are generally quite restrictive and state that colors must be "bay, brown, black, or chestnut." (Bay is essentially a brown color with black "points"—i.e., mane, tail, and legs; see Green 1974 for details of coat colors in horses.) With a few significant exceptions, this rule is

[135]

followed. Coat color is felt to be a very important feature of police horses, as expressed by the patrolmen themselves and by the public who relates to them. Mounted men feel that "uniformity of color is very important" and that "bay and chestnut are the right colors for police horses. We are a paramilitary outfit, and these colors look like what a police horse should be." Others revealed that "dark colors are more traditional; they are more formal; they add formality to the outfit. Riders are all in black and blue, and these colored horses are much more formal than white, roan, buckskin, gray, or palomino." Officers believe that " a bay horse shows more conformity. It looks better for a mounted patrolman. You see the horse's muscularity better, and there is more definition due to the black parts." All feel "it's important that our horses aren't spotted. We want uniformity; it's a military-type thing."

There is total agreement about the lack of suitability of white or light-colored horses for the police force. Mounted police in some cities have them but explain that these horses were donated and are too good to turn down because of economic factors. All officers say, "Bay is our first choice, and we prefer dark horses, but we don't always have our choice." In a city where no white or light horses are now accepted, a patrolman explained, "We wouldn't want a multicolor or white horse in police work. We had one white horse given to us, and it was overruled. It used to be the lead horse at the race track before it was donated to the mounted force." Another officer recalled, "Once we had a horse almost all white; it was silly-looking, and not at all suitable for the police." Others agreed, "Our horses must be bays and chestnuts, not palominos or spotted horses. That would be too much like cowboys and Indians." Several patrolmen speak with disdain of the unusual case of their fellow mounted officer who rides a "flashy light-colored horse"—a golden-colored horse with a flaxen mane and tail. Correlated with this image is the way they portray this particular rider and horse: "He lets his palomino get away with a lot. The horse is out of control; he prances a lot and is excitable. He looks pretty, but although he's the same age as my horse, I keep mine like a gentleman. That guy's horse is crazy!" Another officer says of him, "He lets that horse act wild, and people who know horses can tell this. It doesn't help, and doesn't do the police work any good or help his job to have that horse act wild."

The subject of color as symbol has received attention from anthropologists, particularly in the case of red, white, and black as analyzed in the work of Turner (1967) and the red, yellow, and green of the traffic light as discussed by Sahlins (1976:198–200), drawing on Leach (1974:16–21). In a similar, though at the same time unique, way, the police horse offers a rich subject for analysis, for its color may be seen to operate as a powerful symbolic force. As Sahlins has pointed out, "The whole of nature is the potential object of the symbolic praxis, whose cunning . . . consists in this: that it puts to the service of its own intentions those relations among things existing by their own properties" (1976:196). The horses' colors and what they communicate in society are an apt example of "the suitability of a contrast provided by nature to a distinction present in culture—for instance, between authority and subordination" (Sahlins 1976:196). Relevant to the case of police horses, too, are Firth's statements that "the use of symbols as instruments of control is widespread" and that "symbols as instruments of power and control are most prominent in the public domain" (1975:86).

The uniform darkness of coat color which takes on such significance in police horse specifications serves to communicate authority. The very conservativeness with which the blacks and browns have been imbued in our culture enables them to become symbols of the social order. These colors are generally viewed as more "masculine" than lighter colors. The darkness of the police animals' coats has a certain ponderous quality, a somberness which places them beyond frivolity. The alikeness, the conformity of the dark horses, indicates restraint. And the conformity of each horse to the dark and sobering pattern suggests the collectivity, the unity, of the mounted policemen as members of the law-enforcing arm of society. The dark colors, particularly the bay—composed of both brown and black—confer the same sort of status that accrues to the man in a dark, conservative suit who "dresses for success" to symbolize and communicate his intention to attain or keep his membership in conventional society. Formality, for example, is most intensely symbolized by the black tuxedo. And, whereas light colors often connote a less serious tone, dark automobiles have been traditionally chosen for events important to society, such as weddings, funerals, and politicians' parades. Clergymen, doctors, and lawyers, as upholders of society, tend to wear dark clothing.

According to Sahlins, "the use of the light/dark contrast is truly widespread in human societies, perhaps universally significant, and usually symbolic of fundamental oppositions of the social life—pure and unpure, life and death, sacred and profane, male and female, etc." (1977:175). "It has often been pointed out in Western contexts how light colors are associated with pleasure, dark colors with sadness" (Firth 1975:67–68). According to Radcliffe-Brown, as quoted by Sahlins, "the association of light and dark with euphoric and dysphoric conditions respectively has a psychological basis, for it seems to be universal in human nature" (1977:180).

In the case of the police horses, additional oppositions are apparent and operate symbolically. Here the dark/light contrast can represent the oppositions collectivity and individuality; obedience and fractiousness; and that which is within the realm of order versus that which is outside the realm of order. Light-colored or white horses are, in comparison to dark ones, considered "flashy" and "wild." That is especially true of palominos, light sorrels, and buckskins, which, as mentioned, do not make completely acceptable or typical police mounts. Judging from the general usage of these horses in our society as mounts for showmen, circus performers, and "Wild West" enthusiasts, as well as military leaders, horses of these colors generally denote a certain individualism in their riders. (See chap. 2.) They are apt to be "standouts," commanding special attention. Most particularly in the case of a white horse, as pointed out in the chapter on the White Mustang of the Prairies, the connotation can be that of making its rider a hero, or someone distinctive. In the dark and conforming mounts of the police, on the other hand, the force of collectivity receives emphasis, making these animals suitable to enforcing order in the form of the law. In white or light-colored horses, people uniformly perceive wildness, lack of restraint, contrasting to the conservative subordination denoted by the dark and subdued coat colors.

Departing even further from the ideal image of a police horse is the case of a two- or three-colored horse, whose body is spotted—a pinto, Paint, or piebald horse. Typically associated with American Indians and with the untamed frontier, all informants (both mounted policemen and the public) agree that such horses are the antithesis of police mounts. Even more than white or light-colored horses, which are occasionally tolerated, multicolored mounts are perceived to denote extreme wildness and irregularity. Indeed, for the American Paint Horse Association, which registers such animals, " 'No Two Alike' has long been a slogan descriptive of the unique color pattern of each individual

Paint horse. And the uniqueness of individual Paints is carried over into a unique registry which emphasizes individuality" (King 1978:42).

Sex   There is one specification that is enforced even more rigidly than color in this particular police department, and that is sex. *All* mounts, without exception, must be geldings. To the men, riding a mare for their job is unthinkable. Castrated male horses are the only category acceptable for partners. When pedestrians ask about mares, officers are likely to answer, "This is a macho outfit, too much of a macho outfit to have female horses." Others simply express the common perception that mares are too temperamental: "Mares are fussy when in season, so they are not suitable for use in police work," or "No mares are used, as it would be hard to control them when they come into heat." "There would be management problems," one mountie warned, "so we have no mares. When they were horsing, if the mares were downtown, some would kick your head off if you touched them. When downtown with a bunch of people and you pushed against the mare and that mare was horsing, you know what's going to happen! Maybe mares would be okay for parks. Some cities have mares for patrolling parks, and they are okay except for that period when they come in season."

Patrolmen say that "geldings are not as high-spirited as mares" and believe that "mares would be more frightened in the city." Additionally, there is the certainty that "geldings are more suitable because they have bigger bones." An officer who owns several horses observed, "I have a four-year-old stallion at home, and he is not unreliable. But I would never put a stallion on the street." Another believes "a stallion would be fighting mares and other stallions more than the crowd." Generally officers agreed that "a gelding is more passive. I wouldn't want a stallion *or* a mare. Police horses must have only one thing on their mind—to do what we tell them."

Thus several familiar themes reinforce the image of and give power to the function of police horses. The pervasive notion of the female as wilder, closer to nature, by reason of being more subject to natural physiological processes associated with reproduction, is a deeply rooted and much-discussed idea (see especially Merchant 1980; Ortner 1974). Suffice it to state here that this concept is a factor in establishing castrated males as the only category of horse suitable as enforcers of the law. A gelding is perceived as more orderly, steadier, more dependable, more obedient, more conforming. Viewed as farther removed from wild nature, its will is consequently less its own and so can belong more exclusively to its rider. And significantly, though castrated, geldings are still males, belonging to an essentially male outfit. The notion of the female as part of nature, and of nature as disorder, both presided over by the more orderly and "rational" male element of culture, can hardly have a more blatant expression. The chosen characteristics of police horses, then, are aligned to jibe with the tenor of dominant views and values and thus are legitimized as symbols in representing the social order itself and instrumenting the enforcement of its tenets.

Temperament   "Good temperament" is included in police horse requirements, with the added specification "without biting or kicking habit." The nonaggressive image is sustained and emphasized by constant reference to the horse as an animal that will not attack the general public in the street. A test for this quality is given to potential police horses as newcomers and is rigidly enforced with the regulars in routine daily work. This test is important, for I have seen shoppers in the city pause to stand behind police horses and deliberately pull hairs out of their tails, without provoking the stoic animals to kick. The patience of the horses in this regard is legendary. "Police horses must have good dispositions," mounties say. "They must be good with the general public. They have to have super control, as they are around children as well as grownups all day long." An officer who has trained many police mounts explains, "Kickers and nippers would cause problems. We cull these during training." Nipping is a feature which sometimes crops up because of excessive feeding of treats by the public, but it is held in check by patrolmen, who often have to prohibit offered treats for their mounts because of a habit-forming propensity.

Qualities of temperament which prevent a horse from kicking and biting are not the only unusual characteristics expected from police mounts. The most unique element about them is that both by nature and by training (and by reinforcement when necessary), they must be fearless in the face of city conditions which would ordinarily frighten most horses. Listed under necessary steps in the training of horses in mounted police specifications is the injunction to "test reactions to strange sights and sounds which help to determine if a horse is suitable for city work: street cars, air brakes on large trucks, sewer covers, flags waving, and large crowds."

Who can predict what will frighten a horse in the city, causing him to shy or bolt and run—natural reactions for a member of the equine species? Plastic bags, stirred by the wind, which seem to spark an age-old reaction to a predator, are an ever-present hazard, as are automobile horns, sirens, musicians playing in the street, applause, a Chinese gong used to signal the start of a road race, and the beat of Hare Krishna tambourines, which, his rider says, always spooks one particular police horse. All of these, and many other unforeseen elements, keep the mounted policeman on guard and ever-conscious of the horse's propensity to react to innate fear. Crowd control, often considered the most important function of the horse/rider units, is itself in many ways antithetical to the horse's natural inclination. Untrained, a horse would be more apt to turn and flee from a crowd, rather than move toward it, especially in the case of the noisy and actively moving crowds which he may be called upon to control.

"Nuisance training" to maintain horses' conditioning for the stress which may be elicited by situations encountered on the street is periodically carried out in a riding ring near the police barracks stable. During such sessions, lighted firecrackers are thrown beneath the horses' feet, banners are furled beside them, loud music blares, and balloons are inflated. "On the street," trials consisting of riding the horse past jackhammers and under elevated railways while a train roars directly overhead are said to be the supreme tests for a good police mount. "If they perform well under those conditions, they'll go almost everywhere," officers say. Such training "keeps both rider and horse on edge and ready for whatever they may meet in the city." No matter what a horse's previous experience has been, all agree that "the actual training is on the street. It takes two years for an animal to become a good, dependable police horse." Patrolmen point out that "a horse has to get used to city life; there are so many distractions."

A great deal of the ability to overcome natural tendencies of the horse and carry out police work with an equine partner is attributed to the rider's skill in control. The animal is said to be extremely sensitive to the mental state of the patrolman. An official educational bulletin issued by one municipal mounted unit states: "The most important condition for a well-trained police horse is the rider's confidence and handling ability. Nervousness of the rider is always communicated to the horse." Hence controllability is perceived as the key. It is the power of the policeman over the animal which, in the last analysis, makes the human/horse unit an effective one.

Officers frequently speak of their "very predominant fear" that horses will spook, especially in crowded areas, where they "may spin and go down with the rider." Mounted men are quick to describe the control they feel is necessary to their job:

> It's not like pleasure riding. You must lock your legs in. If a truck with a flag comes along, I know my horse won't like it, and I automatically lock my legs. My responses are automatic. It's not a relaxed ride. If the horse spins, I can react quickly, and it's as if nothing has happened. Two seconds later I am talking to a person who says "My God!" You bet it would be "My God!" if that had happened four years ago, but now it's as if nothing happened.

At one point "we all knew the feeling of fear, but we got over it after training and more experience in the street. At first, when the horse reared and jumped, I was scared and wanted to go back to the cruiser. We're only trained a short time before we hit the street, but we get experience after a while. We get rid of the crazy horses, and we get more training ourselves."

"People ask why we wear spurs. They think you torture the horse. They think you are bad to the horse; they assume this. But I have spurs in case a bus backfires or the fire department comes, to make the horse move. I ask these people, 'Did you ever ride under these conditions?' Sometimes a manhole cover blows up, and the horse jumps from the noise of steaming. We have to prepare for everything."

Pride in a "streetwise" mount is keenly felt by the rider. "My horse has no fear of traffic, even fire engines. One day an ambulance made him huff and puff, but I controlled him." The rider's attitude is given credit for much of the animal's conditioning process:

> Once, my horse wouldn't go near a bus or over a manhole cover. But I had the patience to bring him nearer and nearer. If it does anything, being in a mounted outfit teaches us patience. If the guys didn't have it, they wouldn't be riding today. There is always the element of surprise; you never know until it happens. For example, you are observing a crowd, and a car backfires or a newspaper blows out and wraps around your horse's leg. If you can deal with settling the horse and getting him over that, you are okay. You have to adapt to the unexpected. People

say this is an easy job, but it isn't. It takes terrific concentration to pay attention to the crowd, everything around you, *and* what the horse is doing, all at the same time.

Riding on the street is different than in the corral. It's an entirely different thing. A dressage rider I knew was critical of mounted policemen, claiming we don't ride well. Training for dressage is good, but in an environment like we work in, people ask questions, trolleys go by, trucks backfire, newspapers blow up around the horse's hooves; we are taking radio calls and watching for something which might scare people. There is so much going on at once. You don't realize how much pressure there is at one particular time. Dressage riding would be out of place on the street, as we would be in their arena. We have no time to concentrate on our position on the horse while doing this job.

The last thing a horse wants to do by nature is go into a crowd of one or two thousand people. The horse relies on the rider to get him through it. Some horses never make it in police work because of shying. Through repetition your horse comes to rely on you, and says, "I'll do something for you," knowing you won't get the horse hurt. When my horse starts to shy, I touch him with my hand or foot, and it calms him.

Patience in dealing with their equine partners is stressed by patrolmen:

My horse used to be bad on the street. If something came past him, the horse spun and then would shake. This became a habit. He was very frightened of motorcycles. The horse's habits drove me crazy. But I worked with the horse, and he improved. Now he's one of the best in the barn; he's not afraid of anything. There can be a jackhammer going on in the street, and he will put his nose into it. Even a compressor doesn't faze him. No matter how much noise there is, he is good. He's relaxed, not jumpy; he's really reliable.

Former fears of a horse's shying can sometimes be turned to a mounted policeman's decided advantage:

Now I have no fear. Three and a half years ago, though, after I trained, I was petrified. I lost my confidence. I got my present horse when he was a four-year-old. He had a lot of pep. I was really petrified. When the horse jumped, I felt I had no control. But the trainer told me, "It's not you, it's the horse; work on him, stay with him." Then I was okay. When I was scared, I had lost confidence. Today, I can take him anywhere. He is very active, but I love it. People say, "What a beautiful horse!" His head and tail are up. I'm sitting on him, and I like it! I'm proud of it. When he jumps now, I ham it up. He sidesteps, and I make him sidestep again. People like this. Some people downtown on the street in the evening even say, "Forget Symphony Hall, I would rather stay here and watch this horse." I take pride in the horse. I love it now, where three and a half years ago I was petrified.

Age and Breed　　Two further requirements are briefly dealt with by police specifications for horses. The statement "Breed not too important" is qualified by "as long as not too excitable and high-spirited." So-called "cold-blooded" horses are preferred; Thoroughbreds are considered to be too high-strung. Only a few purebred horses are accepted into the mounted force. Tradition dictates that mixed breeds are far better for police work, being "not as thin-skinned, and less apt to come undone than purebreds." The final specification is listed as "Best age for police horse is 7 years," with the explanation that "this is the best age to acclimate themselves to the work required of police horses. Younger horses are more excitable." Both these qualifications, age and breed, then, once again serve to emphasize the police mount as calm and dependable both genetically, as an individual specimen which may or may not be typical of the particular breed in its background, and through attaining an age signifying adulthood, which is felt to confer a quality of steadiness. Thus by virtue of possessing both characteristics, the police mount becomes even more a model of the conservativeness and propriety of the social order which it reinforces, an order that opposes and restrains the young and the unruly.

The Sound of Hooves: Rhythm, Pace, and Time

The public's perceptions of these carefully chosen police horses in the city, as we have seen, involve to a large degree the sense of sight, translated as "visibility," and to a considerable extent the tactile sense, as well, expressed by the action of patting the animals when they are at close range. In addition to these modalities, the perception of police horses is mediated through the symbolism of sound. City people routinely speak of the "clippity-clop" of the horses' hooves, saying that the sound brings them a deep sense of comfort and well-being, particularly when they hear it at night.

A mounted officer spoke of the frequency with which people on the street ask him and his fellow patrolmen, "Wouldn't the horse rather be in the country than in the city walking on cobblestones?" The question is duly answered with the certainty that "the horse likes to clip-clop on cobblestones. He is used to the city." Particularly in semiresidential areas of the city, where the mounted units are sent out on night shifts for "gang control," people say they "wait to hear the clip-clop," that "it is a reassuring noise." Concerning the clattering of hooves on the street, officers have come to learn that "people know you're around. This is especially true where there are alleys bordered by brick buildings. The noise resounds. They hear you all down the street, and it's reassuring. When you're not in an alley but out on the street, they can see you all down the street, as you are up high. But in the alleyways, it's the sound that indicates our presence and reassures people." Other officers revealed, "People in the districts where you patrol tell us the horse makes them feel more protected. They want to see you regularly during your eight-hour beat and at night to hear you. When they're in bed and hear the clippity-clop, people think they are safe."

The sound of the horses' hooves on the pavement, of course, sometimes influences the tactics which can be used in apprehending a lawbreaker. One officer who had a very strong record of arrests involving suspects breaking into parked cars and stealing equipment revealed that he first uses his vantage point on the horse's back to look over the parking lot and spot any trouble. When he sees suspicious people hanging around cars, he hides and tries to sneak up on them and catch them. "Of course, it's hard to sneak up on someone with the noise of the hooves, though!" Many mounted officers recounted experiences in which they had pursued suspects on horseback, often at a gallop, and the fleeing criminals, after being apprehended, had expressed great fear of the sound of the horses' hooves behind them as they ran. The noise of hoofbeats is a factor in crime prevention. As a mountie said, "If they can't see me, they can hear me, and a criminal says, 'heck, let's go somewhere else.'"

A benign image inspired by the sound of hooves is commonly reported among the general public, however. Older people in particular say that hearing the horses is especially meaningful for them. "I haven't heard a horse in so many years. It makes me think back to the days when I heard it all the time." With a smile spreading over her face, an elderly woman listening in her city apartment said, "I love to hear the horses. It reminds me of the past." Many older city dwellers agree with one man who articulated his response to the sound of hooves: "It takes me mentally back to an era when things were better, when there weren't so many problems as there are now." A mounted officer with extensive experience in a residential area of the city said, "In a car or on a motorcycle, the people don't listen to you as they do on a horse. In the neighborhoods people wait for the clippity-clop. They can hear you with the steel horseshoes on the pavement. They say, 'I'm glad to see you.' There is a slower pace."

The phenomenon of the gait of the horse representing a slower pace, a more natural pace attuned to life rhythms as opposed to artificial mechanized rhythms, a pace more in tune with the past than the present, is a significant dimension of the impact of mounted police on city streets. Engulfed as people are on congested municipal streets by all that represents civilization—industrialization and mechanization and the noise and confusion which accompany them—the horse stands as an incongruous but welcome symbol of a slower time, when all of human life was more in harmony with nature. The overwhelming sense of good feeling inspired by the motion of the horse undoubtedly in large part stems from an almost instinctive reaction to this huge living being, whose slower rhythm and pace are more akin to our own human rhythm, thus meeting our needs and satisfactions better than the machinery of the motorized world which generally surrounds us.

In the case of the police horses, it is actually something as deep as our sense of the passage of time that may be affected. Horses, because of the very rhythmicity of their nature, have been, from the dawn of human thought, closely associated with the marking out of time in human consciousness. It is not coincidence that one of the most persistent symbolic connotations of horses has been their role in drawing the chariot of the sun across the sky, enabling each day to come and go in predictable rhythm (Carr 1965:48; Cooper 1978:85; Howey 1958:114–25; Neiman 1979:321; Rowland 1973:110). Ronald Blythe, whose portrait of rural life in the village of Akenfield often centers on the changes in people's lives that came with mechanization, has articulated the horse's role in demarcating time. "Nothing has contributed more to the swift destruction of the old pattern of life in Suffolk than the death of the horse. It carried away with it a quite different conception of time" (1969:18). Writing of mustangs, Dobie observed: "the more machinery man gets, the more machined he is. When the traveler got off the horse and into a machine, the tempo of his mind as well as of his locomotion was changed" (1952:xiii).

MOUNTED POLICE: A STUDY OF URBAN HORSES

The pace and tempo of urban life are unnatural to the human mind and body, and amidst the din and turmoil the horse seems to represent an oasis, through which people instinctively feel more comfortable by being in harmony with a more natural pace. E. T. Hall, in his recent work on human perceptions of time, writes of a significant episode involving horses which affected his own sense of time. During a horseback journey averaging twelve to fifteen miles per day, he noted that his perceptions became altered, and the experience gave him a "very different feeling than speeding by on a paved highway in one or two hours. The horse, the country, and the weather set the pace; we were in the grip of nature, with little control of the rate of progress. Later, riding horseback on a trek of three or four hundred miles," he discovered that "it took a minimum of three days to adjust to the tempo and the more leisurely rhythm of the horse's walking gait." Once that happened, Hall reveals, "I became part of the country again and my whole psyche changed." Significantly, cowboys, who spend their whole lives around horses, have their own unique tempo of speech, which is not "in sync" with people around them but rather is geared to their own situation. "Dudes and tourists," Hall goes on, "never realized that it was their own urban tempo that was out of sync with the body" (1983:39–40).

With regard to the symbolic association of horses with the passage of time, it is relevant to note an advertisement for Budweiser beer which was frequently shown on national television during 1984. In the scene depicted for this commercial, a horse dramatically in motion across the open landscape is shown to viewers while the announcer simultaneously explains the great amount of time the company takes in order to brew beer of the finest quality. This advertising sequence, still centering on the rhythmic movements of the huge horse, ends with the assertion that because of the slow aging process used in its brewing, Budweiser is the best beer to drink—"time, after time, after time."

The marking out of time is "one of the fundamental applications of order, for no communal human activity can take place without it" (Canetti 1978:397). The regulation of time binds large groups of people together as a society, making possible their participation in shared activities. So again in this sense, the police horse, with its association with the concept of time, comes to represent the social order. Concerning this aspect of being associated with time and social cohesion, it is significant that one of the prominent designated functions of the mounted police is to participate in parades. City parades serve to celebrate the passage of certain segments of time and generally mark a particular seasonal event, being regularly scheduled at a specific date during each calendar year. Parades are often symbolic representations of the values embedded in the force of the social order (Lawrence 1982:233–34), and the regular appearance of the mounted police in such events makes explicit their role as regulators in society. In the official description of the mounted police unit for one city, the statement is made that "participation in a community or city celebration is important" in "displaying its desire to be a part of the citizens of its city."

Another function of mounted police which is related to the horse's slower pace is the unit's frequent designation as honor guard or escort for visiting dignitaries, for special meetings and events, and for funerals. Patrolmen say that city officials consider it one of the mounted unit's most essential duties. Men recall with pride the "special details" in which they have participated. Such ceremonial events as were described to me include visits of United States presidents and vice-presidents, meetings of governors, and visits from many national or foreign dignitaries, such as members of royalty and the pope. Requests for the participation of the mounted unit come to police headquarters from the mayor of the city or governor of the state. City officials make use of the horse/man units at such affairs, according to informants, to add prestige to gatherings honoring the rank of these individuals, and to other special events and ceremonies.

Throughout the history of civilization, there has been a tradition of status being associated with the mounted figure. This association can be traced back to the beginnings of human-horse social relationships, when "the domestication of the horse led not only to a physical improvement of the human condition, but to its ennoblement. This is the prehistoric source of prestige which has attached to the horseman throughout history" (Diolé 1974:209). A horseman has generally been considered elite. Summing it up, horses "signify the past sometimes, and are a utility, but where they shine is in escalating human prestige" (Shepard 1978:230). Ceremonial functions make use of this aura, which is a legacy from kings, knights, and cavalry. In modern times, "there is a certain, and growing, prestige attached to the horse. We have never quite lost the conviction that the horse is a noble animal. . . ." "None of the attitudes and rituals surrounding the use we make of horses are without some reason and foundation in history. The twentieth-century horseman, like his earlier counterpart, still hopes, at least subconsciously, to benefit from the aristocratic past" (Diolé 1974:219–20).

In modern city settings where horses bring prestige to ceremonial and state functions, the natural pace of horses has the dignity of history and the sanction of culture in symbolizing a traditional social order. It is noteworthy that when the sanction of old tradition is desired for our important social events, we often resort to slow pace: consider wedding marches, graduation processions, and funeral corteges. In these events we impose an artificially measured and deliberate tread, and the slow pace denotes solemnity as well as formality. In a similar way, the police horsemen impart formality to the events at which they are in respectful attendance. As discussed in connection with police horses' color, it is this formality which makes them a powerfully symbolic representation of the social order. Dignity and a strong sense of social sanction emanate from the slow and measured rhythm of the horse's pace.

Hoofbeats as Percussion

The beat of horses' hooves resounding on the ground has long been a phenomenon of considerable interest and preoccupation. Almost universally, children at an early age learn to imitate it in both sound and motion. Hoofbeats remain even now in the machine age as the basis of poetry and songs, games, sports, and recreation, as well as of ceremony and ritual, where once they marked out the very tempo of everyday life itself—in peace and war. Hoofbeats are the by-product and symbol of mankind's long and intimate association with horses, and their rhythmicity has become indelibly impressed upon human aural perceptions.

The clatter of hooves is a particularly conspicuous feature of mounted police presence, because of the city context. Although some mounted policemen work in municipal parks, where hoofbeats in roadless areas are more muffled, the majority of patrolmen ride on paved city streets, where every hoofbeat resounds. At night, when the visual effect of the horse/man unit diminishes, the auditory perception seems heightened. Many pedestrians downtown after dark have remarked that the orange reflectors worn on the horses' legs form a kind of dazzling accompaniment of motion accentuating the sounds of hoofbeats in the streets.

Hoofbeats are a unique form of percussion and, when one considers the importance of the role of the horse in human life, both past and present, constitute a phenomenon of considerable significance. Anthropologists generally have not been concerned specifically with this issue, but there are some fascinating exceptions which are relevant for discussion here. As pointed out by Needham, "A type of sound that has attracted attention in comparative ethnography is percussion, that is, noise produced by striking or shaking. The means used to produce this quality of sound are very numerous; they include drums, gongs, bells, rattles, sticks, anklets; also clapping, stamping, striking the palm of the hand against various parts of the body; and many other devices and methods." Referring to the work of Vogt (1977), Needham's list of percussive sounds is expanded to include not only "fireworks, bells, rattles, drum" and "the striking of wooden lances against a target," but also *"hoofbeats"* (italics mine). Needham proposes that there is a universal correlation between percussion and transition—that is, between percussion and certain rites of passage which effect or mark out a transition from one category, status, or condition to another (1981:41; 1967:611). Rhythmic noise, according to Needham, represents "a cultural phenomenon of great importance" (1967:606) and has "universal psychic appeal" (1967:610), being "widely employed as a specially suitable kind of marker" (1967:612).

Vogt, in basic agreement with Needham's hypothesis about percussion, expands it in a meaningful way to include the idea that percussion is associated with transition in the sense of denoting "the passage of solar time." Percussive sounds "are often signalling devices," Vogt observes. "They serve to mark out time in a universe characterized by chronovision," and "in some cases . . . they also symbolize some aspect of the natural world" (1977:242).

Vogt's concept of percussive sounds as "punctuating the passage of solar time" (1977:231) is relevant to contemplate in relation to horses in the present study. Included in the anthropologist's description of "the distinctive patterns of sound in the normal flow of social life" in a Mexican town, along with such things as "the patting out of tortillas at the hearth" and the "predawn explosion of skyrockets on a saint's day," are "the hoofbeats of mules and burros on cobblestone streets" (1977:231). Describing percussive sounds which are meaningful in the social and ceremonial life of Zincantan, "the pounding of hoofbeats of horses that are running in the so-called ritual 'horse races'" is an important element, as is "the whacking together of the stick horses of the ritualists" (1977:232). Apart from utilitarian functions, Vogt considers various sounds to be "integral parts of the accoustic code" (1977:232) and holds that "percussive sounds are transmitting meaningful messages" (1977:233). The "running of the horses" in Zincantan is not a horse race in our sense of the term but rather a rite which calls for swift galloping of the horses "along the path of the sun," enacted as part of the two most important fiestas (1977:241). In this equine event, at noon, when signaled by firecrackers, riders run their horses from east to west, "whirl, charge back to the east, then again to the west" (Vogt 1976:170). A reversal of the "running of the horses" is held at sundown, when the horses are "run along the path of the sun from the west to the east, back to the west, and then returned to the east" (Vogt 1976:171). This pattern suggests that "the hoofbeats transmit messages about the passage of time in the universe" (Vogt 1977:242).

How do these social events involving equines relate to police horses' hoofbeats in a modern city? The frequency and intensity of reactions of city dwellers to the clatter of hooves, and the fact that these responses always focus on nostalgia and a deep sense of comfort, strongly suggest that there is a central theme being communicated by the sounds. The examples cited above give an indication of the range of human perception relating to percussion, specifically the percussion of hooves, and illustrate the possible symbolic usage of such sounds when people relate to horses.

As a kind of secular ritual in the heart of a city, the hoofbeats of police horses, which so many people assert have profound meaning for them, seem to represent the marking out of time and the setting of it at a slower, more natural pace in tune with their own life rhythms. At the same time, it is suggestive that the rhythmic regularity of the beat, the percussion of hooves on the street, so greatly amplified by the metal horseshoes resounding on the pavement, is symbolically associated with the establishment and maintenance of the social order. This association comes about because, by all indications, the beat of hooves in city streets is linked in the hearer's mind with the dispelling of unruliness and disharmony in those streets, resulting in the peace of mind which is so universally described by that hearer.

The regularity of the beat of hooves is greatly reinforced by the predictable and dependable set of characteristics of a police mount, as described previously, and by the uniformed rider who controls the animal and who is already established as part of the social agency to enforce order. The word *beat* itself, as used in police work, means a habitual round or course which is repeatedly traveled when on duty. Though it is not peculiar to mounted policemen to patrol in "beats," it is of interest that the rhythmicity is made even more explicit in the hoofbeat pattern. As mentioned previously, people who live or operate businesses along the mounties' beats become accustomed to the regularity of the horses' presence and complain to authorities when the units are removed. As an interesting aside illustrating symbolic usage (it can be no more than that until more examples are found), there is the case of a renowned English police horse, "Warrior." After his death, one of his hooves was mounted and made into a gavel that was used for restoring order in meetings of an association of World War I Veterans (Campbell 1971:23).

Sources of Power

City police are often viewed by the general public as "holding back the forces of disorder and terror" (Rubinstein 1980:xi). The central focus of my study, both in the gathering of data and in their interpretation, is to illuminate the particular role of the horse in this process and the way in which the equine animal affects the function of the mounted unit as a part of the city police system. Law enforcement, of course, is dependent upon the power which resides in the enforcing agency. Power is expressed by the giving of orders. Orders from an accepted authority are commands which have to be obeyed, unless the recipient chooses to take the consequences of ignoring them or disobeying them, which can be disastrous.

Commands from mounted policemen may be spoken but are often implicit, as well, depending on nonverbal communication. The latter is particularly true in crowd control, when people instantaneously back away from the horse, where they do not do so anywhere near as quickly from foot, motorcycle, or squad car police. The interaction between a mounted policeman and his horse has a specific effect upon people in a crowd, which is qualitatively different from that of a policeman alone or in conjunction with machinery.

Elias Canetti's work *Crowds and Power* contains a deep-level analysis of commands which can be applied to illuminate the process which operates in the case of the horse/man unit of the mounted police.

In essence, Canetti asserts that we as human beings are, from early childhood onward, recipients of commands, or orders, that are imposed from outside ourselves, and which arouse hostility in those who obey them. Commands consist of two parts: (1) the momentum, which forces the recipient to act; and (2) the "sting," which, if the command is obeyed, remains behind in the recipient, sinks deep within his being, and is stored there. It remains unchanged, though it may be hidden, and is produced again as soon as a situation arises in which the former recipient can in turn become the one to issue the command to another, who then becomes subordinate. Thus he passes on to someone else the sting—the "hidden replica of the command he once received and could not immediately pass on" (1978:304, 305, 311).

Canetti applies his theory of command to both animals and people. Commands, he says, "are older than speech," since animals obey them as well. The fact that animals can be trained to obey their human masters without specifically comprehending the language spoken indicates "very ancient roots for the command" (1978:303). Commands predated human/animal contact, and the original command is the one between a predator and its prey, in which the stronger, or predatory, animal causes the prey species to flee. Threat of death lies at the root of such a command, called a "flight command," and this threat remains below the surface of all commands (1978:303–304). The flight command became "domesticated" when a command, instead of threatening death, became linked with the promise of food. "This is obvious in the training of animals. When a horse has done what it is supposed to do, its trainer gives it a lump of sugar." Commands to people are also domesticated when penalties other than death are substituted for noncompliance, so that there is "voluntary captivity"—obedience in return for certain benefits (1978:307–308). "The collective fear of a herd in flight is the oldest and perhaps the commonest example of a crowd state" (1978:309). This statement refers to both animals and human beings, when groups are collectively threatened and herd, or crowd, behavior results (1978:310).

Using as an example the history of the Mongol horsemen's rapid rise to power, Canetti goes on to relate their special success to the closeness with which command was linked to the horse. This closeness depended upon certain characteristics of the horse which suited it to a relationship with people. Fitting these characteristics of the animal itself into his theory, Canetti points out that the horse is a herd animal, "built for flight." Horses originally lived as members of a herd, who were accustomed to fleeing together when threatened by a dangerous animal which preyed on their lives. Danger gave the herd solidarity, and "mass flight was one of the commonest experiences of the horse, and came to be part of its nature" (1978:316). Later, "by taking possession of the horse and taming it, man formed a new unit with it," training it with commands composed of sounds, movements, and pressure which transmit to the animal the will of the rider. The horse understands the rider's wishes and obeys. Among equestrians, "the horse becomes so close to its master that a very personal relationship grows up between them; it is subjection, but of an intimacy only possible in these circumstances" (1978:316–17).

In order to understand this process of the development of a relationship between horse and rider, one must take into account the innate gregariousness of the horse. Domestication of the equine species and its adaptation for the various roles it has assumed in human history and culture were indeed made possible to begin with by the social nature of the animal. The hierarchical structure of herd life, with its well-defined dominance order, means that individual horses respond with obedience to herd members who are above them in rank. The accepted explanation of horse domestication is that the animals adapt and respond to members of the human species who interact with them as they would ordinarily respond to the dominant members of their own species. It is this capacity which makes horses able to respond as acutely as they do to human mastery (see Zeuner 1963:37; Clutton-Brock 1981:15).

In the case of a command among mounted people, as Canetti points out, distance between the giver and the recipient of the order is obliterated. "It is the rider's body which gives direction to the horse's body." Since "space of command is thus reduced to a minimum," the "distant, alien quality which is part of the original character of command disappears." Command is domesticated in a special way with the creation of "a new actor introduced into the history of relationships between creatures—the riding-animal," which responds to the pressure of its master's body. This unique relationship with his horse affects the "command-economy" of the horseman, in that

> a rider can pass on to his horse commands he himself has received from
> a superior. If a goal is set him he does not reach it by running himself,
> but by making his horse run. Since he does this immediately, the order
> does not leave any sting in him; he avoids this by passing the order on

to his horse. He gets rid of the particular constraint which the order would have imposed on him before he has properly felt it. The sooner he carries out his task, the quicker he mounts and the faster he rides, the less sting remains in him. The real art of horsemen, as soon as they take on a military character, consists in being able to train another larger crowd of recipients of commands, to whom they can directly pass on everything they receive from their own superiors. [1978:317]

The Mongols, as examples of some of the world's most skilled horsemen, were noteworthy for their absolute obedience and formidable discipline. The Mongols "bore this discipline easily, for the reason that the section of their people which carried the main burden of it was the *horses*" (Canetti 1978:317).

An understanding of command and crowds and the effect of being on horseback has significant applications for the study of mounted police and helps to shed light on the unit's operation and effectiveness. As previously mentioned, almost everyone who comes into contact with mounted policemen makes special mention of their friendly, outgoing nature and notably the fact that they "seem at peace with themselves and with the world." In contrast to other types of policemen, when mounted on a horse, an officer is in general "not seen as antagonistic and hostile" by the public. It certainly makes sense that this feature of mounted policemen owes its explanation to the spreading of the sting of command to the horse. Police departments are, after all, examples of organizations in which power is distributed according to rank, and orders from superiors are inseparable from the carrying out of daily assignments. With the hostility that Canetti proposes as emanating from receiving orders being in turn transferred to the horse, it is plausible that the mounted officer would thereby be left feeling less frustrated, and consequently more relaxed and "at peace," congenial in dealing with people and patient with the problems of his job. Indeed, that is how he is perceived, and it is this image that makes him so well suited to fulfilling the role of "PR" unit of the police force, the man who deals with the people in the street harmoniously and effectively.

It is this very process of transferring command to the horse that an experienced patrolman articulated when he described to me the importance of a mounted policeman's having a well-disciplined horse. "One patrolman can do so much on a disciplined horse. The name of the game is discipline and control." Important, too, is the physical closeness between the rider, as giver of command, and the horse, as its recipient. This proximity, as exemplified in the case of the Mongol horsemen, means that space and time in the passage of command are obliterated. This lack of opportunity for dissipation of strength between the giver and receiver of orders adds a dimension of power which is nonetheless real for being partly metaphoric. For those who view the instantaneous obedient response of the animal on the city streets see the actualization of command in an explicit way, which becomes a functioning metaphor for the enforcing of social order. This animal/man metaphor is particularly significant in providing a unique contrast in the city context, since, as Ortner points out, "in mechanized society," a "root metaphor for the social process is the machine" (1974:95).

The dispersing of hostile crowds, as noted previously, is considered to be one of the prime functions of the mounted unit of the police force. One of the important features of this accomplishment is that, as patrolmen point out, "when the horse disperses the crowd, no one gets hurt. When regular policemen do this, some people can get hit by sticks. It's a real problem; the Civil Liberties gets involved. But there are no injuries when horse patrols are used. One or two people may get stepped on, but that's not serious. It's not necessary to use violence when the horse clears the way." It would certainly appear that something about the process of passing the command down through the horse turns away the wrath of the crowd, even as its members recoil from the animal as though in fear. The potential "sting" of being ordered to disperse seems to dissipate before any substantial anger can be built up.

In this regard, all patrolmen who have been involved in handling the problem of hostile crowds and mass demonstrations are struck by a common experience, which seems to them strangely inconsistent. They note that within minutes of exhibiting great anger and antagonism toward the police as the agent opposing them, members of the crowd often are suddenly pacified to the point of becoming friendly, approaching the mounted pair and usually patting the horse and even chatting with the mounted officer. One patrolman described his experience with this phenomenon when a protest was being staged involving large numbers of hostile participants:

There were fifteen thousand demonstrators taking over a downtown hotel. The crowd was out of hand, like a madman. They said they

[156]

would not move; when asked peacefully, they refused to move. They wouldn't let any cars through the downtown area. The foot patrol could do nothing about it. It was our job to disperse them and open up a path to let traffic get through. The crowd was screaming and hollering and was extremely angry. It was like a tidal wave. But six of us on horses broke them up and got them to move, even though they at first refused. Afterwards, when the crowd had been dispersed and cars were getting through again, I got the horse on the sidewalk. Right away some of the demonstrators came over; they would pat the horse and shoot the breeze as though nothing had happened. They were hostile to foot officers. But they didn't seem the least bit angry when they came over, whereas they had been swinging and hollering and threatening to throw bottles shortly before.

Passing the command through the horse, then, strengthens it and gives it efficiency but at the same time makes it more palatable and almost benign.

Whether in subduing and controlling crowds or in accomplishing other routine duties which serve to prevent or oppose the unruliness that undermines the social order in the city, the horse/man unit is undeniably effective. Its effectiveness must depend in large measure upon the unique nature of the interaction between man and animal and, as discussed, the way command is transmitted. It depends, too, on the manner in which the patrolman and his mount are perceived by those who are affected by their presence—the general public and the actual or potential offender. As mentioned, there is a strong symbolic factor inherent in the human as conqueror of the horse, establishing by example incontrovertible dominance and authority. The stage is thus implicitly set for further subduing and acquiescence.

People are generally cognizant of the fact that the equine species runs the gamut from wild to tame, and that the police animals represent a special case of horses held in check in a city environment, which are uniquely acquiescent and subservient to man's will. The wildness of horses is a commonly used metaphor in daily life and experience, even for city people. In this regard it is relevant that the horse as a species is known to be much more resistant to taming than, say, domesticated ruminants such as cattle (Zeuner 1963:329; Clutton-Brock 1981:86). "Great daring and ingenuity" were required to achieve domestication of the horse (Diolé 1974:210). "It requires no mean skill on the part of man to assert his dominance over such an animal [wild horse] and break it in for riding" (Clutton-Brock 1981:86). It is common knowledge that each individual horse has to be "broken" in a more or less laborious process of training. Knowing that a background of extensive training and conditioning is part of each horse/man unit's preparation, and that the horse has gone against its own wilder nature to conform to a city context, engenders an enhanced respect, which fosters obedience to similar restraint.

On a deeper level, an even greater equine transformation has taken place, in which mankind has replaced the herding nature of the horse with a substitute relationship with the human species, the rider in a sense taking the place of the horse's own conspecifics. The flightiness, the fleeing instinct, so much a part of the animal's "original mode of being," has been ostensibly eliminated in adapting the horse for civilization. Natural equine behavior traits have been overcome and replaced with conditioning which binds the horse to the rider and makes it of use for human purposes. Just as the collectivity of the herd or society is stronger than the sum of its individual members, now the unit of man/horse, comprised of two species in dynamic interaction, has a strength more than equal to the sum of what each would be alone. It well may be the strength of the collective force of the equine's former gregariousness which has now been subverted into the relationship with the rider that gives such unusual motivating power to the horse/man unit.

Patrolmen are aware of the submerged herd nature of their mounts. As one said,

> Your horse will concentrate when by itself with you. When other horses are there, sometimes he doesn't concentrate. He wants to go to the other horse. Trying to catch up to the other horse, he is distracted. He might even run out in front of a bus through wanting to catch up with the other horse. Maybe they can't stand each other, and will kick or bite each other when in the paddock, but they still want to be next to each other.

Mounted policemen indicated that "if one horse bolts, the other may do it; if one shies at something, the other may shy at it too." But the gregariousness is sometimes turned to advantage: "Horses work better together in certain situations. If one horse is afraid in parades, rears and tries to bolt, he can be put between two calm horses and in this way finish the parade. He may still prance, and get into a lather, but at least he finishes out the parade." Or, "If there's a metal bridge that looks scary to some horses, and the first horse goes over it with no problem, the horses that follow will usually go over it okay."

Rhythm: Horses and Crowds

It is possible that there is an age-old subconscious connection between the gregariousness of equine animals and the origination of human crowd formation. Crowds of people are characterized by a sense of unity, which results from shared belief and a solidarity which emanates from conviction. The communal excitement of such a group molds its members into what Canetti calls "the rhythmic or throbbing crowd" (1978:31). Looking backward to the dawn of human society, it may have been the sound of multitudinous herds of hoofed animals, whose "rhythms are often richer and more audible than those of men," which gave our ancestors the concept of associating the noise of rhythmically resounding beats with the idea of strength in numbers. For "hoofed animals flee in herds, like regiments of drummers." By applying the example of animals to themselves and coming together in numbers which were made to seem greater through similar sounds they could produce in unison—a process which the participants soon transformed into patterned movement, or dance—the early hunters evoked among members of the group the feeling of confidence, strength, and "invincible unity." For each member to perform identical bodily motions at precisely the same time became symbolic of their feeling of being merged into one entity (Canetti 1978:31–32). Such gatherings, characterized by repetitive movements and sounds which transformed them into a rhythmic or throbbing crowd, were a means both of achieving and of expressing an ideological consensus.

This theoretical connection between human perceptions of hoofed animals such as horses and the formation of crowds provides background for understanding the deep-level reactions that may occur when mounted police are called upon to deal with crowds. When the horse is ridden by the patrolman, the animal has of necessity already undergone an individualization process, which has separated it from its herd. Its herding instinct, so to speak, has been overruled and replaced with obedience to the rider's will. In an analogous way, in order to disperse a crowd, the rhythm and continuity of that crowd must be broken up and its collective spirit of oneness destroyed. In a sense, people must be returned to the status of individuals. When the horse/patrolman unit

[159]

comes upon the scene to disperse the crowd, these implicit interactions between the animal and its rider give the pair a force rooted in metaphor, which makes it stronger and more effective in crowd dispersal than any other type of police agent.

Effectiveness: Nobility, Power, Predictability

The horse is very frequently referred to as "noble." City dwellers and city visitors seeing the mounted police in their midst use this word, as do the patrolmen themselves. Treatises on domestication refer to the equine as man's noblest conquest. As explained by one authority,

> In the relationships between man and horse there is an ambivalence; man, having dominated the beast, feels he has a certain control over the horse's performance and behavior, and he assumes a sense of power and mastery from his position above and astride the animal—in the rider's seat. Yet the horse's majestic beauty and its mobility demand respect. There is always the tacit understanding that the horse is bigger, nobler, and more powerful than the one holding the reins. Between steed and rider, there exists an exchange of strength and integrity that is the basis of their compatibility. [Neiman 1979:348]

The interchange of power referred to in this passage has no clearer example than the horse/man unit of the police, which experience has shown to be "big, visible, mobile, and intimidating" ("Veterinarian Crusades" 1980:1074). From earliest times mankind has utilized the power of animals for his own varied purposes. The police horse is a noteworthy example of the use of animal power in which that power itself, not just man's control of it, becomes a motivating force in the effectiveness of authority. The horse has an input of its own in an exchange of power with its rider, and, though it does man's bidding, the dimension of this input is an essential element in the thrust and action of the mounted unit. As a motorcycle policeman who stopped to talk with a mountie expressed it, "I wouldn't want to be a mounted cop. I'm afraid of horses. These horses are powerful. At least with a bike you can turn it off. With the horse you can't. It keeps going."

The dynamic interaction between patrolman and mount can be better understood when we take into account the unique situation of a police officer in our society. "Signs of danger and trouble suggest withdrawal and flight to most people, but for the policeman they are signals of obligation and opportunity. He must be prepared to advance when others withdraw" (Rubenstein 1980:290). There is a parallel here between rider and horse, in that the training and discipline of an officer which enable him to go against his own instincts can be strengthened by the corresponding situation in which he is responsible for making sure his mount maintains *his* training in going against *his* natural instincts. A police instructor stressed this principle in explaining the schooling of police horses: "You must make the horse face his fears quietly over and over again, until his conditioning takes the place of his instinct."

On the street, a mountie confided, "a horse's defense is to run to get away. He will even run from a newspaper. He's basically a coward, and won't attack anyone. He will help you, though, but you have to prod him to go after someone." Indeed, it appears true that "thousands of years of obedience have not been sufficient to reassure the horse. . . . There seems always to be a thin layer of panic just beneath the surface of the horse; a nervousness always on the verge of being translated into a kick or bolt" (Diolé 1974:217). In the simultaneous conquering of the instincts of both—man and horse—each counter-commands the other, continually forcing conditioning to overcome instinct and fear. From the dynamic interaction involved in this process, the horse/man unit takes on power and strength.

The close relationship between police horse and rider, which depends upon communication at many levels, explains the functional importance of the "one rider-one horse" tradition. This practice is listed in official mounted police regulations as "the general rule," which "sometimes has to be changed for various reasons such as (1) a sick horse, (2) one that has to be shoed, and (3) one that may be injured." Without exception, mounted patrolmen are adamant that their horses be exclusively their own. Men say, "You get to know your own horse. You are with the horse a long time each day, more than a jockey is, or a pleasure rider. He does what you tell him. He will sneak a look at you if he is doing something wrong. When you know him, you are always in command." As another mountie explained it, "Your horse knows you. You call out 'Hey!' and he flicks one ear. If your horse tries to sneak something, all you do is say 'Hey!' sharply, and he shies away from what he was going to do."

Patrolmen agree that "it's a real nice feeling to have a horse you can trust and he trusts you." One described his especially dependable police mount as "the Rock of Gibraltar; he'll really put out for you."

Predictability is an essential component: "When you've been on the same horse a couple of years, you know what he's going to do." Officers contend that "it's very important to match the rider to a horse he likes. One rider may have a horse that works well in the street for him, but another rider may not like the way that horse does things. When my horse was laid up and I rode another, it was just not the same. A man may be happy on the street with his horse, while the same horse makes a tedious day for another rider." An officer was proud to make known that "my horse had thrown two other riders before I got him. He is nervous and has a lot of energy, but I have no trouble with him at all. It took me six months to calm him down and get him to relax."

Expenditure of personal effort with a mount is important to the men. "You put a lot of work in on a horse, and you get pretty attached. You become like one. You know all his habits, how he will react on the street, and you are ready for his reaction without hardly thinking about it." A great deal of resentment was felt by those men who had "put a lot of time and work into a horse and then had to turn it over to another guy."

All patrolmen expressed the sentiment that "I don't want anyone to ride my horse. The horse can pick up a bad habit in a day, and it takes months to get him over it. He can get headshy if the rider slaps him on the head, for example." One officer, who told me, "My horse seems to move with me. We're as one, instead of partners," feels that

> other riders would have a very difficult time with my horse. The horse knows when a stranger is on him and will try the rider out, and get him off quick. These guys, and everybody on the mounted unit, tease me about this, but no one else has ever worked a full tour of duty on him. He gets uppity with other riders on him. He dances and becomes high-strung. With a different set of aids he becomes unglued and is unruly. The guys razz me about saying this, but no one ever gets on him. I would quit the unit if they took my horse away.

On the street, an officer explained to a pedestrian, "If someone else rides my horse, he gets belligerent. He won't let anybody other than me on him." Another mountie admitted, "My horse has quirks and this is good, because I don't want others riding him. They would teach him bad habits. You form an affection with the horse." One officer "left the unit and came back. If my horse had been sold," he said, "I wouldn't

There is often a close bonding between a mounted
policeman and the horse that is his working partner. Photo
by author.

have come back. I came back because I got my old horse. There is a
feeling 'It's mine,' a possessiveness, I guess. I take care of him. If
someone treats him differently, he may spoil him, he may ruin the
horse for me. It's a personal thing. You have comfort and safety in your
own horse." An officer who showed me his injured horse at the barracks was "very upset to have to ride another mount all summer. I
would much rather ride my own horse."

It is clear that familiarity and mutual trust lead to a quality of
predictability which is vital to the horse/man unit's efficiency and success in working on city streets. The great amount of discipline necessary for their tasks is enhanced by the control that depends on previous
knowledge about how the other member of the horse/man team will
respond to difficult or unusual situations. The frequent articulation by
the officers of the idea that they put in an inordinate amount of time and
work on their horses, and their resentment of sharing the animals with
other riders indicate the high degree to which a mountie may project
himself into his horse, so to speak. There is in some cases a merging of
self with the animal, the investing of one's identity as well as energy in

the animal. Such relationships facilitate the occurrence of closeness of command between rider and horse. As previously discussed, the physical closeness of horse and rider enables command to spread instantaneously. This process is increased even more by the intimacy of bonding of a nonphysical nature, which is facilitated by the exclusivity which exists between a specific horse and his accustomed rider.

Other Police Agents' Views of Mounted Police

Mounted policemen often remind themselves and communicate to others the fact that no such bonding takes place with automobiles and motorcycles. Mounties know, too, that they are often viewed with bad feeling by other police personnel. Mounted men say, "Patrol officers in a car have envious feelings toward us. They feel the guys on horses are elitist. They think we are here to look pretty, and that we don't do anything. They complain we don't take enough radio calls, do enough crap calls (like family fights), and that we're not subject to the same controls as they are." Many mounted patrolmen expressed the idea that "they think we are prima donnas, glory seekers, so they resent us." One officer patrolling on his horse in a shopping area explained, "The walking and car police may do the basic work, but tourists still say to us, 'You guys do wonderful work.' The guy in the police car is working hard, but he gets no thanks. He sees us get all the credit, and he's boiling inside." It is common knowledge among the mounties that "if a police car and horse are together on the street, people will invariably come to the horse, so the guys in the cars don't like us."

One of the officers who speaks of his work on horseback as "a nice job" shared the view that "we have the animosity of the policemen in cruisers and the bike guys; they say the mounted police get all the attention." His fellow mountie agreed: "It's like looking at someone with green eyes; the mounted police get a lot of attention they don't get." There was the common complaint that "in spite of our high arrest record and proven effectiveness, regular police claim we in the mounted unit are 'pretty boys' and are on the street to get our pictures taken." As another officer put it, "There is professional jealousy. It's the same throughout the country. The high echelons think we are useless. But once they use us, and see what we can do, they are horse lovers overnight."

When I talked directly with police officers from other units, these perceptions of the mounted unit were confirmed. In particular, regular policemen told me that "the mounties are generally hanging around doing nothing" and claimed that "their only usefulness is in looking pretty, and being good for riot control." One foot policeman disparaged their effectiveness by saying that the horses would fall if they galloped on city streets, especially in going around corners, as the animals have no traction on pavement. It is noteworthy that several officers admitted that though mounted police are good for show, crowd control, and riots, they personally are scared to ride horses.

The notion of having a symbolic, almost decorative, role dominates other units' perceptions of the mounted police. Because the mounties are aware of this situation—almost without exception each officer told me about it, spontaneously bringing up the subject in conversation—these views seem to reflect back upon the men. This process serves to magnify the concept that theirs is a special outfit, that indeed they *are* elitist, and that the extra attention they receive and the admiration they elicit from the public are assets which can be utilized as decided advantages.

Personalized Social Relations: Accessibility

Citizens in contact with the mounted units praise the accessibility of this type of police agent. They say the individualized quality of the encounter makes them feel comfortable and protected to a much greater degree than is the case with other police units. The fact that there is no intervening machine is noted as an overwhelming advantage in communicating with police and in imparting to people a unique sense of security. In this regard, mounties like to tell the story about taking their horses to a handicapped children's hospital to allow interaction between the animals and the youngsters. On the same occasion, they said, "a big company brought a robot for the children. At the end of the affair, the lieutenant took a poll as to how the horses and the robot were rated, 1 to 10. The final vote was horses: 10, robot: 2!"

For young and old, horses in the city soften the effects of the sense of alienation which is so prevalent in urban society. Relating to a man on a horse, who is exposed and available for direct communication, and whose own association with an animal so beloved by the great percentage of the citizenry is evident, becomes a social event of importance, full of meaning. Children take delight in the police horses, feeling that they represent at least one element in the midst of the confusion of the adult world of the city which is special for them. To the elderly, especially, the presence of the horse/man unit in a metropolitan area suggests a world in time before the advent of machine-based industrialization, in which, as Firth remarks, there was "much greater emphasis than today upon social relationships of a personalized character" (1975:40). It is this same loss that is lamented by a villager of Akenfield, who speaks for his fellows in regretting that now, since the passing of the horse, "nobody walks about in it (the community). You don't say you saw your neighbor, you say you passed his car. People wave and toot where they used to talk" (Blythe 1969:128).

Informants indicate that mounted patrolmen frequently fill their need for the kind of social interaction often denied them in city life. Indeed, one of the goals of the mounted unit, as set forth in its official guidelines, is that of "maintaining a high degree of community involvement," in "relations with both residents and merchants as well as visitors to the city." Under "good public relations" in the description of the mounted force, it is spelled out that the "horse serves both rider and community well and is a bond between the policeman and the community." People in neighborhoods where a mounted patrolman is assigned say they enjoy knowing "we can spot the man on the horse right away. We get to know him on a first-name basis. It's more personal, he is part of the neighborhood, not like someone driving through in a car." A mounted officer recognized that "you can work in a cruiser for ten years and get no response from people. But you go out just once with the horse, and people come out of the woodwork." Another mountie observed that "people really relate to the mounted guy. They remember him and speak to him. They ask, 'How's the horse?' They never remember the cruiser guy and don't greet him. They never ask him, 'How's the cruiser?' "

A mounted man knows that

> people along my beat wait each day to meet me in their area. Kids wait with their parents to feed the horses carrots. People in residential areas set up their backyards to water the horses. They don't even care about cutting up the lawn. They don't object to the horse manure; in fact, they gather it up to use on their garden. They say, "I'm glad to see you," which they never would say to a man in a car or on a motorcycle. If the cop on a bike said "Hello," they would think he was crazy, yet they expect it from the mounted man. Getting to know people helps, because they may tell us about a bad gang of kids or other situation we

ought to know about in the neighborhood. In these places unruly gangs take off when we come.

"I never heard of anyone who doesn't love horses," a mountie told me, "except for Henry Fonda in *On Golden Pond.* In the movie, when his wife told him he was her knight in shining armor, he answered her that he didn't like horses. But riding the horse, you meet people, and they all love horses." "People feel so positive about horses," patrolmen indicated, that "there is seldom anyone who will hurt our horses." Men say, "If anyone hurts the policeman, it's okay with the public, but if it's the horse, people will stop them." "People go after the cop, not the horse; they may throw rocks at him, but not at the horse." An experienced city police official explained, "In the many years our mounted force has been in operation, only rarely has a horse been shot at. One of these, which a sniper hit a few years ago, recovered okay and received hundreds of get-well cards during his convalescence." It is also noteworthy that "people don't steal police horses as they do cars and bikes." A few minor incidents occur, such as the one that involved "a crazy man, who took the saddle and bridle off of a tethered police mount and began taking them apart. When caught, he said he only wanted the horse to be free."

"Severe maliciousness against horses is rare," the officer in charge of the mounted police force in one city told me,

> but during hostile mob demonstrations against forced bussing in our city, it did occur. Someone put cyanide into apples and placed them along the area where the police horses were generally tied up during certain parts of the day at the time of the rioting. We received an anonymous call early in the morning, and when we investigated, we did find some apples scotch-taped together with cyanide pellets inside. If it involves the horses, we are more apt to get warning calls with information. Piano wire is sometimes strung across a street to obstruct motorcycles, or nails in cardboard are put out so squad cars will get flat tires, but in these cases we are never notified.

"The positive attitude the public has toward the horse is very important," a mounted police lieutenant explained. "The presence of the horse itself makes people *feel* more protected." For example, he believes that

> even though two officers and a sector car may *actually* afford the most protection, the horse makes you *feel* more protected. If people see the horse, especially at night, they feel well about it, and psychologically

they don't know that a sector car is more protection. When they see you, and hear the clip-clop, they think they are safe. The public perception is that the real police is the mounted police, whereas the sector car generally does a great deal of the work.

Others agree, arguing that "what the public perceives is important. People have a positive feeling on observing the horse. People that have twenty sector cars drive by and are not impressed at all see one horse and have a terrific sense of well-being. They feel they are protected. The fact that a sector car might be more practical and efficient has no bearing."

A mounted officer has learned from his daily experience that "there is a special feeling about a horse." In trying to explain, he suggested, "It's inbred from childhood. Maybe it's related to cowboys or something. The public seems to zero in on the horse. It gives them a sense that everything is all right." Experiences of city police departments have uniformly indicated, as all mounties are aware, that "if citizens complain about lack of police protection, they always bring up not seeing the horse out on the streets." It is a known fact that "people love them. Some politicians want to get rid of the mounted unit, but as soon as they make this known, people start screaming and yelling. They protest vehemently." I was repeatedly told that "an overwhelming public outcry is immediately forthcoming when financial cutbacks reduce the number of mounted police on the street or threaten to eliminate the mounted force entirely." In a brief informal history of its mounted unit released by one city for educational purposes, this reaction is summed up: "Throughout the years there have been suggestions from austerity-minded city officials that the Mounted Unit in this city should be abolished because of the expense involved. However the citizenry has always turned out in legion and protested the proposed suggestion with such vigor, that such recommendations were abandoned." The "good will and mutual respect between the department and the public" is cited as one component of the successful work of the mounted force.

The Police Horse as Symbol

As we have seen throughout this study, the cognitive process which operates at a deep level with regard to the mounted police has a heavy impact on the effectiveness of the horse/man unit in the city and the importance of its role within society. Focusing on the horse and the horseman in this study has revealed a strong symbolic element in action. Described in Firth's terms, "There is a coding of experiences in symbolic form which serves to organize the individual's relation to the society" (1975:85). The horse/man unit is a complex image and is a clear example of the power which resides in the structural arrangement of certain carefully chosen components and the force which can result when that image stands in a particular relation to society.

Commenting on the "apparent universality of animals as images of the profoundest symbolic significance," Willis sees this universality as grounded in the concept that "the animal is both within us, as part of our enduring biological heritage as human beings, and also, by definition, outside and beyond human society." Thus the symbolic animal is "necessarily a dualistic image" (1974:9). Though Willis's reference is to animals in a different context from that of the contemporary police horse, nevertheless this idea of a two-sided image is relevant in shedding light on the meaning of the horse/man unit. The dualism in this case involves the paradox of a large herbivorous animal's being transformed into an instrument of city life. He is like us in being a live entity referred to by name, or as a pal, sidekick, son, or partner, yet he has become almost, though significantly not quite, like a machine in carrying out daily functions which expedite the social processes of industrialized society. The horse, unlike the machine, has a volition of its own, and though the animal is virtually always subservient to man, those exceptional occasions when he is not are of quintessential importance. Through its dual image, the horse/man unit brings into being a contrast between civilization and nature, between order and chaos, which is balanced in a special way. That, I believe, is the root of the very prevalent reaction to police horses—the contradiction described earlier—in which there is both fear and admiration. There is fear of the disorderly element, the instinctual nature which lies deep within the animal, but respect for the way in which this life force is held in check, commanded, and controlled.

Unlike the rodeo bucking events, for example, which, as described in chapter 3, leave so much room and scope for wildness in the tame/wild duality that is symbolized by cowboy and bronc, we are confronted in the police horse with a decided overweighting on the side of the tame—i.e., civilization, as represented by the city. Culture triumphs over nature as the horse's innate wildness, fears, and herding instinct are controlled by the rider for human purposes. As Douglas has pointed out, "The more value people set on social constraints, the more value they set on symbols of bodily control" (1973:16). In the case of the mounted police, as we have seen, symbols of human control over nature are carefully manipulated, arranged, and utilized in the operation of a law enforcement agency whose reason for being is the preserving of social constraints through the force of benign authority.

In reference to the mounted police, it has been observed that "to city dwellers unaccustomed to contact with horses, the sight of so large an animal has a restraining influence" (Neiman 1979:1970). In carrying out the dictates of law and order in a city, mounted police symbolically reflect the value society places on restraint. In all the many ways which have been discussed in this study, assertions are metaphorically stated by making use of what Cohen calls "the resources of the dynamic unconscious" (1980:63), in the sense that restraint, reflected in the police horse, represents civilization.

With regard to the question posed at the beginning of this study concerning the horse's affinity for city life, the answer is that the equine animal has made a remarkable adjustment to the urban setting. As an illustration, one mounted officer related a story of city-adapted mounts who "when taken out to the country, with pasture and trees, became neurotic and had to be brought back to the city." Police horses are considered useful only in densely populated areas. Unlike many horse-related phenomena in our society, they do not belong to the rural life, to the open fields and plains, or to the West. As visitors from those areas are fond of pointing out, "I love to see these horses in the city. It's unusual for us. We don't have mounted police where we come from."

Under conditions vastly different from those of its natural environment, deprived of the grassland ranges to which the equine species in its evolution has been inextricably linked, the horse as a police mount occupies a niche which allows symbolic expression of its composite image. Its duality enables it to represent the balance between civilization and chaos. There is the paradox of culture (as city) now being joined to nature (as the horse) in the way of a centaur: mind and reason are wedded to, and yet override, the inborn qualities of wildness and instinct. The horse has been transformed by the city, yet in one sense it remains aloof. It has a longer history than machines, and, throbbing with life, it has a vital connection, a close and dynamic interaction with mankind which is of another order.

REFERENCES

Baskett, John
    1980   *The Horse in Art.* Boston: New York Graphic Society.

Blythe, Ronald
    1969   *Akenfield.* New York: Pantheon.

Campbell, Judith
    1971   *Police Horses.* North Hollywood, California: Wilshire.

Canetti, Elias
    1978   *Crowds and Power.* New York: Continuum.

Carr, William G.
    1965   *Man and Animal: Man through His Art,* vol. 3. Greenwich, Connecticut: New York Graphic Society.

Clutton-Brock, Juliet
    1981   *Domesticated Animals from Early Times.* Austin: University of Texas Press.

Cohen, Percy S.
    1980   "Psychoanalysis and Cultural Symbolism." In *Symbol as Sense,* ed. Mary LeCron Foster and Stanley H. Brandes, pp. 45–68. New York: Academic.

Cooper, J. C.
    1978   *An Illustrated Encyclopaedia of Traditional Symbols.* London: Thames and Hudson.

Diolé, Philippe
    1974   *The Errant Ark: Man's Relationship with Animals.* New York: Putnam.

Dobie, J. Frank
    1952   *The Mustangs.* Boston: Little, Brown.

Douglas, Mary
    1973   *Natural Symbols.* New York: Vintage.

Eliade, Mircea
    1978   *The Forge and the Crucible.* Chicago: University of Chicago Press.

Firth, Raymond
    1975   *Symbols: Public and Private.* Ithaca: Cornell University Press.

Green, Dr. Ben K.
    1974   *The Color of Horses.* Flagstaff, Arizona: Northland.

Hall, Edward
    1983   *The Dance of Life.* Garden City, New York: Doubleday.

Howey, M. Oldfield
    1958   *The Horse in Magic and Myth.* New York: Castle.

Hughes, Robert
    1984   "A Vision of Four-Legged Order." *Time* 124, no. 21:132–33.

King, Henry
    1978   "The Paint Horse." *Western Horseman* 43, no. 10:42, 84

Kroeber, T.
    1970   *Alfred Kroeber: A Personal Configuration.* Berkeley: University of California Press.

Lawrence, Elizabeth Atwood
    1982   *Rodeo: An Anthropologist Looks at the Wild and the Tame.* Knoxville: University of Tennessee Press.

Leach, Edmund
    1974   *Claude Lévi-Strauss.* New York: Viking.

Lévi-Strauss, Claude
    1966   *The Savage Mind.* Chicago: University of Chicago Press.

Merchant, Carolyn
    1980   *The Death of Nature.* New York: Harper & Row.

Montagu, Ashley
    1978   *Touching.* New York: Harper & Row.

Needham, Rodney
    1967   "Percussion and Transition." *Man,* n.s. 2:606–14.
    1981   *Circumstantial Deliveries.* Berkeley: University of California Press.

Neiman, LeRoy
    1979   *Horses.* New York: Abrams.

Ortner, Sherry B.
    1974   "Is Female to Male as Nature to Culture?" In *Woman, Culture, and Society,* ed. Michelle Z. Rosaldo and Louise Lamphere, pp. 67–87. Stanford: Stanford University Press.

Rowland, Beryl
    1973   *Animals with Human Faces: A Guide to Animal Symbolism.* Knoxville: University of Tennessee Press.

Rubinstein, Jonathan
    1980   *City Police.* New York: Farrar, Straus and Giroux.

Sahlins, Marshall
    1976   *Culture and Practical Reason.* Chicago: University of Chicago Press.
    1977   "Colors and Cultures." In *Symbolic Anthropology,* ed. Janet L. Dolgin, David S. Kemnitzer, and David M. Schneider. New York: Columbia University Press.

Shakespeare, William
1972   *Macbeth*. New York: Amsco.

Shepard, Paul
1978   *Thinking Animals*. New York: Viking.

Turner, Victor
1967   *The Forest of Symbols*. New York: Cornell University Press.

"Veterinarian Crusades for Mounted Police Unit"
1980   *Journal of the American Veterinary Medical Association* 177, no. 11:1073–75.

Vogt, Evon Z.
1976   *Tortillas for the Gods*. Cambridge: Harvard University Press.
1977   "On the Symbolic Meaning of Percussion in Zinacanteco Ritual." *Journal of Anthropological Research* 33, no. 3: 231–44.

Willis, Roy
1974   *Man and Beast*. New York: Basic.

Zeuner, Frederick E.
1963   *A History of Domesticated Animals*. New York: Harper & Row.

Horses in Human Experience

5

In its close association with mankind, the horse's complex nature and diverse attributes have enabled the animal to become far more than a worker and helper, vehicle of transport, or tool for sport. Potentiality for dynamic interaction between people and horses, as we have seen, arises from the social nature of both the equine and human species, which allows the development of a unique form of complementariness. From the beginning of horse-human contact, the particular qualities that this richly symbolic animal has stood for in the human mind have deepened the relationship which developed, infusing it with mental and spiritual dimensions which have carried the animal far beyond utilitarian considerations in the human value system. The horse's remarkable capacity to exert a transforming influence upon people with whom it interacts gives it power in making it a vital force in the life and culture of certain societies.

Gypsies

Gypsies, for example, as mentioned in the preface, perceive themselves as partaking of their group identity only if they are in some way in relationship with horses. As is the case with the Crow Indians, the animals are part of their sense of self, essential to their feeling of cultural belonging. For traditional Gypsies, the nomadic existence to which they are so passionately committed is closely connected to horses, which, in a literal sense, have from earliest times made this life possible. For true Gypsies, even now, "life revolves around the horse," and greeting between friends is not "I hope you will live happily" but rather "May your horses live long" (Seth-Smith 1979:312; Clebert 1963:102). Respect and admiration for the equine animal are natural to a Gypsy, for the horse "has been his stock-in-trade, mode of transport and constant friend for centuries of wandering" (Boswell 1970:183).

The trademark of the traditional Gypsy life of wandering is the colorfully decorated horse-drawn caravan that serves as home. "The horse is considered too noble an animal to be piled high with household goods." "His position does not allow him to do anything but draw a cart" (Block 1939:118). The role of the horse is central to the Gypsy way of life, enabling people to move as their culture dictates, set apart both physically and ideologically from the demands and constraints of regular sedentary society. For Gypsies are "the least domesticated of civilized peoples"; to make them settle down is "like harnessing a lion to a plow" (McDowell 1970:9).

"Perfect credentials" for a Gypsy include being "born in a caravan," having "a horse collar for a crib," and being literally "suckled by a mare" (McDowell 1970:18). Like other nomadic groups, Gypsies have generally evoked hostility from populations with fixed residence, being viewed as pariahs and dangerous characters by settled peoples with whom they come into contact in their journeying (Clebert 1963:xv-xvi). There is constant pressure upon Gypsies to abandon the vagabond life; nomadism is actively discouraged and often declared illegal. Forbidding Gypsies by law to trade in horses is one way, for example, that certain governments attempt to "make the footloose Gypsies settle down" (McDowell 1970:100).

To Gypsies themselves, however, the nomadic life, made possible by their horses, is the only way of living worthy of man. Their own term for non-Gypsy translates as peasant, or farmer, in the pejorative sense of "clod-hopper," "yokel," or "bumpkin." Their perceptions of themselves are as "Lords of the Earth" (Clebert 1963:xvii).

Gypsies' use of the horse, as a central symbol in their culture, reflects many of the themes revealed in the human-horse studies which make up this book. Like the American cowboys, who look down upon workers in other occupations, particularly farmers, as degraded, and the Crow Indians, who as mounted nomads once became "lords of the Plains," Gypsies' involvement with horses is associated with an imperious quality and a view of themselves as proud and free.

[175]

As described in connection with the White Mustang of the Prairies, a quality which the horse seems almost universally to stand for is freedom. Riding or driving horses gives people—both literally and figuratively—a sense of freedom from the constraints of conventional society. The cowboy riding the range perceives himself in this way, and popular thought often makes use of the Plains Indian mounted on his pinto as the very image of this kind of liberation. Close association with horses signifies proximity to, and harmony with, nature, as evidenced by the cowboy and the mounted Indian. Clebert could have been referring to both Crows and cowboys when he wrote of the Gypsies' "love of freedom, the reaction against the monotony and routine, the taste for novelty, for the unexpected, and for risk" (1963:91). Gypsies are united in their "love of freedom, in their eternal flight from the bonds of civilization, in their vital need to live in accordance with nature's rhythm, [and] in the desire to be their own masters" (1963:xix).

Contemporary Crows, as we have seen, find freedom from the dictates of the dominant culture and a slower and more natural pace, which they feel is intrinsic to their native identity, in their interaction with horses. In the context of rodeo, the quality of freedom is measured by the wild-to-tame transition, symbolized by the range of events from wild horse race and bronc riding through calf and steer roping. And it is again this very element of freedom—signified by the potential wildness of the horse appearing to be completely under control—that, through implicit contrast, gives the horse/policeman unit its power and force of authority.

In their tenacious orientation toward horses as symbols of the only life that suits them, Gypsies are reminiscent of modern-day Crows, who need to be surrounded with horses. Because "the Gypsy is primarily and above all else a nomad," ritual nomadism survives as a definite characteristic. Even when Gypsies become sedentary, "they at all times give the impression of camping" (Clebert 1963:201). "Horse-fetishism" can still be found among Gypsies. "Even now when he lives in a modern house or trailer caravan a Gypsy will surround himself with the horse *motif:* he will have china horses in his cupboards, chrome-plated horses on the bonnet of his scrap lorry, a horse-shoe tie pin, horseman-type boots and clothing. If he can possibly afford it he will keep a few horses in a field somewhere, although he has no real work for them to do" (Boswell 1970:183).

[176]

Gypsies, like Crows, cowboys, rodeo contestants, and mounted policemen, often show a strong sense of identification with their horses. A Gypsy who was employed in the cavalry during World War I wrote poignantly, "Remember that we are a lover of horses—they've been our friends." He noted that the war horses were "just as down-hearted as men were at times" and revealed, "I always thought that the horse had thinking periods. When he was left alone he used to think, and he used to fret, and no doubt about it, horses would remember their original life, and where they'd come from. And then to come into battle. And it was just like me. I had come from a free life. And then to come under this military discipline." Later, "when I was put in the infantry I lost all interest in soldiering. I lost my pal—my horse" (Boswell 1970:91–92).

In the words to a Gypsy song, a familiar theme of identification with the free spirit of the horse is also articulated. A non-Gypsy man asks:

> Girl, wilt thou live in my home?
> I will give thee a sable gown,
> And golden coins for a necklace,
> If thou wilt be my own.

And the Gypsy girl answers:

> No wild horse will leave the prairie
> For a harness with silver stars;
> Nor an eagle the crags of the mountain,
> For a cage with golden bars.
>
> [Leland 1882:81–82]

Expressive of horse-human unity, too, is the Gypsy horse broker, who, in order to be effective, must "be able to make a horse show his paces handsomely." He is required to be "a good runner," regulating his pace to the trot of the horse. His task requires that "both man and horse move their legs to the same rhythm" (Erdös 1959:2).

Typically, Gypsies are engaged in occupations which can be adapted to nomadic life, earning their livelihoods as peddlers, traders, fortune tellers, exhibitors of trained animals, musicians, dancers, blacksmiths, and metal workers. But "to employ oneself with the horse is the noblest profession and only occupation worthy of a Gypsy." "He is before everything a horse-dealer." In addition to its use as a draft animal, the horse is essentially an object for barter with people in the outside world. "The true business of the Gypsies, who are not content just to buy and resell the animals," is "in concealing the animals' defects," in "making up" horses in order to sell them. The Gypsies' "greatest art and reputation consists in 'putting right' the beasts which they show at fairs" (Clebert 1963:103).

Thus a central focus in Gypsy culture is the transformation of the horse. The equine animal, as in other diverse horse-owning societies, becomes a measure of certain vitally important qualities—in this case, cunning, ingenuity, the ability to outwit non-Gypsies, and, above all, intimate knowledge of the horse that makes possible its manipulation for personal advantage. According to one scholar, Gypsies generally have an exhaustive store of information concerning the stock of horses in the country where they wander, which they put to use in the purchasing and selling of animals according to availability and demand. Buying for a trifle an uncared-for and run-down nag in which the Gypsy sees potential, and feeding it up for a few months before selling it for a threefold price, is the art of the trade (Erdös 1959:1).

Gypsy "horse-copers" are noted for the tricks of the trade, which are used with consummate skill so that "a horse entrusted to Gypsies for a time comes from their hands unrecognizable" (Clebert 1963:104). So-called horse-faking involves many artifices. "Gypsy horse-traders may prick and prod placid horses with a hedgehog before taking them to auction, so that in the market they will start prancing and gambolling at the slightest touch." To make a horse appear lively, pebbles are put in a bucket and "clanked in front of it until it gets completely mad." Then "it would be enough, at the market, to show a horse the bucket, even from a distance, for the laziest of steeds to be transformed into a mettlesome colt of hardly controllable fieriness." A broken-winded horse may become saleable after it is given pumpkin or henbane mixed with elderberry, is force-fed on fat, or is subjected to bleeding. Ginger may be stuffed into a horse's anus to make it hold its tail high, giving it an elegant carriage. These are examples of the many procedures known to horse-copers which are used to "transfigure even half-dead jades into the fiercest of steeds" (Erdös 1959:3–4).

To conceal an aged horse's hollow eyes, a Gypsy horse trader will pierce the skin above the eye, insert a straw, and blow it up with air (McDowell 1970:100). To make an old horse look younger, its teeth can be bored and filled in to resemble a colt's, or the teeth can be rasped off to disguise advanced age. Gypsies routinely belittle a horse to the seller to obtain it at a lower price. They may even resort to surreptitiously cutting an animal with a knife and showing its blood to the owner in order to induce him to sell it quickly at any price before it dies (Erdös 1959:4). Gypsy horse dealers are said to change the color of horses they have stolen by rubbing the animals with secret concoctions or administering medicinal powder in their feed. "The transformation makes all investigations [of theft] unavailing," and "once the danger of discovery is past, the gypsy applies remedies which soon put the horse right again and give it as silky a skin as it had before." Gypsies are highly skilled as blacksmiths, as well, and know how to conceal a horse's lameness by shoeing (Block 1939:157–58).

Throughout their history, Gypsies have in fact been closely associated with the art of blacksmithing. Traditional legend dictates that the cause of their unremitting wandering over the earth can be traced to the guilt of a Gypsy smith who, in biblical times, forged the nails used for the crucifixion of Christ (Clebert 1963:2–5; Seth-Smith 1979:311–12). The Gypsy blacksmith as a shoer of horses is relevant in representing another link between horses and the crucifixion—as in the previously cited legend that the nails used to fasten Christ to the cross were subsequently made into a horse's bridle rings (see p. 179). According to Clebert, Gypsies as a culture are closely related to the history of the forge (1963:12–15), and it is noteworthy that magical powers were once almost universally ascribed to the art of the forge and the worker in metallurgy. This belief is rooted in the transformation of matter which takes place in the working of metals, and to the smith's mastery of fire as the element through which nature is changed (Eliade 1978:8–9, 79). Thus through the powers attributed to them, smiths are often identified as magicians and healers. "Even shoeing smiths are implicated in this connection, since they profit both from the prestige of the blacksmith and from the symbolism which has crystallized round the horse, a psycho-ceremonial animal." The horse, from antiquity, has frequently appeared as an important instrument in human belief systems involving myth, ritual, and ceremony (Eliade 1978:104; Clebert 1963:97–98).

Hoofbeats: Transition and Renewal

Turning now from the topic of "Gypsy gold," as a symbolic condensation of characteristics of the horse-human relationship that serves to illustrate many of the themes common to the studies which constitute this book, to broaden the scope of discussion, we are logically brought from the forge to the objects created by the blacksmith. Horseshoes are almost universally linked with beneficent magical forces. They derive their powers partly from the supernatural faculties ascribed to blacksmiths, who, in performing the transmutation of mineral substances which once shared in the sacredness attached to the earth, are laborers who, in modifying the state of matter, replaced the work of Time itself by accelerating natural processes (Eliade 1978:7–8, 169, 171).

Additionally, it is the horseshoe shape conceived of as an arch, a bifurcated set of horns, a lunar crescent, or a serpent—all objects with special power to protect against evil spirits—which makes it a talisman of luck. The iron and steel themselves also have this safeguarding power (Lawrence 1968:137–38). Of course, the close proximity of the metal shoe to the horse, often considered to be a magical or sacred animal, is instrumental in making the horseshoe the "favorite amulet of Western civilization" (Lawrence 1968:100). I believe that since the Christian era there has been a symbolic association of the horse, who routinely has nails driven into its feet, with Christ, whose feet were nailed to the Cross. Though I have never come across an explicit statement of it, I look upon this association as a powerful implicit metaphor in the post-Christian image of the horse.

On a more pragmatic level, I suggest that another explanation of the horseshoe as a good-luck symbol is the biological power inherent in the area between the horse's hoof and the shoe. There, continual growth takes place, for the hooves normally continue to elongate during the life of the animal. It seems natural that this area would be perceived as a place of origin for the flow of rhythmic energy and dynamic renewal. The attached shoe delineates and "orders" the growth of the horse's hoof and keeps the horny material from wearing off, cracking, or growing unevenly. Long hooves are purposely maintained on certain show horses to make them lift their legs higher. This heightening of the so-called action of the legs increases the force and impact of the particular gait being executed.

Extremely significant, I think, is the fact that the metal shoes nailed to the horse's hooves accentuate the sounds made when the animal is in motion. It well may be that the almost universally favorable response to this clip-clop accounts for the widespread belief in the horseshoe as a good-luck charm. For the rhythmic sound, over the centuries, has frequently calmed and reassured as well as pleased us. It has filled us with awe, as well. In the Bible, the horse, clothed with thunder, "paweth in the valley" (Job 39:21), and hands became feeble "at the noise of the stamping of hoofs of [his] strong horses" (Jeremiah 47:3). In diverse religious traditions, there appears the symbolic concept that the very earth itself is felt to quake under the feet of the horse (Howey 1958:167, 207).

Previously discussed (chap. 4) in relation to hoofbeats as percussion is Needham's intriguing proposal that percussion is associated in human experience with the state of transition. With the inclusion of hoofbeats as a type of percussion, I suggest, comes a concept of the association of horses themselves with transition. In this regard it is noteworthy that there is indeed a connection between the percussive act of drumming and the horse for healers in certain Asian cultures. The Yakut shaman changes the rhythm of his drumming while chanting a hymn containing the lines "The horse of the steppe has trembled!" "Come, then, O horse of the steppe, and teach!" (Eliade 1974:230–31). " 'The drum is our horse,' the shamans say" (Eliade 1974:233). "The drum is called the 'shaman's horse' "; often it bears a likeness of the horse or is made with a horse's hide that represents that animal. A drum may be referred to as a "shaman-horse"; the stick with which the drum is beaten may be called the "whip" (Eliade 1974:173,174). In one rite the drum is pierced three times with a stick; then "the drum turns into a three-legged mare that carries him into the east" (Eliade 1974:470). Sometimes even "burning horsehairs is equivalent to evoking the magical animal that will carry the shaman into the beyond" (Eliade 1974:469).

The meaning for the shaman is that through the beating of the drum which becomes his horse, he takes a symbolic journey. He passes out of the everyday world and beyond the reckoning of ordinary time. He experiences a "coming out of oneself" that "makes the mystical journey possible"; metaphorically "the horse enables the shaman to fly through the air, to reach the heavens" (Eliade 1974:467). Thus, brought into being by percussion, the horse empowers the shaman to leave the boundaries of this pragmatic world and enter into another domain. In other words, he is able to pass from one state to another by means of the drum-turned-horse. Expressed in equine terminology, the "beliefs, images, and symbols in relation to the 'flight,' the 'riding,' or the 'speed' of shamans are figurative expressions for ecstasy, that is, for

[181]

mystical journeys undertaken by superhuman means and in regions inaccessible to mankind" (Eliade 1974:174). By means of the horse, the shaman undergoes the experience that allows him to transcend both time and space. Not only a figurative but sometimes an actual horse can be the instrument of transition for a healer. A horse is held nearby during a certain curing ceremony, for example, in which the shaman calls the soul back to the body of a sick person in order to make him well. The animal is part of this ritual because "the horse is the first to perceive the return of the soul and shows it by quivering" (Eliade 1974:217). Thus the sensitive nature of the horse enables it to instantaneously mark the transition from illness to health, with the implication or potential of also indicating the transition between death and life in a case in which the patient had been moribund but is revived during the shamanic soul-returning procedure.

Just as the horse is perceived as carrying the healer on mystical journeys, it has almost universally been thought of as the animal that "carries the deceased into the beyond; it produces the 'break-through in plane,' the passage from this world to other worlds" (Eliade 1974:467). It is well known that in many human societies, including that of the North American Plains Indians, horses have been customarily sacrificed at the grave of the deceased in order to insure transportation to the next world. In its association with death and with the assumed afterlife—as examples of the most dramatic of changes in human status—the horse is clearly linked with transition and with the rites of passage which mark transition. Even in our contemporary society, there remains the ritual of the saddled but riderless horse, with boots facing backward in the stirrups, as a central feature of military or state funerals. The horse's slow pace, as discussed previously, adds to the somberness of the occasion. The aura of finality is measured out in the slow beat of the horse's hooves, which prolongs society's parting tribute to the dead individual.

Because the horse was the main implement of war throughout much of human history, its association with destruction has made it a symbol of death. The horse, with its rapidity of movement, may also be an image of death in the sense that it stands for the swiftness of the passing of life. But more importantly, at death there is a return to the earth, and I believe that the horse, with its slower pace, symbolizes this reversion to the rhythm and harmony of the natural order.

Not just in death, but in other experiences of human life involving changes, a pattern can be found in which horses are often associated with various states of transition. Eliade states that "the horse and its rider have held a considerable place in the ideologies and rituals of 'male societies.' " The horse's ability to carry a person from one world to another explains why the horse "plays a role of the first importance in certain types of masculine initiation." Initiates may be required to shoe a horse or participate in symbolically "killing" and then "reviving" a horse (1974:467; 1978:104). Similarly, "the ritual of shoeing and that of the death and resurrection of the 'horse' (with or without the rider) on the occasion of a marriage marks both the fiance's break with bachelordom and his entry into the class of married men" (Eliade 1978:104).

Probably through sexual connotations that are ascribed to the horse because of its dynamic force and rhythm, potency, and the phallic symbolism of being ridden, horses are closely associated with rebirth, "the renewal of the world and life" (Eliade 1974:79–80). Horses have been sacrificed, for example, "at the full moon following the summer solstice; the purpose is agrarian—'that the wheat may grow' " (Eliade 1974:197). In many societies, bridal horses not only stand for the transition of the newly married woman, but also, related to the sun as a creative force, equine animals in this context are an "unspoken prayer for the fruitfulness" of the bride who rides them (Howey 1958:100–101).

Stick-horses or hobbyhorses commonly represent the equine animal in the rites and ceremonies or festivals which are associated with transitions in many societies. Traditional beliefs and customs which survive today in some parts of the world associate the hobbyhorse (or similar horse figure) with the change in season. In England and Europe, for example, the hobbyhorse fertility rite exists in the form of a dance still performed annually to rid the countryside of winter's frost. It takes place at the end of winter, when people are anxious about the arrival of spring. "The ritual contest between winter and spring is symbolized by the ceremonial beheading and resurrection of the horse" or in a "mock wedding ceremony." The "process of stomping out the old and bringing in the new is acted out in an amusing play featuring the horse" and represents the ultimate triumph of spring over winter (Lonsdale 1981: opp. 89, 103, 165).

Themes of transition as expressed by actual horses are also articulated by hobbyhorses. In the initiation of a shaman, "a horse-stick

A May Day ritual of ancient origin still performed in
Cornwall features the hobbyhorse which periodically "dies"
and then rises exuberantly back to life, symbolizing the transition from winter to summer. Photo by author.

takes on life and becomes a real horse" (Eliade 1974:118). Dances with
hobbyhorses are often connected with weddings. In one South Pacific
society, a trance-dance is traditionally performed. "The dancer starts
out riding the hobbyhorse. But as he enters more deeply into the
trance he becomes the horse—prancing, galloping, stomping and kicking." For the Bambara of Mali, "a wild ride on a divine and chaotic
hobbyhorse marks the culmination of the sixth and final state of a life-
long initiation process." The stick-mount symbolically enables an initiate to engage in spiritual union with God. Eventually the initiate
shows signs of "autonomous control of the reins of destiny," and he
becomes a kind of chief of cavalry. In riding the hobbyhorse, the
initiate searches for knowledge and ultimate immortality. "In the
dance, the desperate kicking, running, rushing, jumping and bucking of
the hobbyhorse represent to the Bambara a warrior coursing into battle on his steed to fight for the life which has no end. The candidate who
goes on to penetrate the secret of immortality ascends to God through
the celestial skies, as if borne on a winged horse and swift winds"
(Lonsdale 1981:165–68).

The term *hobbyhorse* is derived from multiple and complex roots (see Cawte 1978:3–9; Howey 1958:90), but what is relevant here is to note the origin of our current usage. According to one source, a hobbyhorse is something a person clings to tenaciously, in the same way the English common people refused to give it up when the Puritans outlawed the appearance of the hobbyhorse at festal occasions (Howey 1958:90). Most significantly, even in our pragmatic, machine-oriented world, *hobbyhorse* is still used to indicate a diversion or interest that in the figurative sense has the power to carry a person away to another world!

As we have seen, horses, whether hobby- or actual, seem in many instances to be associated with transition and boundary marking in human life experience. It is tempting to try and relate this phenomenon to the intense attachment for horses often formed by teen-aged girls in our society, an obsessive commitment that seems to approach horse-fetishism in many cases. This attachment between girls and horses has been remarked upon by many observers and often glibly attributed to sexual motivation alone, though it is undoubtedly a more complex and multifaceted interaction. I suggest that, in addition to other factors, the horse could indeed be associated with marking the passage from childhood to adolescence for certain individuals.

The unique symbolic significance of the equine animal, as I have described in the section on the horse in rodeo, lies in the fact that it has, in its many forms which range from wild to tame, the capacity to represent and display all stages in the transition between nature and culture. This transition is, of course, the basic and ultimate change of status that brings into being the entity we call human society, in which individuals have passed from a state of nature to become a group which is characterized by the possession of culture in all its various manifestations. Thus it is not surprising that many forms of horses, actual and symbolic, have profound meaning within society and are instrumental in demarcating certain life stages and time sequences in human existence.

Victor Turner has called attention to the relationship between liminality and a symbolic connotation attributed to animal forms. The "classical prototype" for this association he suggests, is Cheiron, the centaur, "half wise old man, half stallion." As a teacher "in his mountain cavern—epitomizing outsiderhood and liminality"—the centaur had the important role of instructing the adolescent boys who were to become social and political leaders of Greece. "Human wisdom and animal force meet in this liminal figure, who is both horse and man" (1974:253).

The theme of association between horses and liminality is suggested by the studies of human-horse interactions which constitute this book. Contemporary Crow Indians, for example, are able to hold onto past traditions and values by means of horses yet also use them as a bridge to the present. The animals are related to an ethnic separateness, or outsiderhood, which the society wishes to retain, yet at the same time they represent a kind of emergence into modern times. The White Mustang is a liminal figure, set apart as he is, beyond the control of man. Civilization is closing in on him, however, so that his domain of freedom is in jeopardy. Unable to fit into the new order according to which the West was taking shape, he became an anachronism. His position at the threshold of the tamed frontier was untenable, and that made him a victim to be sacrificed.

In the cowboy world of both ranch and rodeo, horses at certain stages in training seem to represent liminal states. Such animals can be transferred from one domain to another—that is, by "making a bronc into a partner" through training or by "conquering" a mount in the arena through a high-scoring ride. Cowboys and rodeo contestants often identify with rebellious stock, perceiving themselves, like the horses, as nonconformists, outsiders in relation to the rest of society—"a breed apart." The police horse, which is often viewed as the epitome of a "wild" animal under the restraints of taming, can nevertheless quickly revert to unruliness on city streets. So there is a kind of perpetual liminal status for the horse, as it represents various states between chaos and order. For people who interact with police horses, as described, the animals often signify the comfort derived from nostalgia for simpler times. These city horses, like the mounts of contemporary Crows, which "help to fight the machine age"; like the White Mustang, whose world was the unfenced prairie; and like the broncs that recreate the West that cannot be won again, represent the values of the past. Yet all seem somehow poised upon the boundaries of change.

Rhythm and Motion

As we have seen earlier, Needham's proposal that percussion is associated with transitional states in society has been expanded in my work to include the concept of hoofbeats as percussion and horses as symbolically associated with transition. Considering the high rate of occurrence of percussion, and the importance it assumes in almost all types of human society, the subject merits more than routine consideration by anthropologists. The prevalence of drumming and other forms of syncopation in the context of so many cultures gives testament to its relevance in people's lives and suggests deep-level meaning. The satisfactions that are obtained appear to be no fewer in our contemporary society, in the light of the extremely large number of people who can be observed listening to a "beat" of some sort during virtually every waking moment. And one avenue of inquiry which is sure to lead to fruitful analysis would be the disparity, and even conflict, between successive generations that is overtly expressed by a "different tune"—a different form of rhythm which becomes the separate domain of each age group.

All peoples, no matter what their culture and society, seem to have a deeply ingrained sense of rhythm, to possess a *beat*, as it were, which serves to articulate the intensity of life in many dimensions. In our relatives, the primates, are found the beginnings of this peculiar urge which has flowered in human society. Chimpanzees are known to beat "drums" in the form of tree trunks (Reynolds 1965:15, 132–35; van Lawick-Goodall 1971:19, 170, 176) and to enact a kind of ritual dance which is rhythmic in nature (van Lawick-Goodall 1971:52–54). From the time of our earliest human ancestors through the present industrial age, a rhythmic beat, and the bodily response it elicits, have been associated with social life. Mankind has a special propensity to express and communicate rhythm through the medium of the body: "To dance is human, and humanity almost universally expresses itself in dance" (Hanna 1980:3). Dance is a unique art, in which the body makes patterns in time and space (Royce 1977:3). In dance, action and awareness merge (Hanna 1980:3).

Horses appear to merge action and awareness in a way that gives them a unique place in human consciousness. Many different types of animals, such as performing bears and dogs, have been trained to dance. But it is the horse, both by its very nature and through arduous training, which, to a much greater degree, partakes of the human kinetic and spatial rhythm, sharing those qualities that make us dance. A horse's rhythmic motion and extension through space are inborn as well as contrived by man. They belong to the realm of nature as well as that of culture. When it is running free, we marvel at the equine's graceful movements and admire the prancing and dancing which are part of its inherent repertoire. From the dawn of human awareness, people have been captivated with equine motion, depicting it in cave art and carvings with all its spectacular beauty, appreciating it for its own sake long before our species became charioteers and riders. D. H. Lawrence has pointed out "how the horse dominated the mind of the early races. You were a lord if you had a horse. Far back, far back in our dark soul the horse prances. . . . The horse, the horse! The symbol of surging potency and power of movement, of action, in man" (1981:60–61).

Ever since the human partnership with horses began, an affinity with the equine animal, some sense of a common rhythm, has made the horse important at many intervals. At the most fundamental level, it may be that the sound of horses' hoofbeats echoes our own heartbeat, the pulse of life itself. Even before birth, hearing a rhythmic beat may be important. Needham believes that "the distinctive response to percussive sound derives from imprinting in the womb, when the developing consciousness is unremittingly subjected to the reverberations of the mother's heartbeat" (1981:48).

Clip-clop, whether made by a real horse or a symbolic or fabricated one, is a sound we have grown accustomed to and made part of our lives. Children, even those who are raised far away from actual horses, become entranced with the sound. They are apt to "play horsie" as soon as they can toddle, exhibiting what seems to be an inherent patterned trotting motion, universally expressed by the same rhythm of motion, perhaps to the accompaniment of slapping the thigh or clapping. Next come the stick-horses, or hobbyhorses, which bring toddlers the added joy of being astride, however meager may be the likeness to a true equine. Formed and bridled equine heads now provide a set of reins, imparting a feeling of control. Vertical motion is exaggerated; indeed, the derivation of the word *hobbyhorse* may come from "to toss, to move up and down" (Howey 1958:90). Youngsters provide the locomotion; yet, trotting or galloping, they become like grotesque centaurs, already merged with a power they could never possess alone—"carried away" with the joy of motion.

Undoubtedly the pleasures of juvenile horse replicas reflect the fact that we are born remembering and longing for the rhythmic rocking of our prenatal life. Many authorities on childhood have attested to this vestigial need. Babies, of course, are almost universally rocked. In

[188]

early childhood, multitudes of children are preoccupied with rocking horses, finding joy in the motion of their own bodies in tune with the motion of the rocking horse, and in the accompanying fantasies of galloping away on spirited chargers to an enchanted world. I have noted with the coming of each consecutive Christmas, particularly in the most recent years, that the rocking horse as a yuletide symbol becomes ever more prevalent. Beyond the fact that toys in themselves stand for Christmas, and that a rocking horse is a popular and spectacular toy, I suggest that the horse figure here, as in other contexts, represents renewal—both in the birth of Christ and in the transition into the New Year which will soon take the place of the old one. Signifying the annual holiday season, which recurs regularly on a cyclical basis, the rocking horse thereby marks the passage of time, adding to the symbolism with its own back-and-forth motion. It represents, too, a return to the old traditional values, which is part of the spirit of Christmas, turning us back toward simpler times. The farther into the machine age we progress, and, I suspect, the more troubled the times, the more significant this toy becomes as an expression of our longing for a slower pace. At any rate, childhood is itself a transitional state, and all kinds of horse effigies carry us through it.

The merry-go-round entrances not only children but all who have a flair for being young. Here are gaily colored and caparisoned mounts—prancing with arched necks, flaring nostrils, and bared teeth. They strain at motion, legs frozen in a flying gallop, epitomizing the swiftness and grace of equine movement that fascinates us. The machinery empowering them is hidden in a dizzying array of color and mirrors, poles, stripes, and garish portraits. Patrons rush to be the first, to beat the other riders, scrambling to mount the up-and-down steeds—those with another dimension of rhythm and the illusion of autonomy—rather than the static horses, which move only in the forward direction, merely impelled by the platform. No one but the infirm or the unimaginative contemplates riding in the chariots. For most, it is the vertical rhythm and forward surge combined, the plunging into space, which bring an unexplained but almost universal form of ecstasy.

Always, the carousel equestrian rides to the accompanying time of music, music that sets the beat, punctuates the ride, becomes one with the continual circular course that substitutes for the beat of the horses' hooves. Mesmerized with the rhythm as they circle, riders merge with mount and music in an orgy of motion as they are whirled through

[189]

A spirited carousel horse, galloping with arched neck and flowing mane, epitomizes the swiftness and rhythmic grace of equine motion, and may carry its rider on a symbolic journey. Photo by Gary Sinick.

space. How poor and empty a merry-go-round ride would be without music—always that special type of calliope sound, strong and pulsating, surging music that gives life and breath to motion, that makes a beat for its spinning. Elation makes riders giddy as they revolve in syncopated time on steeds who respond to a giddyup beyond their own voicing. On the charger that becomes large as life, a carousel equestrian becomes a lord, a knight, even a king or queen—high status, here as always, accruing to the horseman. Transformed by a carnival world, we are nobility, but we rule in transit, without responsibility for a fixed kingdom. We are at the same time like a Gypsy nomad, whose horse is gold, for we have left behind the constraints of a static society. Luck will bring us the gold ring, and another ride. Real time is suspended now, for carnival time is mythic: we can be carried through it without the reckoning of its passage. Though we are transported onward by a make-believe horse, we have not progressed to the actuality of the next

[190]

stage; we have only gone through the motions. We have engaged in an allegorical journey, but we have remained young.

Whether in effigy or in living form, horses are perceived as dancers. A popular song centering on a horse who is ready to enter the Kentucky Derby communicates to the young Thoroughbred that the race represents the chance of a lifetime, and urges the horse toward fulfillment of its destiny with the words "it's high time you joined in the dance." A horse who would not submit to man is celebrated in familiar verse as the "broncho that would not be broken of dancing" (Lindsay 1980:466–67). And a farmer who nostalgically describes working behind a team of horses recalls their stride and motion:

> A dance
> is what this plodding is.
> A song, whatever is said.

[Berry 1980:89]

When people dance, it is sometimes called "hoofing," and those in a dancing group may be referred to as "hoofers" (Knoll 1982:1). Musical rhythm is in the equine repertoire, part of what we admire and share with horses. As Shakespeare wrote of a mount in *Henry the Fifth,*

> When I bestride him, I soar, I am a hawk: he trots the air;
> the earth sings when he touches it; the basest horn of his
> hoof is more musical than the pipe of Hermes.

[1942:728]

A poem celebrating the elation of riding, echoing the horse's gait, ends with the line "But set our days in measure with the song the saddle sings" (Grover 1929:52). Some of the steps of the most popular of all Mexican dances, the jarabe, "imitate the clicking of hoofs and the pawing and prancing of spirited horses. Historians have interpreted the jarabe as a perpetuation of the imitative motions made by native Mexicans upon first seeing the horses brought into their country by the conquistadores" (Dobie, Boatright, and Ransom 1965:248–49). Listening to the cavalry song "Garryowen," we both feel and hear the sound of the horse's trot and our own rhythmic response, and we come to understand the sweeping away and sense of abandonment which are the élan of the cavalry charge. Hearing strains of the "William Tell Overture" makes even the most sedentary listener seem to be galloping

[191]

over land which resounds with hoofbeats. Riding a living horse, we post, or rise rhythmically to the trot, or move our bodies in harmony with the horse's canter. As Highwater writes in his analysis of dance, "Bodily movement is man's most expressive act" (1978:25). The human response to the equine animal's motion becomes a metaphor for the rhythm of life—prenatal rhythm, sexual rhythm, seasonal rhythm, the slowing rhythm of death—hoofbeats on frozen ground.

There is universal fascination with the horse's kinetic qualities. Like the dancers in many diverse societies who draw power from the animal through imitation of its pace and postures, we share in our horses' motion and take it unto ourselves. We breed horses for special gaits and glory in their sound and sight. High-stepping Hackneys must "hit their chins with their hooves." The smooth and ambling gait of Tennessee Walking Horses that enables the rider to sit without posting creates a mount for those who would ride effortlessly. Our five-gaited Saddlebred Horses surpass nature in the elegance of the two artificial gaits—the slow-gait and the rack—for which they are trained. The Morgan Horse Association is plagued by controversy between its two factions: those who would leave the muscular little utilitarian-bred horses, famous for hard work and versatility, to their own natural gaits, and those who would breed and train them for a high-stepping gait resembling that of Saddlebreds. The latter group spurns the value of a "daisy-clipper"—a horseman's derogatory term for animals who do not raise their hooves up high.

Gait, analysis of motion, and the way a horse places its feet on the ground have always interested people. As I have pointed out in the second chapter, the White Mustang always paced. His lateral gait was one of the distinguishing characteristics which set him apart and imbued him with symbolic meaning. Kroeber, in his anthropological studies, wrote of the "flying gallop"—a way of depicting a horse running with full extension of its legs—which was characteristic of many societies and cultures, as wholly symbolic, "used in art because of its suggestion of great speed" (1948:497). Though horses cannot actually run in this position, it was only when the camera proved this fact that artists began to portray horses running in a realistic manner. Until that time, only the bushmen's keen eyes enabled them to paint galloping animals with the legs appearing as they are actually used (1948:502). With the photographic work of Muybridge, whose abridged book *Animals in Motion* (1957) was first published in 1887 under the title *Animal*

Locomotion, and with the analysis of Stillman, who produced *The Horse in Motion* (1882), every detail of the horse's locomotion at all gaits and in all types of use, and the laws that govern movement, came under scrutiny.

Motion is the quintessential element of our use and enjoyment of horses. Horse races reward the swiftest with some of society's most impressive accolades. Hunters and jumpers must take the hurdles according to a rigid set of standards and patterns. Style in bucking horses, as explained, exhibits a range of diversity from the natural buck of an energetic horse to that induced or exaggerated by the bucking strap in rodeo. In bronc-riding contests, there is opposition, a dance of rebellion between horse and man, but still there is the effort to attain harmony, as the rider gears his body rhythm to that of the mount. Satisfaction is derived in most other horse sports by the degree to which the rider succeeds in getting in tune with his horse's rhythmic movement through space.

Circus horses perform various complex feats, particularly dance routines, and always to the accompaniment of music. The liberty horses, with their dance steps in unison representing collectivity, have already been described. Additionally, there are the classic great white equine creatures that canter so steadily, dependably, around the ring, always with the same faultless and modulated rhythm, providing an unfailing background, a living beat, as it were, for the acrobats who use them as easily as though their broad backs were a staging. Here, athlete is counterpoint to athlete; man and beast in harmony create the beauty of artistic expression. Still more training is given to equine animals "high-schooled" for dressage, taught elaborate repertoires comparable to the most complex dance. Lifetimes are occupied with the perfection of prancing routines, quadrilles, and jumps. The Lipizzan stallions, world-famous as "dancing white horses," are the most intricately trained of all steeds and ultimately learn to execute the "capriole"—a dramatic leap into the air—after years of arduous preparation. Such feats depend upon a kind of kinetic interaction between equine and human bodies, as well as the merging of wills through reciprocal communication channels. Such a combination is unique to man's relationship with horses.

A recent phenomenon which vividly reinforces the concept of the symbolic nature of the human-horse relationship is a dramatic exhibition first presented at horse shows in 1983. This act, entitled "Adagio for Horse, Rider, and Dancer," is a "pas de deux" performed by a talented black male dancer and a dressage horse ridden by a skilled female equestrian. Breaking with "the time-honored principle of inequality between man and horse, the idea that man is always master and the horse subservient to him" ("Adagio" 1983: 31), the "Adagio" presents man and beast as ultimately being equals and partners. Sometimes the man's movements match the horse's, and sometimes they contrast, but they always express harmony through the intense coordination that is achieved.

In the dance, man and animal first confront each other in fear and hostility; then they move toward graceful harmony which expresses mutual respect. The performance is said to represent "the whole American ideal coming together—man and woman, human and animal, black and white, work and art" ("Adagio" 1983:32). Audience members are often moved to tears, and generally respond with standing ovations. Explaining the warm-up exercises he does to make his muscles stand out before entering the arena, the dancer admits, "I'm a very small object out there compared to the horse, and I need all the definition I can get" (Hancock 1983:9). An observer wrote that when their steps match, "you had never noticed before that a man could seem as large and powerful as a horse, or a horse as compactly beautiful as a man." When asked, "How did it feel, dancing with a horse?" the dancer revealed, "When we were dancing, it didn't feel like it was a horse. We were two beings. And I don't know if he thought I was a horse, but he responded to me" (Hancock 1983:9).

A newspaper reporter summed up the "Adagio": "Man *is* the ethereal, not-of-this world being that classical ballet portrays him to be. But he is also flesh, blood and muscle, a creature of earth, and one of the moods of our time is to rediscover that earthly relation. And when the man is at the peak of physical perfection, as Antonio is, any incongruity you feel when the two bodies first begin their steps quickly dissolves" ("Adagio" 1983:32). Thus this performance illustrates once again the process which seems to be universal to mankind—that of using the animal as a being against which to measure ourselves and the human predicament.

Horses and the Human Relationship to Nature

Most significantly, this innovative performance expresses the spirit of the present era of ecological awareness, in which we are rethinking the human relationship to nature, questioning our role of dominance over other forms of life, which has thus far in our existence proven so disastrous. A new consciousness impels us to balance our old hostility toward other forms of life against a potential status of complementariness. In articulating these timely dilemmas, which must be solved before it is too late, the horse, as man's ancient servant but also his ally and friend, is symbolic of the range of interrelationships which bind mankind to the natural world and from which we must now choose.

Horses extend their human riders into the world without enclosing them, something machines seldom do. Through this process people become a part of the equine animal's forward thrust, reconfirming the human status as part of nature. Symbolizing nature by virtue of their rhythmicity, horses also represent freedom, power, and romantic beauty. Horses are often likened to the sea, with its rhythmic waves and tides, the recurrent ebbing and flowing, its surging power, and the vastness that connotes wildness and freedom. As with horses, the motion and sound of the ocean calm and reassure us, relating us to the cosmos. Many myths and legends tell of horses originating from the sea, and people from diverse cultures share the idea of an affinity between horses and the ocean.

Frequently, too, tales embody the concept of horses' being born from the wind, the swiftness of the wind being the horse's only rival in speed of flight. From the wind horses have been perceived as acquiring their unrestrained wildness and the dual capacity for being quiet and docile as a summer breeze or wild and powerful as a winter tempest. Horses, too, as "fiery steeds," are associated with flames and are classically perceived in connection with the chariot of the sun. The similes used for horses share the dominant quality of rhythmicity, and several of these—the sea, wind, and fire—are also elements which symbolize crowds (Canetti 1978:75–90) by virtue of this quality.

Horses, like the wind and the sea, belong to the realm of nature; yet they also belong to the domain of man. Embodying simultaneously the spirit of both spheres, horses are unique in the complexity and duality—and often the contradictory elements—of the values they express. In their mobility and wildness, their perpetuated capacity to revert to the feral state, horses always represent freedom. Their power and strength are a reminder of the capacity for rebellion against restraint which may once again surface even after so long a history of obedience. For his many purposes, mankind has ever subdued the wild

Lord Grosvernor's Arabian with a Groom by George Stubbs (1765). As a beautiful and powerful animal, long domesticated but still retaining a certain potential for wildness, the horse symbolizes the range of interrelationships which bind mankind to the natural world. Courtesy of Kimbell Art Museum, Fort Worth, Texas.

spirit of the horse, reenacting the conflict between nature and culture with a wild-to-tame transformation. To make it useful in human society, the inherent fears of the equine animal, considered as its instinctual nature, must be overcome. Jung wrote, "The horse is dynamic and vehicular power: it carries one away like a surge of instinct. It is subject to panics like all instinctive creatures who lack higher consciousness" (1983:188).

In symbolic usage, then, human reason drives the animal force of instinct, and man and horse relate in complementariness. The archetypal conquest of wild and chaotic nature by the rational and ordered forces of culture is clearly articulated in the legend of Alexander the Great and his horse, Bucephalus—one of the most famous pairs to share a special man-horse relationship (see p. 64). As a boy, Alexander alone was able to conquer and ride a powerful and previously intractable horse that had defied all of the expert horsemen in his father's kingdom of Macedonia. This extraordinary feat was possible because Alexander had noticed that the horse was frightened of his own shadow, which was cast in front of him. Through the simple expedient of turning the animal toward the sun, the horse was no longer afraid and performed obediently for this wise handler (Plutarch 1980:257–58). Thus Alexander, manipulating the forces of nature through his own rationality, was able to infuse the fearful animal with confidence, thereby winning himself a bold steed who would become a fitting partner for his conquest of the world.

In bending the horse to the purposes of civilization, mankind has ever been confronted with the equine instinct of fear, which motivates the animal to shy or bolt. Like the cavalry horses of bygone times, police horses in modern cities can be trained to overcome their instincts in going toward the very sights and sounds which in the natural state would be most terrifying. That such a feat is possible is testament to the order, conformity, and obedience that have been imposed upon the horse, and in an allegorical sense it is through the enactment of this conquest that power accrues to the mounted man, grants him authority, and often makes him a hero.

In virtually all of its relationships with people throughout history, the horse has elevated the human status. By first providing power and mobility, the animal transformed the total fabric of life for horse-owning societies, as exemplified by the Crow Indians of the American Plains. In the saga of the winning of the American West, it was the frontiersman who had conquered the horse who ultimately extended his domain over a continent. Domination of nature is closely related in our value system to our own progress away from our instinctual selves. In contemporary society, "we allocate honour and prestige to people of science and industry who excell in understanding and controlling the powerful domain of nature. We also honour people who overcome animal urges, curbing these in accordance with moral codes" (MacCormack 1980:6). *Curbing,* of course, comes directly from horsemen's terminology for use of a bit which checks a horse. Its frequent use in everyday language reveals the way in which a rider's control of his horse symbolizes the social constraints which regulate human behavior by overcoming its animal, or instinctual, component. The horse in the city—the police horse—epitomizes this representation.

Studies of the horse in Crow Indian culture, the White Mustang of the Prairies, rodeo horses, mounted police, and horses in human life experience, which make up this book, reveal the multifaceted nature of the horse and the depth of its involvement in society, as well as the many diverse meanings with which it is endowed for various peoples. In living closely with the horse, and engaging in dynamic interaction with it, people transform the horse but are also transformed *by* it. Because of the significant roles which the equine animal often plays in people's lives, and through the process of becoming a creature esteemed as something of high value, the horse often imparts back to people a sense of identity which helps to define their status in the social order. As expressed in the reference to horses as "Gypsy gold" (see p. ix), often the horse seems to embody those elements of life that seem most meaningful within a certain culture. Knowledge concerning the specific human-horse relationships characteristic of a group gives insights leading to a richer understanding of that people's ethos and values. It is clear that there is an important and intriguing relationship between hoofbeats—representing both actual and symbolic horses— and a particular society's perceptions about themselves and the world around them.

REFERENCES

"Adagio: Exploring the Human-Equine Relationship."
  1983   *The Horse Digest* 1, no. 9:31–32.
Berry, Wendell
  1980   *A Part.* San Francisco: North Point.

Block, Martin
1939   *Gypsies: Their Life and Their Customs.* New York: D. Appleton-Century.

Boswell, Silvester Gordon
1970   *The Book of Boswell: Autobiography of A Gypsy.* London: Gollancz.

Canetti, Elias
1978   *Crowds and Power.* New York: Continuum.

Cawte, E. C.
1978   *Ritual Animal Disguise.* Totowa, New Jersey: Rowman and Littlefield.

Clebert, Jean-Paul
1963   *The Gypsies.* London: Vista.

Dobie, J. Frank, Mody C. Boatright, and Harry Ransom, eds.
1965   *Mustangs and Cow Horses.* Dallas: Southern Methodist University Press.

Eliade, Mircea
1974   *Shamanism.* Princeton: Princeton University Press.
1978   *The Forge and the Crucible.* Chicago: University of Chicago Press.

Erdős, Kamill
1959   "Gypsy Horse-Dealers in Hungary." *Journal of the Gypsy Lore Society* 38, nos. 1–2:1–6.

Grover, Edwin Osgood
1929   *The Animal Lover's Knapsack.* New York: Crowell.

Hancock, Elise
1983   "A Standing Ovation in Madison Square Garden." *Johns Hopkins Magazine,* February, pp. 7–11.

Hanna, Judith Lynne
1980   *To Dance Is Human.* Austin: University of Texas Press.

Highwater, Jamake
1978   *Dance: Rituals of Experience.* New York: A & W.

Holy Bible, The (King James Version)
n.d.   New York: Cambridge University Press.

Howey, M. Oldfield
1958   *The Horse in Magic and Myth.* New York: Castle.

Jung, C. G.
1983   *The Essential Jung,* ed. Anthony Storr. Princeton: Princeton University Press.

Knoll, Adrienne
1982   "International Hoofers: Shall We Dance?" *Brown Daily Herald* 116, no. 1:1.

Kroeber, A. L.
1948   *Anthropology.* New York: Harcourt, Brace.

HOOFBEATS AND SOCIETY

Lawrence, D. H.
   1981   *Apocalypse.* New York: Penguin.

Lawrence, Robert Means
   1968   *The Magic of the Horse-Shoe.* Detroit: Singing Tree.

Leland, Charles G.
   1882   *The Gypsies.* Boston: Houghton, Mifflin.

Lindsay, Vachel
   1980   "The Broncho That Would Not Be Broken." In *Best Loved Poems of the American West,* eds. John J. and Barbara T. Gregg, pp. 466–67. New York: Doubleday.

Lonsdale, Steven
   1981   *Animals and the Origin of Dance.* New York: Thames and Hudson.

McDowell, Bart
   1970   *Gypsies: Wanderers of the World.* Washington: National Geographic Society.

MacCormack, Carol P.
   1980   "Nature, Culture and Gender: A Critique." In *Nature, Culture and Gender,* ed. Carol MacCormack and Marilyn Strather, pp. 1–24. Cambridge: Cambridge University Press.

Muybridge, Eadweard
   1957   *Animals in Motion.* New York: Dover.

Needham, Rodney
   1981   *Circumstantial Deliveries.* Berkeley: University of California Press.

Plutarch
   1980   *The Age of Alexander.* New York: Penguin.

Reynolds, Vernon
   1965   *Budongo: A Forest and Its Chimpanzees.* London: Methuen.

Royce, Anya Peterson
   1977   *The Anthropology of Dance.* Bloomington: Indiana University Press.

Shakespeare, William
   1942   *Henry the Fifth.* In *The Complete Plays and Poems of William Shakespeare,* ed. William Allen Neilson and Charles Jarvis Hill, pp. 710–46. Boston: Houghton Mifflin.

Seth-Smith, Michael
   1979   *The Horse.* London: Octopus.

Stillman, J. D. B.
   1882   *The Horse in Motion.* Boston: Osgood.

Turner, Victor
   1974   *Dramas, Fields, and Metaphors.* Ithaca: Cornell University Press.

van Lawick-Goodall, Jane
   1971   *In the Shadow of Man.* Boston: Houghton Mifflin.

Index

INDEX

White Stallion of the Prairies. *See* White Mustang of the Prairies
Wild horse race, 86–87
Wild horses, 42, 57, 82–84, 88, 177. *See also* Mustangs
Wildness of horses, 121, 169, 195, 196; as metaphor, 157; and mounted police work, 133; scoring of, in rodeo, 83, 90
Wild-tame duality, 62, 63, 79–80, 81, 82, 83, 88, 94, 96, 97, 101, 102, 107, 113, 121, 157, 169, 185, 197

Wild West show, 68–69, 79
Winning of the West, x, 61–62, 63, 82, 186, 197–98
Wintering of horses, 6, 18, 21, 41, 46, 49–51
Wissler, Clark, 3, 8, 12
Wister, Owen, 70–71
Women: and broncs, 96; relationship to horses, 16–17, 37–38; and rodeo, 33, 95–96